At His Crossroad

Igor Kovač

Editor

At His Crossroad

Reflections on the Work of France Bučar

 Springer

Editor
Igor Kovač
University of Cincinnati
Cincinnati, OH, USA

ISBN 978-3-319-78330-7   ISBN 978-3-319-78331-4   (eBook)
https://doi.org/10.1007/978-3-319-78331-4

Library of Congress Control Number: 2018941578

Printed on acid-free paper

This Springer imprint is published by the registered company Springer International Publishing AG part of Springer Nature.
The registered company address is: Gewerbestrasse 11, 6330 Cham, Switzerland

Preface

Every nation has its Goethe, Nelson, and Jefferson. And France Bučar is Slovenian Thomas Jefferson. Both were intellectuals, both were lawyers by profession and their life-paths led them to politics, where they have made their greatest historical mark – forming a new nation. As Jefferson's works are well known and are being translated into many languages, this so far could not be said for Bučar and other statesmen from arcane countries. However, their thoughts and ideas could be interesting and inspiring for broader global readership and scholarship.

Thus, as the Head of the American Slovenian Education Foundation (ASEF), I am thrilled to see this publication translated in English. The ASEF's aim is to enhance American and Slovenian education activities, contributing to diversity of ideas by fostering academic exchange between the USA and Slovenia. Such a volume is beneficial not only for the vocation of ASEF but for the social science academia and broader intellectual community. Ideas and accomplishments of non-Anglo-Saxon authors have long been overlooked in both natural and social sciences. ASEF has recently been highly supportive of Dr. Edi Gobec book entitled *Slovenian American Inventors and Innovators*. It turns out that Dr. France Rode, the lead inventor of the first sophisticated pocket-size HP-35 calculator, and Ed Repic, the leader of the Rockwell's Space Exploration Team and major contributor to the design of Apollo 11 – the first spacecraft from the Earth that landed on the Moon in 1969, were both Slovenians. Still, what about social sciences, can a Slovenian author offer something unique in this field as well?

France Bučar and the present volume provide an affirmative answer to this question. Although my interest lies in computer science, Bučar's work tangents my curiosity. Namely, his provocative thoughts push me to rethink about the fundaments of my own work. His innovative system theory drives natural scientists to think anew about the assumptions, which we make – how can we model the (ir)rational individual and his action.

Furthermore, although national identity and national interest are essential variables for Bučar, I recall his numerous speeches and articles, in which he encouraged Slovenian students and professionals to move abroad. He opposed a narrative, which is still very characteristic for other Slovenian intellectuals, fearful of brain-drain, lamenting the fact that many young Slovenian intellectuals are moving abroad. Bučar's understanding of national interest was different. Slovenian young intellectuals need to face their knowledge, ideas, and capabilities with their global peers and global competitors. Yet, they cannot do this from Slovenia, where the research resources are very limited. They can only reach their full potential in a stimulating environment. Moreover, only by achieving their full potential they can really be the new intellectual elites that post-communist country needs to succeed in its transition, reforms, and modernization. Thus, Bučar stands shoulders above other bigoted proponents of "Slovenian national interest." His fusion and synthesis of different ideas is extraordinary and deserves attention from intellectuals deriving from both, natural and social sciences, across the globe.

The following essays about Bučar views and the translation of Bučar 2006 book *At a New Crossroads* are applauding endeavors of presenting a so far unknown author with a relevant idea and interesting background story to a highly demanding English-speaking audience. The volume will not disappoint you. However, one should remain critical and engage with the argument presented by Bučar for several reasons. First, this is what our devotion to academic excellence instructs us to do. Second, this is what Bučar would want us to do – advance our knowledge by criticizing one another. Third, only by engaging and juxtaposing a diverse set of theories, one can sort out the wheat from the chaff. In this vein I wish for many discussions to be stirred due to this publication.

Stanford, CA, USA   Jure Leskovec

Acknowledgment

I am grateful to many people and organizations that have devoted their time and energy toward this edited volume. First, to France Bučar, who for two decades gracefully shared his ideas with me. The present book is my eulogy for the great man he was. To the Bučar family, particularly Janez, whose indispensable encouragement and goodwill presented an oasis of positive thoughts in the early stages of this project.

Moreover, I cannot stress enough the appreciation for humbleness, openness, and commitment of the members of the American Slovenian Education Foundation (ASEF). This organization, which I am a part of since 2014, is dedicated to building bridges between American and Slovenian academia. My ASEF colleagues have intellectually adopted the present work, so it is as much theirs as it is mine. It personifies the very purpose of ASEF and my colleagues have unselfishly recognized it as such.

I would like to thank all the contributors for their essays. In a short period of time they took on a great endeavor. Their papers provide an excellent evaluation of France Bučar and link him to different research questions they have dedicated their careers to.

I would also like to express my gratitude to Simon Ozvatič and Celjska Mohorjeva družba press, who have published the original text of *Na novih razpotjih* and have granted the permission to publicize the translation. Kelly Daugherty from Springer has been extremely helpful throughout the project. A special thank you is in place for Lorraine Klimowich at Springer, who trusted in me and gave me the opportunity to make this project a reality.

Without Aleš Lampe, who translated the Slovenian text into English, and Erica Johnson Debeljak, who has fought through the language editing, this book would not be the same. Furthermore, Slovenian Research Agency has also supported the translation.

Lastly, I would like to thank my colleagues at the University of Cincinnati. I held several fruitful discussions with them that also enabled me to shape this book. And thank you my peers at the Slovenian Paneuropean Movement. You are my political reality check that every "crazy scientist" needs.

Introduction

Igor Kovač

Professor France Bučar was born on 2 February 1923 in Bohinjska Bistrica, Slovenia. Being one of the six children of a local shoemaker, the local priest recognized his brightness and persuaded the family to send him to Ljubljana to attend the elite Catholic Classical College. When he enrolled to study law, the Second World War broke out and Bučar was first arrested by the Fascist occupiers and spent several years in the concentration camp in Gonars, Italy. In 1944, while on a train to another, this time German, concentration camp, he escaped and joined the partisans. After the war, he completed his law studies and became Secretary of the Republican Chamber in the Assembly of Slovenia – a republic in former Yugoslavia. In 1959, he was awarded the Eisenhower Fellowship and in 1963, became a professor at the University of Ljubljana's Law School. He was banned from lecturing in 1976, and in 1978 dismissed from the university due to criticism of the social-political situation in Yugoslavia. He worked as a dissident, writing against Marxist and Leninist narratives, arguing for socio-political-economic reforms, emphasizing ethics as a main feedback loop in his system theory. In 1988, he wrote an article outlining the plan for Slovenian independence and on the first free elections in Slovenia; in 1990, he became a member and afterward also the president of Slovenia's first parliament. He wrote the Slovenian constitution and in 1991 declared the independence of his country. Bučar continued to be socially active as the president of a nongovernmental organization – Slovenian Paneuropean Movement – until 2012. He passed away on 21 October 2015.[1]

The present book is a commemoration of this great man, with whom I had the privilege to work with for more than a decade. Although Bučar was an extremely prolific writer, his work was rarely translated and published abroad. Yet, this should not dim the scientific and policy contributions of his thoughts. This is the quintessential motivation and the point of the present publication – to present an overlooked author to the scientific and broader intellectual community.

---

[1] For Bučar's Biography see Pesek (2016), and for his Bibliography see Bučar (1993).

I can identify three reasons why his works were missed. First, time-space continuum: Bučar lived in a totalitarian state, with limited links with foreigners. This is also one of the reasons for the lack of other Eastern-European authors being published in the West. Still, Bučar did manage to forge relations with the likes of Otto von Habsburg (1912–2011) – the head of the House Habsburg and a long-term member of the European Parliament. It was Otto who invited Bučar to deliver a speech in the European Parliament in 1988 – presenting an argument for Slovenian independence and the dissolution of Yugoslavia. However, these relations were polity-oriented, and although they were relationships among intellectuals, their purpose was not academic but political. Nevertheless, it was exactly in the "independence period" that his, so far, the only, English book translation was published – *The Reality and Myth* (1989). The translation was a product of its time – Slovenian struggle of independence – and such was its substance and objective as well. Yet, some characteristics of his deeper theory were displayed between the lines; as Lucy Despard (1990, 194) wrote in her Foreign Affairs review of the book: "The Reality and the Myth is a general treatise on the communist system and its inability to adapt to reality without giving up its essence, the monopoly of power."

Second, history is written by the victors: capitalism and liberal democracy have won the Cold War. Similar to the previous reason, this can be viewed also as a general cause for the lack of English publications of Eastern-European authors. Although Bučar was a crucial individual in the Slovenian independence movement, which made him a sort of micro-level victor, he was still a part of the world which needed to undergo substantive modernization and reforms to implement democracy and capitalism. Thus, on the macro-level, and in the eyes of the West, he was a part of society that needs to be educated about the aforementioned terms. Therefore, a general narrative was that books should be translated into Slovene, not the other way around. In this context it was easier to publish English translations of Vaclav Havel and other play, prose, and poem writers, which were cultural not sociopolitical texts.

Third, every man is the smith of his own fortune: Bučar had several characteristics which impeded translation of his books. Besides being (overly) humble – not taking his own initiative to publish a translation in English – two other reasons are most significant. First, his texts are difficult to read, thus being less attractive. Bučar possessed many admirable qualities, but a good writer he was not. This does not mean that he was not clear or concise, his style was just inelegant. As such, the translator and language editor did an extraordinary job in the present volume. Second, there are many books to choose from – none serving as a sort of Bučar's trademark. As like so many great minds (e.g., Alfred Thayer Mahan) before him, Bučar did not write a single piece that would encompass his theory in detail. There is no single book dedicated entirely to explain his system theory, where he outlines his assumptions, independent variables, dependent variables, conditional variables, and intervening variables, and draws a causal map of logical connection of all those elements. Bučar briefly outlines his theory in several of his works. Therefore, the question arises, if translating Bučar becomes feasible, which book should be translated in order to encapsulate Bučar best for the wider global intellectual audience?

I have struggled with this issue extensively and at the end was left with two options – *Porušena harmonija sveta* (2003) and *Na novih razpotjih* (2006). At the end, I have decided for the latter, for several reasons – making it a better fit for the purpose of this publication. First, it is less Slovenia-focused than the former. Second, Bučar dedicates more space to describe his theory. Third, he applies his theory to a variety of issues, compared to the alternative, where he deals only with positivist meta-theory or philosophy. As such, the project *At a New Crossroads* had commenced.

So, what is it about? After the 2008 financial crisis, the question of ethics in politics, economy, and in broader social issues has come to the forefront. *At a New Crossroads* addresses the role of ethics in society, where Bučar normatively redefines national identity as the crux of his novel understanding of ethics. Using system theory, he addresses the problems of globalization and governance, presenting a postmodern synthesis of the logic of free flow of capital and global citizenship, with national and cultural identity. Speaking to contemporary society, he shows how society and ethical life are reproduced. Bučar provides us with new tools to think about national identity and global politics.

Why Read Bučar?

The present book is divided into two sections. First is a selection of essays, where scholars address different dimensions of France Bučar. These supplementary essays derive from the questions and premises that Bučar makes. They further explain, critically assess, or apply his thoughts. Second is the English translation of his book – *Na novih razpotjih*, or in English – *At a New Crossroads*.

I argue that the publication widens the diversity pool of the literature in three ways. First, in the theoretical sense – Bučar displays a unique system theory and novel ethical suggestions. His normative ethics is different from pragmatic or utilitarian approaches common to the Anglo-Saxon world (e.g., Dewey and Tufts 1932; Sidgwick 1981). Second, as analyzed above, few scholars from former Communist Eastern Europe have been published in English, and thus, their thoughts are arcane to the wider academic world. Such a publication can enrich the global intellectual community. Third, few scholars had the opportunity to put their thoughts and theories into practice. France Bučar is one such example. Bučar wrote the Slovenian constitution and declared its independence as its first president of the parliament. Since the book has been originally published in 2006, it is a product of both – Bučar's ideational capacity (Bučar as a scholar) and the political experience that he received during his years in office (Bučar as a politician). I believe that this type of scholarly work and these types of authors help bridge the divide between academia and practice.

As I display below, Bučar indeed developed a unique system theory, which has its own scholarly merit, and operationalizes ethics as a source of human and states' behavior. These two elements should be appealing for any academic and intellectual desiring "food for thought." Furthermore, the first section of the present book – the essays on

Bučar – analyzes and applies his system theory to a variety of issues. As such, this section presents the first comprehensive classification and study of his work in English.[2]

What Does Bučar Say?

Bučar's theory starts with a critique of the contemporary society and polity. Yet, he is not tossing anathema over them but uncovers two repugnant social dynamics, both rooted in positivism, which is, throughout his book, the main antagonist. First, herding, which Bučar defines as mindless acceptance of leveling-out of all cultures and personal identities. Thus, human rights are not based on ethics but in positivist desire to equate and measure society; for doing that one needs a unit, which should be the same everywhere – a human individual. Furthermore, he attributes the success of herding to apathy – a characteristic of intellectual and spiritual laziness. The phrase "nothing can be done" is for Bučar ethically contested. Second, nostalgia, which Bučar determines as a wish to return to traditional society, rejects the new civilizational circumstances and dimensions. "It was better before" state of mind dims prudence in seeking relevant and applicable answers to today's problems. Moreover, ignoring complexities and oversimplification does not offer desired solutions. Therefore, the author presents a prescription: a reconceptualization of individual and national identities, based on a novel understanding of ethics. Reason cannot reveal every dimension of human existence. For Bučar, ethics is an alternative source of human action and rationality, which is not rooted in positivism. Although he does not want to moralize, his work sets grounds for a new type of postmodern ethics. The greatness of his work lies in its skillful development of social critique without succumbing to the creation of a new ideology; yet, the book still offers solutions, although the Bučar is humbly reluctant to call his suggestions so.

Bučar reaches his conclusions through the analysis of different social issues, where he employs system theory. However, he argues that this scientific tool does not paint the whole picture, and consequently it cannot offer solutions to contemporary problems. As he claims in his Introduction to the present book – tools of the past are not applicable for today's issues. Thus, he presents an alternative – his unique system theory, where ethics is presented as the main feedback loop. Yet, doing so Bučar does not deny rationality, quite the contrary, his system theory is a rationalist zenith. Namely, it is an intellectual epiphany to admit to the limits of human intellect and science and incorporate other dimensions of human mind and existence. Similar to other authors (e.g., Ferry 2002), Bučar calls for openness toward the absolute transcendence.

---

[2] Elsewhere I have examined Bučar within the International Relations Theories (Kovač 2013); yet, this piece has been published in Slovene. Moreover, I have built upon Bučar's ethics – labeling it "geopolitical ethics" (Kovač 2014); however, this was only partial usage of Bučar's theory.

For Bučar this absolute is the new understanding of ethics, which he pinpoints in anti-collectivizing globalization, new individual identity, and recreation of national identity. The crux of his ethics is preservation of individual and cultural uniqueness. The individual and the nation are for Bučar sanctuaries. As it is ethical to oppose murder, or destruction of unique personal identity, in interpersonal relations, so too it is ethical to prevent genocide, or destruction of unique cultural-national identity, in international relations. Therefore, the other – person, culture, and nation – does not become the adversary but a value in and of itself. In this sense Bučar follows Emmanuel Levinas (2003). Yet, unlike Levinas, who was a personalist, Bučar's thoughts mainly concern European history and the EU; therefore, he is more interested in international relations. Nevertheless, he was influenced by Richard Coundenhove-Kalergi's (1923) statement that you are European, because you are German, French, Slovene, etc. For Bučar the individual must not neglect his own culture and national identity, for this deed equals to suicide or murder. Thus, it is not only a categorical imperative for an individual, but for nations as well, to preserve their and other unique cultural-national identities. As such, Bučar supplements the ethical considerations of classical realists (e.g., Niebuhr1932; Carr 1939; Morgenthau 1948), which argue that there are two sets of ethical norms – for individuals and for states. Contrary to them, Bučar remarkably applies the same ethical norms on two different images of analysis (Waltz 1959) or different levels of agencies (Wendt 1999). Moreover, he replaces the "top-down" globalization logic, which rejects any kind of differentiation, and advances the notion of "global citizenship," with a "bottom-up" ethical-cultural logic, where cultural identities are redefined so that the more one is, e.g., Spanish, the more one is European, and consequently the more one is cosmopolitan. As such he adjusts and furthers the idea of Constitutional Patriotism (Habermas 1997).

Thus, Bučar's theoretical starting point is synthesis, which has deeper philosophical grounds. Hay (2007) argues that we cannot prove ontological positions, or the relations between ontology and epistemology; rather, researchers adopt a specific position which makes most sense to them. Following Hay, Bučar may be classified as a scientific realist – foundationalist ontology (believing that the world is out there independent of the mind); however, the path to the real world may lead using positivist or interpretivist epistemology. Therefore, Bučar's meta-theoretical starting point is favorably set for synthesizing. On the ontological level, Bučar opposes the dialectics between material and ideational, and between agency and structure. For him these are all elements of the real world; therefore, the real question is how we can uncover them. As such, Bučar opposes the meta-theoretical thesis-antithesis pink-ponk, as scientific added value may be found in both – positivist and interpretivist research designs. There are few works deriving from either positivist or interpretivist camps that would commit to finding a new proposition with synthesis (e.g., Ragin 2000). However, in the last decade there is an increasing understanding on both sides for the need for such an inquiry (Lebow and Lichbach 2007). Yet, scientific realism enables Bučar to distinguish himself not only by being aware of the need for such studies but actually to conduct such an intellectual endeavor.

Most scholarly works referring to synthesis in Political Science come from a meta-theoretical standpoint labeled as scientific realism. It has gained traction in the recent years (e.g., Jackson 2011; Psillos 2005) particularly in its structural morphology – critical realism of Roy Bhaskar (e.g., Bhaskar and Hartwig 2010) and his followers (e.g., Kurki 2008; Wight 2006). However, these works remain on the level of philosophy of science and present little practical and operational suggestions for politics. Bučar, on the other hand, offers exactly the latter. He starts with a real-world problem and dives into resolving it using his analytical method – system theory. Through this analysis, he reveals the deficiencies of existing positivist system theories and presents his own system theory. Moreover, he unveils also his meta-theoretical positions and ultimately reaches suggestions for concrete steps on how to move forward in resolving the issue at hand. Thus, the work fills the gap in the synthesis literature in Political Science – making synthesis applicable for politics. Furthermore, due to his palpability, Bučar becomes appealing to the wider intellectual and policy audience, not only to academia.

Although critical to positivist philosophy, Bučar uses system theory – a typical positivistic concept – as his method of inquiry. This paradox is resolved when Bučar introduces ethics into the system theory, thus presenting a synthesis of positivist and interpretivist notions. With the rapid development of science and innovation after the Industrial Revolution, many concepts and their relations became opaque, which also reduced their effective utility. Thus, positivist philosophy developed a useful tool for modeling: general system theory – which was quickly adopted by natural sciences (e.g., Bertalanffy 1928) and subsequently also by social sciences (Parsons 1951). The system approach was a new type of organizing knowledge and it also opened space for new research questions. It emphasizes holism – system's elements form a distinctive unit, which is not only a conglomerate of its parts – and applies the logic of self-correcting and self-regulating feedback loops. Therefore, a particular system theory is determined by the structure of its constitutional elements (hierarchy or heterarchy) and the nature of the process and communication between these elements. Based on these two variables one can determine the uniqueness of Bučar's system theory compared to other authors. Several different types of system theory were developed after the general system theory: e.g., dialectical system theory (Čančer and Mulej 2010), theory of living systems (Miller 1978), soft systems theory (Wilson 2010), and critical system theory (Payne 1992). Some of these were already used in Political Science. Yet, none of them encapsulates Bučar's system. Thus, Bučar advances the system theory scholarship, as well as the scope of Political Science.

One of the first and most renowned applicants of system theory in Political Science was developed by David Easton (1953). Using a very simple system theory, defined by system's inputs, their conversion into the system, system's output, the feedback loop from the output to the input again, and the environment, which influences the feedback and the input into the system (Easton 1965), he analyzed political process and developed a definition of politics as the authoritative allocation of values for society. Easton stressed the structure of system's elements; the processes were limited to the feedback loop and the environment influence on the input of the system, their nature was not considered. Such a system theory suffered from a "black box" problem. This was addressed by Easton's fellow behaviorist Karl Deutsch, who opened the "black box" and created a more complex structured system theory, one that contains many subsystems – elements, with a variety of dyadic feedback loops – relations among elements (Deutsch 1963). This internal social dynamic is similar to the dynamics in an organism; hence, the title of his book – *The Nerves of the Government*. As in an organism, there is a clear hierarchy in government among the subsystems and who reports to whom – feedback loops. If Easton stressed structure, the followers of Deutsch began to focus on the relations and process among the subsystems. Therefore, the system theory inquiries in Political Science became increasingly close to cybernetics and applied to the study of communication. "The poster child" of such an approach was Niklas Luhmann. Luhmann is concerned with the communication among subsystems and between the system and the environment. Yet, he understands communication digitally – exchanging information, where interpretation of the information does not play a role (Luhmann 1977). As such, Luhmann may be characterized as anti-humanist, since he once stated that he is not interested in humans (Luhmann 1995).

Bučar's system is an antipode to Luhmann's. Although both built upon Deutsch, in fact Bučar said several times in his interviews that his biggest influence was indeed Karl Deutsch, Luhmann's and Bučar's system theories are worlds apart. Bučar supplements Deutsch and contrasts his theory from Luhmann's with two points. First, the individual – the system and subsystems are operated by individuals; therefore, a system theory should not exclude the individual. As such, for Bučar the key in understanding how a system functions is to understand the individual and his role in the subsystem. Therefore, the elements in the system should be defined based on the individuals or elites leading them. Second, related but distinct, ethics – since one cannot understand an individual and his actions without ethics, Bučar's analysis leads him to identify ethics as the crucial missing component of existing system theories. He understands ethics as the crucial feedback loop and corrective mechanism within the relations among subsystems and the system itself. Thus, Bučar normatively deducts prescriptions how system and individuals operating with a specific subsystem should work, and consequently also develops a distinguished system theory. Therefore, Bučar "brings the individual and agency back in" to the system theory. At this point the descriptive and prescriptive nature of his theory twist and its normative nature is displayed. Namely, through the descriptive analysis, Bučar argues that existing scientific concepts are inadequate to tackle contemporary problems. Yet, in order to ameliorate the sociopolitical situation, we need to create new analytical tools, such as his new system theory.

As Bučar presents a new synthesis of fundamental elements of the system theory – structure and relations – he also synthesizes when it comes to the understanding of ethics. Namely, he introduces a new type of postmodern ethics; not one where traditional (nation) and modern (individual) only co-exist, but one where they are integrated and create a new notion altogether. To merge the two, Bučar uses Weber's (1919) "ethics of responsibility" as a mechanism for their fusion. To look at the consequences of one's deeds, and follow the ethics of responsibility, requires a bold mind; yet, the latter is difficult to be acquired and consequently difficult to be expected from majority of people. Thus, Bučar subscribes to an elitist understanding of politics. In a Pareto (1935) sense – where spiritual, cultural, intellectual, political, economic, and other elites operate the social subsystems – the ethics of responsibility lies first and utmost with these elites. If the "Denmark elites are rotten," then also Denmark democracy, nor its people, cannot function as they normatively should. When Bučar applies his ethics into his system – as the main corrective mechanism or the crucial feedback loop – he positions himself next to Habermas's (1990) discourse ethics (universal obligation of communicative rationality). Still, the difference is that Bučar uses synthesis to supplement such a relational approach with constitutive approach – arguing that some fundamental ethical principles are not relational, agency-, or system-specific, but reflect the absolute. Thus, he applies Hans Küng's (1991) global ethos (four commitments: to a culture of nonviolence and respect for life, to a culture of solidarity and a just economic order, to a culture of tolerance and a life of truthfulness, and to a culture of equal rights and partnership between men and women) anew. As such, Bučar's ethics resembles ideas of Levinas (2001) and his ethics of "the other," where constitutive and relation dimensions of ethics are considered. Still, one could argue that Bučar applies Levinas to Political Science and more particularly to International Relations, since he talks about national and cultural identity and defines them as the absolute. These notions are not adversary to one another but complimentary. Therefore, they are considered ethical in and of themselves, and it is an ethical imperative to preserve them. Such bold statements also have clear policy implications: For example, it is a categorical imperative for all the nations and its leaders to prevent any genocide or cultural cleansing.

Organization of the Book

The following chapters are divided into two parts. First, four essays examine the present work of France Bučar. As he has applied his system theory onto a basket of issues, so too the conglomerate of scholars and issues tackled in these essays are interdisciplinary – ranging from Political Science, Economics, Law, and the Philosophy of Science. Two of the essays are theory oriented, and two are more practical or applicative in nature. Peter Verovšek examines different branches of Critical Theory and classifies Bučar within them. Mark Hamilton discusses system dynamics of Bučar's system theory. Urška Velikonja applies Bučar's system theory to the question of the ethics, rules, and regulations in financial economics. Finally, Matej Drev connects Bučar to the issue of artificial intelligence and inequality.

The second part consists of the English translation of the original text of Bučar's book *Na novih razpotjih*, or in English – *At a New Crossroads*. Moreover, to meet the terms of the Slovenian Research Agency, who has supported the translation, two reviews may be found in the appendix in their original form.

In his chapter Peter Verovšek provides a context for reading Bučar. He compares his ideas to those of the Frankfurt School, Praxis School, Ljubljana Lacanian School, and other Critical Theory authors. He concludes that Bučar is much closer to Habermas than to the likes of Žižek. Still, he also makes an argument, same as Mark Hamilton in a later chapter, that Bučar is in a way related to Max Weber due to their mutual commitments to synthesis.

The chapter reveals the richness and diversity of Critical Theory, and particularly the extent of theorizing within this paradigm in former Yugoslavia. Verovšek is fully aware that the members of Praxis School, as well as Bučar, suffered tremendously under totalitarianism. His objective and narrative are not to write an apologia for a communist regime as if the state was open for free exchange and development of ideas, but to point out the unbelievable amount of theory development in an unlikely time and space – the heyday of totalitarian state.

Moreover, what is intriguing is the fact that Verovšek does not, and in fact could not, include all branches of Critical Theory pursued in Slovenia. In fact, such an endeavor would require its own book-length manuscript, and the author rightfully sets certain time-frame limitations. Unfortunately, many interesting ideas consequently did not make the cut. In my mind, the most significant of them were the Christian Socialists – Andrej Gosar, Vekoslav Grmič, Edvard Kocbek, and Janez Evangelist Krek. Christian Socialists were extremely influential social movement in Slovenia before the Second World War and greatly impacted Bučar's ideas. What is unparalleled is the political power that Christian Socialists had in Slovenia. Whereas in Germany they obtained low single digests at the elections; in Slovenia, their score moved around a third of the votes. Furthermore, it is worth pointing out that Bučar was labeled as the last Christian Socialists by Slovenian media and intellectuals, among them also Rudi Šeligo – Slovenian writer, playwright, essayist, and the former Slovenian minister of culture.

Verovšek's contribution opens several future research questions. First, if one defines Bučar as a critical theorist, then how does that reconcile with the role of agency and freedom that Bučar stresses? Or more generally, is there room for agency in Western Marxism? Second, following the first skeptical question, since Bučar emphasizes the role of individuals – their responsibility and freedom – would it be more appropriate to classify him within the liberal camp? Third, deriving from both previous questions – is there potential for a synthesis between Marxism and liberalism (e.g., Kandiyali 2013), and is Bučar the link?

In his chapter Mark Hamilton neatly explains the history and utility of the system theory in analyzing a complex world. Furthermore, he displays how Bučar's system theory is convenient for policy makers. Nevertheless, he points to a paradox-like problem when it comes to Bučar's theory, which Hamilton labels as optimism.

Namely, Hamilton argues that although Bučar's theory is very applicable for policy makers, Bučar himself seems to neglect the policy-making process. Thus, Bučar implies that if the diagnosis of the state of the system is performed well, then solutions or an exact pathway of reforms flow logically and automatically from such an analysis. For Bučar if all the feedback loops are in place, the system will be able to adapt and change appropriately. As such, paradoxically, although he stresses the role of individuals and elites which operate the subsystems, Bučar underestimates the problem of decision-making process. To make the paradox even greater, the suboptimal reactions of the system may not happen due to the ir(rationality) of individuals, or the bureaucratic nature of decision making (Allison 1971), or human corruption, which are all the causes that Bučar deals with, but they can occur due to a more fundamental issue, the very nature of micro-politics. Namely, to reach a desired outcome several policies, deriving from the same diagnosis as well as fulfill the ethical criteria, may be pursued. "God draws straight lines with curves" is a saying that applies to politics. It is uncertain what the best policy choice is, no matter how long and strong the list of criteria one makes. Politics is not digital in nature. Identifying a problem does not mean I have identified its solution. Yet, Bučar appears to treat it as such. Strangely, since one would not expect this from someone who is critical of positivism.

Therefore, I think a more appropriate adjective to label Bučar with would be naïve, or idealist, not optimist. Nevertheless, Hamilton also makes an appealing comparison between Bučar and Polanyi. Both authors see the divide between a market economy and the nation-state as artificially generated. When Bučar makes a case for state-private enterprise partnership, what would strike a chord with geoeconomy (e.g., Csurgai 2017), intelligence (e.g., Potter 1998), and cybersecurity (e.g., Harknett and Stever 2009) literature, he resembles the "Market Society" argument of Polanyi.

In her chapter Urška Velikonja applies Bučar's theory on a contemporary legal debate in the United States – nonenforcement of legal provisions. The essay attests the general applicability of Bučar's system theory – not only can it be used in different fields of scientific inquiry, but it also cuts across cultural and geographical fault lines.

It is important to note that the topic of the paper is not concerned with the nonenforcement due to the incompetence or any other malfunction of an individual or subsystem. Instead, what Velikonja does is explain nonenforcement as a strategic political behavior or action of a subsystem and/or individual. She eloquently refers to the literature on power and draws parallels with Bučar.

Bučar's theory becomes of great value in explaining the nonenforcement, since he positions ethics as one of the sources of behavior, also legal (non)action. American legal tradition struggles in developing a theory of nonenforcement. Since it equates law with ethics, there is no room for a normative justification of nonenforcement. Yet, Bučar enables it. He positions ethics not only as a component of legal subsystem but also as a part of politics. Ethics is the main feedback loop for all subsystems. Therefore, politics and law are not juxtaposed against each other in a check and balance relations but are rather two subsystems in partnership with each other. Thus, ethics and normative behavior, stimulus of one's action and justification for it, can derive from either of the two - politics and law - or in fact both. Structurally the same argument, but with regard to the relationship between politics and economy, is presented by Hamilton and applied by Drev in their chapters respectively.

Velikonja builds upon Bučar in setting several recommendations in how to deal with legal nonenforcement.

In his chapter Matej Drev analyzes the coming challenge of artificial intelligence for the labor markets. The issue at hand is that the challenge is specific to individual economic sectors: some sectors are more exposed than others. More importantly, the challenge does not present itself gradually, but abruptly. Namely, once the challenge arises – new technology is developed for a specific sector – it immediately replaces the human workforce. As such, a danger of instant inflow of unemployment is created. Therefore, in order to avoid the negative externalities of development of this technology, the state needs to be ready to tackle sudden spikes of unemployment, since the market itself will not have the capacity to correct the situation in a timely manner.

As such, Bučar's argument of state-private enterprise partnership, which he develops in chapter 7 of his book, becomes extremely relevant. Drev applies Bučar's ideas onto the challenge posed by artificial intelligence and develops several policy recommendations. Moreover, Drev draws parallels to Polanyi, which was also pointed out by Hamilton in this volume.

Literature

Allison, G. T. (1971). *Essence of decision*. Boston: Little Brown.
von Bertalanffy, L. (1928). *Kritische Theorie der Formbildung*. Berlin: Gebrüder Borntraeger.
Bhaskar, R., & Hartwig, M. (Eds.). (2010). *The formation of critical realism: A personal perspective*. London: Routledge.
Bučar, F. (1989). *The reality and myth*. Antigonish: St. Francis Xavier University Press.
Bučar, F. (1993). *Prehod čez rdeče morje*. Ljubljana: Založba Mihelač.
Bučar, F. (2003). *Porusena harmonija sveta*. Dob pri Domžalah: Miš.
Bučar, F. (2006). *Na novih razpotjih*. Celje: Celjska Mohorjeva družba.
Carr, E. H. (1946). *The twenty years' crisis, 1919–1939: An introduction to the study of international relations*. New York: Macmillan and Company.
Csurgai, G. (2017). The increasing importance of geoeconomics in power rivalries in the twenty-first century. *Geopolitics, 23*(1), 1–9.
Coudenhove-Kalergi, R. N. (1923). *Pan-Europa*. Vienna: Pan-Europa Verlag.
Despard, L. (1990). Yugoslavia: Socialism, development and debt; The reality and the myth. *Foreign Affairs, 69*(4), 194.
Čančer, V., & Mulej, M. (2010). The dialectical systems theory's capacity for multi-criteria decision-making. *Systems research and behavioral science, 27*(3), 285–300.
Deutsch, K. W. (1963). *The nerves of government; Models of political communication and control*. London: The Free Press.
Dewey, J., & Tufts, J. H. (1932). *Ethics. New York: H. Holt and company*.
Easton, D. (1953). *The political system. New York*: Knopf.
Easton, D. (1965). *A framework for political analysis*. Englewood Cliffs: Prentice-Hall.
Ferry, L. (2002). *Man made god: the meaning of life*. Chicago: University of Chicago Press.
Habermas, J. (1990). *Moral consciousness and communicative ethics*. Cambridge: MIT Press.
Habermas, J. (1997). *A berlin republic: writings on Germany*. Lincoln: University of Nebraska Press.

Harknett, R. J., & Stever, J. A. (2009). The cybersecurity triad: Government, private sector part-
    ners, and the engaged cybersecurity citizen. *Journal of Homeland Security and Emergency
    Management*, 6(1), 1–14.
Hay, C. (2007). Does ontology trump epistemology? Notes on the directional dependence of ontol-
    ogy and epistemology in political analysis. *Politics*, 27(2), 115–119.
Jackson, P. T. (2010). *The conduct of inquiry in international relations: Philosophy of science and
    its implications for the study of world politics*. London: Routledge.
Kandiyali, J. (2013). Marxism and liberalism: A new synthesis. *Res Publica*, 19(4), 387–391.
Kovač, I. (2013). Filozofija Franceta Bučarja znotraj tokov mednarodnih odnosov: "geopolitična
    etika" in post-pozitivna znanstvena paradigma. *Anthropos*, 45(3–4), 31–55.
Kovač, I. (2014). EU in the struggle for global governance: geopolitical ethics. *International
    Journal of Diplomacy and Economy*, 2(1–2), 118–138.
Kurki, M. (2008). *Causation in international relations: Reclaiming causal analysis*. Cambridge:
    Cambridge University Press.
Küng, H. (1991). *Global responsibility: In search of a new world ethic*. New York: Crossroad.
Lebow, R., & Lichbach, M. (Eds.). (2007). *Theory and evidence in comparative politics and inter-
    national relations*. London: Palgrave Macmillan.
Levinas, E. (2001). *Alterity and transcendence*. New York: Columbia University Press.
Levinas, E. (2003). *Humanism of the other*. Urbana: University of Illinois Press.
Luhmann, N. (1977). Differentiation of society. *Canadian Journal of Sociology/Cahiers canadiens
    de sociologie*, 2(1), pp. 29–53.
Luhmann, N. (1995). *Social systems*. Palo Alto: Stanford University Press.
Miller, J. G. (1978). *Living systems*. New York: McGraw-Hill.
Morgenthau, H. (1948). *Politics among nations: The struggle for power and peace*. New York:
    Kopf.
Niebuhr, R. (1932). *Moral man and immoral society: A study in ethics and politics*. New York:
    Charles Scribner's Sons.
Pareto, V. (1935). *The mind and society*. New York: Harcourt, Brace and Company.
Parsons, T. (1951). *The social system*. London: The Free Press.
Payne, S. L. (1992). Critical systems thinking: A challenge or dilemma in its practice?. *Systemic
    Practice and Action Research*, 5(3), 237–249.
Pesek, R. (2016). *Bučar*. Celovec: Mohorjeva.
Potter, E. H. (Ed.). (1998). *Economic intelligence and national security*. Ottawa: Carleton
    University Press.
Psillos, S. (2005). *Scientific realism: How science tracks truth*. London: Routledge.
Ragin, C. C. (2000). *Fuzzy-set social science*. Chicago: University of Chicago Press.
Sidgwick, H. (1981). *The methods of ethics*. Indianapolis: Hackett Publishing.
Waltz, K. N. (1959). *Man, the state, and war: A theoretical analysis*. Columbia University Press.
Wendt, A. (1999). *Social theory of international politics*. Cambridge: Cambridge University Press.
Weber, M. (1958). Politics as a Vocation. In H. H. Gerth & W. Mills (Eds.), *From Max Weber:
    Essays in sociology* (pp. 129–158). New York: Oxford University Press.
Wight, C. (2006). *Agents, structures and international relations: Politics as ontology*. Cambridge:
    Cambridge University Press.
Wilson, B. (2001). *Soft systems methodology*. New York: Wiley.

Contents

Contributors

Matej Drev is an applied economist, having obtained his Ph.D. in Public Policy and Management from Carnegie Mellon University. Formerly a faculty member at the Georgia Institute of Technology, he now serves as a strategy and corporate finance consultant with one of the world's premier management consulting firms.

Mark Hamilton serves as Professor of Multidimensional Security and teaches Conflict Analysis and Resolution at the Inter-American Defense College (IADC) in Washington, DC. He earned his M.A. in International Development and Ph.D. in International Relations at American University, where he still serves as an adjunct faculty member. Hamilton's research examines multidimensional approaches to peace and security and explores why and how young people are mobilized into violent and nonviolent movements, grounded by his systems modeling and diverse field experiences in Latin America, South Asia, and Middle East.

Igor Kovač is a Ph.D. candidate at the University of Cincinnati and in 2018–2019 predoctoral fellow at the Institute for Security and Conflict Studies at the George Washington University. His dissertation project develops a new theory of persistence imbalance of power – Pervasive Hegemony. Kovač received his MAIS at Diplomatic Academy of Vienna in 2012. Moreover, in 2010 he also received a MS in Sport Science from University of Ljubljana. His research projects are tied to security studies, grand strategy, power, geopolitics, political economy, intelligence, and cybersecurity.

Jure Leskovec is an Associate Professor of Computer Science at Stanford University where he is a member of the *InfoLab* and the *AI lab*. He has joined the department in September 2009. He is also working as Chief Scientist at *Pinterest*, where he is focusing on machine learning problems. Leskovec has cofounded a machine learning startup Kosei, which was acquired by Pinterest, and in 2008/09 he was a postdoctoral researcher at Cornell University working with Jon Kleinberg and

Dan Huttenlocher. He has completed his Ph.D. in Machine Learning Department, School of Computer Science at Carnegie Mellon University under the supervision of Christos Faloutsos in 2008.

Urška Velikonja is a Professor of Law, Georgetown University Law Center. She graduated first in her class at the University of Ljubljana School of Law with an LL.B. degree in 2002 and received her LL.M. from Harvard Law School in 2003. She received her J.D. *magna cum laude* from Harvard Law School in 2009. Prior to entering academia, Velikonja clerked for Judge Stephen F. Williams of the US Court of Appeals for the D.C. Circuit and worked as a banking and finance associate with an Austrian law firm in her native Slovenia. She previously taught at Emory University School of Law. Professor Velikonja writes primarily about securities regulation and enforcement. Her recent scholarship has appeared in the *Yale Law Journal*, the *Stanford Law Review*, the *California Law Review*, the *Cornell Law Review*, and many other journals. Professor Velikonja's work is regularly discussed by regulators and has been featured in major newspapers, including the *New York Times*, the *Wall Street Journal*, the *Economist*, the *Financial Times*, and other media.

Peter J. Verovšek is Lecturer (Assistant Professor) in Politics/International Relations in the Department of Politics at the University of Sheffield. His forthcoming book, *The European Rupture: A Critical Theory of Memory and Integration in the Wake of Total War*, develops a narrative theory of remembrance as a resource for political change and analyzes the role that collective memories of Europe's age of total war played in the origins and development of the European Union. His work on critical theory, collective memory, European politics, and transitional justice has been published in *Perspectives on Politics*, the *Review of Politics*, *Political Studies*, *Memory Studies*, *Constellations*, the *European Legacy*, *Millennium*, the *Journal of Cold War Studies*, and the *Critical Review of International Social and Political Philosophy*.

Part I
Reflections on France Bučar

Eastern Praxis and Western Critique: France Bučar's Critical Systems Theory in Context

Peter J. Verovšek

The former Yugoslavia was the site of unorthodox thinking on multiple fronts during the postwar period (1945–89). Within international politics, Josip Broz Tito's "non-aligned movement" attempted to find a third way within the bifurcated Cold War system, which forced most states to choose between the capitalist, democratic West supported by the United States and the communist, authoritarian East under the leadership of the Soviet Union (Willetts 1978). Yugoslavia's orthogonal social and political position was also visible within its domestic policy, which sought to split the difference between the two dominant socio-economic systems by developing a "self-management market socialism" that relied "on markets to guide both domestic and international production and exchange, with the socialist element coming from the 'social ownership' and workers' self-management of enterprises (Estrin 1991, 187; see also Howard 2001; Flaherty 1992)."

Beyond politics, the intellectual environment in postwar Yugoslavia displayed similar non-conformist tendencies. Although the Communist Party continued to make use of the tools of repression and censorship after Tito's 1948 break with Joseph Stalin, "southern Slavic" theorists were able to develop a variety of theoretical syntheses that departed from the orthodox scientific Marxism-Leninism professed by the rest of the communist bloc. These idiosyncratic interpretations often united Marxist ideas with a decidedly non-Leninist humanism (Gruenwald 1983). Although many of these unorthodox thinkers eventually ran into trouble with the authorities and ended up as dissidents, they were able to develop and publish their ideas in a much more open atmosphere than those working in the Soviet Union or elsewhere in the Warsaw Pact.

France Bučar's work must be understood within this broader geopolitical and intellectual context. Bučar was an engaged politician and thinker during the communist period, becoming even more visible in the aftermath of Slovenian independence,

P. J. Verovšek (✉)
Department of Politics, University of Sheffield, Elmfield, Sheffield, UK
e-mail: p.j.verovsek@sheffield.ac.uk

© Springer International Publishing AG, part of Springer Nature 2019
I. Kovač (ed.), *At His Crossroad*, https://doi.org/10.1007/978-3-319-78331-4_1

in which he played a crucial role (e.g., Bučar 2007). As a citizen of a small nation, he was keenly aware of the dangers posed by the development of the state, with its "merciless suppression of everything that did not conform to the prevailing characteristics of the dominant nationality." This awareness grounded his support of European integration and of the Pan-European movement, whose Slovenian chapter he helped to refound in 1992. However, he also remained cognizant of the continued importance of the nation as a reservoir of national solidarity and belonging. He therefore argued (Bučar 1993, 34): "The Europe of the future is not only an extension of the present national state into a higher supra-national level. It needs a complex rearrangement which does not negate the national state but adds a series of new structural elements of greater complexity, characterized by the spirit of these complex times."

These comments about the complexity of the post-Cold War world also testify to Bučar's attempts to link his political activity to his intellectual work by developing his own approach to critical systems theory. In the intellectual sphere – just as in the political realm – understanding the environment in which he was working is crucial. Bučar's evaluation of Yugoslavia's experiments in self-management socialism is particularly interesting. He emphasizes the continued dependence on the state to assume the "burden of general education, as well as to provide social security as a condition for effective social production and general social stability." Adopting language reminiscent of one of his primary intellectual touchstones, the German economic historian and sociologist Max Weber (1958, 129–158), Bučar expresses his doubts regarding the ability of self-management to effectively match up to the imperatives of the economic system by noting that the "development of science and technology led to a situation in which the use of such indirect means to satisfy social needs was no longer possible (Bučar 1978, 418)."

Unlike the orthodox thinkers within the Soviet Union and its broader sphere of influence, Bučar was able to explore theoretical resources beyond the works of Karl Marx and Friedrich Engels. He retained at least some of this intellectual freedom even after his expulsion from the Communist Party in 1963. Ironically, this dismissal actually allowed led him to engage even more deeply with the groundbreaking work of Weber than he otherwise could have. Additionally, unlike Western interpreters, who had to overcome their aversion to Weber's post-World War I reactionary nationalism (especially in Germany) or had to separate his ideas from the influential but "erroneous" interpretations his English-language translator Talcott Parsons, Bučar was free to explore Weber's thought without such preconceptions (Cohen et al. 1975, 236).

My goal here is not to provide an analysis or even an outline of Bučar's critical systems theory; this has been done elsewhere (Kovač 2013). Neither is it to explore the impact of Weber on his thought in detail. Instead, I aim to situate Bučar and his work in the broader context of postwar socialist Yugoslavia. Understanding this geopolitical and intellectual environment is crucial because it shaped the conditions of possibility for his synthesis of Marxist emancipatory criticism with Weberian systems theory.

In particular, I aim to bring Bučar into conversation with the most important movement that sought to bring Marx together with Weber from the Western side of the Iron Curtain, i.e. the Frankfurt School of critical theory. In addition to its intrinsic importance to the history of twentieth century continental political thought, and the surprising historical connections of this movement to those within communist Yugoslavia, this comparison is also interesting because – like Bučar – the primary postwar exponent of critical theory, the philosopher and sociologist Jürgen Habermas, sought to combine systems theory with social criticism.

My argument is organized as follows. I start by tracing out the broad contours of the unorthodox interpretations of Marx that flourished in postwar Yugoslavia, focusing on the "Praxis School" and its ties to western scholars of the "young Marx." I pay particularly close attention to the links between Habermas and the Frankfurt School. In the second section, I examine how Bučar's engagement with Marx and Weber relates to the famous debate about systems theory that took place between Habermas and Niklas Luhmann in West Germany in the 1970s and 80s.[1] I argue that certain aspects of Bučar's critical systems theory bear a striking resemblance to Habermas's own attempts to integrate Weberian insights into his own version of critical theory. I conclude by reflecting on how Bučar's work can be understood as a combination of Eastern praxis with Western critique.

The Intellectual Context of Postwar Yugoslavia

Although many intellectuals within the communist bloc "questioned the uncompromising dogma that passed for Marxism in these countries," one of the most visible and interesting was the movement of Yugoslav dissidents collectively known as the Praxis School. The work of this group is preserved in the eponymous journal they produced between 1964 and 1974, whose board brought together an interdisciplinary selection of theorists from Serbia, Croatia and Slovenia (Massey 1991, 224).[2] Their version of humanist Marxism drew on the discovery of the so-called "young Marx," i.e. the Marx that emerged as a result of the discovery of his previously unpublished texts in the first half of the twentieth century. In these early philosophical writings, Marx builds on the concept of alienation (*Entfremdung*) to develop a critical social theory that is at odds with the more economic, "scientific" Marxism propounded by orthodox thinkers within the Soviet Union and the rest of the Eastern bloc. As Marx's "Economic and Philosophical Manuscripts" of 1844 and his other previously unknown texts became available, they were enthusiastically welcomed in the West because they provided a basis for the conceptualization of "a non-Leninist Marxist society (Massey 1991, 224; Bell 1962, 355–392)."

---

[1] Although I will focus on these two variants, many other interpretations of critical systems theory exist. For an overview, see Bausch (2001).

[2] The journal actually had both a domestic and an international edition. The foreign contributors include Jürgen Habermas, Lucien Goldman, Herbert Marcuse, André Gorz, Norman Birnbaum and Donald Hodges, among others.

Although the work of the Praxis School was eclectic, it fit within this broader movement – which also included the Western Marxism of the Frankfurt School – that read Marx primarily as a social theorist. Its members, including Gajo Petrović, Mihailo Marković, Rudi Šupek, Svetozar Stojanović, Veljko Rus and the other regular contributors to the journal, sought to reinterpret Marxism as "a body of thought which is uncompromising in its rejection of all forms of human alienation, exploitation, oppression and injustice, regardless of the type of society – bourgeois or socialist – in which these phenomena occur." More concretely, "the consistent and thorough realization of the goal of workers' self-management was the overriding passion of the Praxis theorists (Sher 1977, 258–259, 263)."

Although the members of the group ran into trouble with the authorities – leading to the shuttering of their house journal in 1974 – their work gained critical acclaim in the West, opening the door for intellectual dialogue across the Iron Curtain (Cohen 1974, 32–33). Most notably – and most importantly for my purposes here – they managed to draw the attention of the thinkers working within the Frankfurt School of critical theory. These Western Marxists saw "the Yugoslav writers associated with the journal *Praxis* /as/ their kindred souls. Better yet, their writings bore the stamp of authenticity, of first-hand experience (Massey 1991, 228)."

This mutual interest – which was spurred by the Praxis School's own desire to compare their own attempts to create a humanistic socialism in Yugoslavia to the social democratic, welfare state experiments of the West – was formalized in a number of ways. For example, Herbert Marcuse, a core member of the *Institut für Sozialforschung* (Institute for Social Research, the institutional home of the Frankfurt School), who later became the doyen of the New Left in the United States, is listed as a member of the Advisory Council to the journal "Praxis" in 1967 (Massey 1991, 236). On an intellectual level, the connection between the two groups was institutionalized through the establishment of a joint international "summer school" of leftist social and political thought.

Originally organized on the Croatian island of Korčula between 1963 and 1968, the meetings were banned after Tito's crackdown on the Praxis School and the dismissal of eight of its members from the University of Belgrade (the so-called "Belgrade 8"). However, just at this time the Inter-University Centre for Post-Graduate Studies was founded in Dubrovnik with the express intent of sponsoring international conferences and discussions between East and West. Taking advantage of this opportunity, Gajo Petrović, a Praxis contributor from Zagreb, asked Jürgen Habermas to coordinate and codirect a summer "seminar-conference" under the general title "Philosophy and Social Science" that would recreate the discussions that had previously taken place on Korčula. Habermas enthusiastically agreed, both due to his own interest in developing a "humanist Marxism" and as "a gesture of solidarity with our Yugoslavian colleagues." Habermas's international stature meant that for a certain period these summer meetings were "the only place where the Belgrade 8 could give public lectures and participate in public discussions in Yugoslavia (Bernstein 2017, 272)."

The debates of the summer "conference-seminar" quickly moved beyond Marx to include thinkers like Weber, Parsons and Luhmann, integrating these Western thinkers into Yugoslavian philosophical discourse. In addition to discussions about the key touchstones of twentieth century social and political thought, the Dubrovnik meetings also brought many leading thinkers to Yugoslavia. Over the years, the speakers included Claus Offe, Charles Taylor, Richard Rorty, Steven Lukes, Anthony Giddens, Gayatri Spivak, Cornelius Castoriadis, Agnes Heller, Axel Honneth, Seyla Benhabib, Nancy Fraser, Andrew Arato, Jean Cohen, Rainer Forst and Judith Butler among many, many others (Bernstein 2017, 273).[3] These international theorists brought with them the leading methods and approaches of contemporary social science in the West, including debates about positivism and systems theory. This intellectual cross-pollination surely played a role in helping Bučar to develop his own unorthodox approach to critical systems theory.

In addition to contributing to the broader intellectual milieu of Yugoslavia, these developments also played a role in shaping Bučar's narrower environment within Slovenia. Indeed, one of the most important intellectual debates in Yugoslavian social and political thought occurred in Slovenia at the annual meeting of the Yugoslav Association of Philosophy and Sociology in 1960. Although Tito's break with Stalin had occurred in 1948, scientific interpretations of Marx that subordinated ideas to material conditions continued to dominate the country's educational institutions and ideological apparatus. At the meeting, which was held in the Alps at the resort town on the shores of Lake Bled, Mihailo Marković emphatically rejected this orthodox approach.

Although Yugoslavia's vibrant intellectual culture prevented him from pointing to a single strain of opposition to Soviet Marxism, Marković was able to divide its opponents into two groups. The first sought a "positivist reduction of philosophy to a quasi-objective science." By contrast, the second – represented by Marković and the other thinkers of the Praxis School – wanted "to develop Marxism as a critical science (Marković 1976, 71–72)."

Regardless of their internal disagreement, representatives of both positions found common cause in their rejection of the official, more dogmatic interpretations of Marx (Petrović 1967, 319; Šupek 1972, 328–331). In the subsequent discussion, these unorthodox thinkers were able to defeat "the dogmatists." They did so in large part through their "experimentation with a diversity of ideas, ranging from those of the American pragmatists to the Vienna Circle of logical positivists (Massey 1991, 232)."

Unfortunately, we do not know if Bučar himself was present on this occasion. However, his mixture of heterogeneous intellectual resources is undoubtedly indebted to the discussions of the 1960 Bled congress (Sher 1977, 280).[4] Bučar's own critique of positivism, which seeks to preserve certain quantitative aspects of

---

[3] These meetings continue to this day. However, as a result of the Yugoslavian civil war, since 1992 they have been held in Prague under the auspices of the Institute of Philosophy at the Academy of Sciences of the Czech Republic in cooperation with Charles University. I am proud to be a regular participant at these meetings, which continue the tradition of the Praxis summer school, even though my name has been misspelled (Verošek instead of Verovšek) in the official list of participants published for the 25th anniversary of the relocation of the conference to Prague. See The Prague Conference: Directors, General Themes, Plenaries, Workshops (2017).

[4] Bučar's name is not included in a partial list of participants, but he may still have been present.

the study of society and politics while stressing the role of the individual and of ethical conduct, displays some similarities to Marković's rejection of this approach in favor of "emancipatory practice (or simply praxis) /.../ understood as an integral (individual or social) activity abolishing the bounds of human freedom and self-realization (Marković 1987, 119)."

In addition to mentioning how Bučar's thought fits within his broader intellectual environment, it is also worth considering how it diverges from it. Although his critical systems theory pushes against much of the philosophy and social science as practiced in postwar Yugoslavia, it also differs from the dominant approach in Slovenia (Stamm 2005). Although Slavoj Žižek is in many ways a singular figure – it might even be better to call him a singular global phenomenon – his blend of Marxist critical theory and psychoanalysis inspired by the work of Jacques Lacan is hardly unique in the Slovenian capital of Ljubljana. On the contrary, it is part of a broader Lacanian school that seeks to theorize "a dynamic freedom that enables us to question the very presuppositions of the circuit of Capital." In addition to Žižek, this group includes other Slovenian philosophers such as Mladen Dolar and Alenka Zupančič. In considering them as a part of a unified movement, Benjamin Day argues, "The Slovene Lacanians are perhaps the only proper 'school' of neomarxist thinkers to emerge since Habermas built a following and, even then, the Slovenes are much more coherent as a group in terms of their intellectual framework and politics (Day 2004, 1)."

What is interesting about this group in light of my discussion of the importance of Habermas and the Frankfurt School to the history of the Praxis School are the differences between these two approaches to critical theory. On the one hand, the Frankfurt School attempts to blend psychoanalysis with Marxism through the work of Sigmund Freud. Building on the Vienna-based thinker's faith in the power of the "talking cure," the Frankfurt School contends that self-awareness of an existing social pathology (*Sozialpathologie*) is the first step to generating a rational solution to it (Freud 1990, 8). In particular, Habermas argues that this "Freudo-Marxists" approach to critical theory builds on psychoanalysis as the "methodology of self-reflection" in the sense that it "terminates in a transformation of the affective-motivational basis, just as it begins with the need for practical transformation (Habermas 1971, 214, 241–242)."

By contrast, what might be called the Ljubljana School of "Lacano-Marxism" is much less rationalistic. Instead of seeking solutions in "ideology critique" (*Ideologiekritik*) or in accounts of "reflective unacceptability" that seek to show the members of a society that – upon proper consideration – they would not agree with certain existing social practices, the Slovenain Lacanians show much less faith in the power of self-awareness to bring about social or psychological transformation (Geuss 1981, 62). On the contrary, they argue that social pathologies of the kind identified by the Frankfurt School are not supported ideologically, but through fetishes that "enable/e/ us to carry on participating in social practices we no longer necessarily believe in." As Žižek puts it in "Welcome to the Desert of the Real!" (2002), "this is how we are believers today – we make fun of our beliefs, while continuing to practice them, that is, to rely on them as the underlying structure of our daily practices (Day 2004, 12; Žižek 2002, 71)."

This is not the place for an in-depth analysis of the differences between the Frankfurt and Ljubljana Schools of critical theory. However, this comparison – even in the brief outlines I have provided here – is important for situating Bučar's intellectual project. More specifically, it is notable how much closer his philosophical approach is to that of the Frankfurt School than to the Slovenian Lacanians despite his physical proximity to the latter. In contrast to the Ljubljana School, and in a manner much more reminiscent of his colleagues in Frankfurt, Bučar's approach is based on reason and maintains a certain faith in the potential of human agency. Much like the Frankfurters and the Praxis Group, Bučar is also more interested having theory speak to practice than his compatriots from Ljubljana.[5]

Additionally, following Weber, whose thought also hugely influenced German critical theory, Bučar is wary of the rise of instrumental reason (*Zweckrationalität*) and of the potential for "autopoietic" (literally, "self-creating") economic and administrative systems to override the normative steering-capacities of human agents within modern legal-rational regimes of rule (*Herrschaft*). In this respect too, his work is more reminiscent of the Frankfurt School, and particularly the work of Habermas, than of the Slovenian Lacanians. This connection – to which I now turn – further emphasizes his unique position within the intellectual context of postwar Yugoslavia and post-independence Slovenia (Day 2004, 2).

Towards a Critical Systems Theory

Habermas's work represents a particularly interesting Western parallel to Bučar's approach, given the Frankfurt theorist's own attempt to combine the insights of systems theory with Marxist social critique. This interest is most visible in his high-profile dispute (*Streit*) about systems theory with its main twentieth century exponent, Niklas Luhmann (Habermas and Luhmann 1971). At the most basic level, this debate, like Bučar's own work, addresses the "alternative between an emancipatory social philosophy and /.../ social technology (Knodt 1994, 81)."

In contrast to Habermas's attempts to preserve humanity's discursive control over the forms of technical or instrumental rationality that he interprets as the main causes of alienation in the late modern world (in this sense his work can be seen as an attempt to update the young Marx's analysis of *Entfremdung*), Luhmann argues that these autopoetic systems not only "produce and change their own *structures*," but are also closed to interference by social agents due to the fact that "everything that is used as a unit by the system is produced by the system itself." Despite this internal logic, Luhmann contends that such systems do retain a sensitivity to the outside environment. Although they do not "create a world of their own" externally, each system "operat/es/ within a world of its own" internally (Luhmann 1990, 3).

---

[5] This shared desire is also the root for another similarities between Bučar and the Frankfurt School: their mutual interest in American pragmatism. See Rehg and Bohman (2001).

The descriptive differences between the positions of Habermas and Luhmann point directly to their core theoretical and ethical disagreements. On the first dimension, Habermas argues that social action ought to be governed by discursive political agreement, whereas Luhmann contends that late modern societies are too complex for this kind of consensual decision-making, requiring impersonal systemic regulation instead. On the second dimension, Habermas holds that systemic regulation along the lines Luhmann defends violates human agency, creating a democratic deficit by reducing social policy to mechanical control. By contrast, Luhmann argues that given the irreducible pluralism within modern societies, which makes normative agreement impossible even in cases where the simplicity of social processes still could potentially be governed by collective human agency, only impersonal, positive laws governed by systemic processes can act as sufficient safeguards of individual and community rights (Bausch 1997, 315–316).

These conflicting positions – one based on Marx's emancipatory social theory, the other on the autonomous control of objective, self-regulating systems – can be summed up in two quotations from the central protagonists. On the one hand, Luhmann insists, "The basic reality of society can no longer be said to lie in its capacity to generate and sustain interaction system. /.../ In view of this, moralistic demands for more 'personal participation' in social processes are hopelessly out of touch with social reality." On the other hand, Habermas notes that if Luhmann is right, then "individuals henceforth belong only to the environment of their social systems. In relation to them society takes on an objectivity that can no longer be brought into the intersubjective context of life, for it is no longer related to subjectivity." Given that this situation represents an untenable "dehumanization of society," Habermas seeks to segregate certain aspects of life from the operation of functional systems (Luhmann 1982, 78; Habermas and Henrich 1974, 60).

Although Habermas resists Luhmann's application of systems theory to almost all areas of late modern social life, he agrees that such impersonal structures do indeed regulate much of contemporary social life. In fact, he even agrees that they must do so given the complexities of a fully industrialized world. The best example of such socially necessary systemic regulation is visible in the economic realm, where the mechanism of the market does generally provide the best solutions for providing and pricing most socially necessary goods. Thomas McCarthy notes that Habermas's "strategy is to enter into a pact of sorts with social systems theory: certain areas are marked out within which it may move about quite freely, on the condition that it keep entirely away from others (McCarthy 1985, 28)."

Unlike Luhmann, Habermas argues that social control governed by discursive agreement – a domain he refers to as the lifeworld (*Lebenswelt*) – must always preserve both the right and the ability of individuals acting together to subject such systems to regulation when they produce undesirable outcomes or interfere in areas of life that the community has decided should not be subject to systemic control.[6]

---

[6] For more on how this process plays out in the example of markets, see Jütten (2013). In certain respects, Habermas's argument is similar to Sandel (2013).

This desire to retain the power of human collective agents – usually achieved through political mechanisms – to determine the scope of systems is at the heart of Habermas's thesis of the "colonization of the lifeworld" (*Kolonializierung der Lebenswelt*) and his rejection of technocracy (Habermas 1984/1987; Habermas 2015). This form of control over autopoetic systems is the product of collective discursive decision-making, i.e. of institutionalized political decisions, a topic that has dominated Habermas's work since 1990.

The basic contours of Habermas's reply to Luhmann, as well as his desire to construct a "'two-level concept of society' that integrates the lifeworld and system paradigms" is very similar to Bučar's basic approach (McCarthy 1985, 27). Bučar does not phrase his rejection of systems theory in Habermas's language of the lifeworld, of course. He does, however, seek to provide some mechanisms for control by human agents over and above systemic concerns. The main difference is that whereas Habermas's approach is collective and discursive based on his theory of communicative action, Bučar's is much more individualistic.

This crucial difference can be seen in the crucial role that Bučar gives to the individual. Habermas stresses the importance of collective social structures – usually mediated through political institutions and law – in allowing "the people" to stand up to colonization by systemic forces. By contrast, "For Bučar, the individual plays a central role /.../ as human beings are the only ones that connect and understand both the material world and the world of ideas (Kovač 2014, 122)." By stressing the power of the individual vis-à-vis the system, he seeks to combine the logic of the system, which is based on power, with individual ethics. This fusion of agency and structure forms the essence of Bučar's (2003) "geopolitical ethics".

At a purely theoretical level, Bučar's approach seems to overestimate the ability of the individual to shape and in some sense "govern" autopoetic systems. However, when he transposes this approach to international relations, Bučar replaces the individual with the nation. In recognizing the need for individuals to come together and create a form of "higher agency" that can oppose systemic forces at the international level, Bučar's (2007) theory starts to become somewhat more "realistic".

This change also brings Bučar somewhat closer to Habermas's position. However, one crucial difference remains. Whereas Bučar retains a positive, optimistic vision of the nation and of national identity to ground collective consciousness, Habermas argues that the experience of two World Wars has discredited nationalism as a legitimate source of social cohesion (Bučar 2003, 64–68). Habermas therefore disavows the use of any prepolitical or cultural characteristics that are often used to ground collective identity, arguing instead for a "constitutional patriotism" that binds individuals together into a political community through their collective respect for the democratic procedures preserved within constitutional practice (Müller 2007; Müller 2000, Ch. 2). Although I cannot resolve this disagreement here, it is clear that regardless of their differences, Bučar and Habermas present two interesting yet divergent approaches to critical systems theory.

Conclusion

In this chapter I have sought to situate France Bučar and his critical, personalistic approach to systems theory in its broader intellectual and political context. I argued that understanding the geopolitical and intellectual environment of postwar Yugoslavia is crucial because it shaped the conditions of possibility for Bučar's synthesis of Marxist emancipatory critique with Weberian systems theory. In order to complete this task, I outlined some of the most important strains of social and political thought in the former Yugoslavia, focusing in particular on the *Praxis* Group and the work of the Ljubljana School of Lacano-Marxism. The former movement is particularly interesting, as it forms both an intellectual and an institutional link between Marxist thinkers in Yugoslavia and those working in the West.

The Frankfurt School, and particularly its primary postwar exponent, Jürgen Habermas, are a particularly interesting counterpoint to Bučar's work, given their mutual interest in combining an emancipatory reading of the early Marx with Weber's insights into systems theory. Despite similar interests and influences, however, Bučar and Habermas end up endorsing very different forms of collective action to oppose the impersonal forces the increasingly globalized system. Whereas Bučar looks to the nation, bound together through a culturally-rooted self-consciousness, Habermas seeks to ground collective action in legitimate procedures that take the views of all those affected by the system into account, without regard to pre-political forms of identity.

There are many possible reasons for these differences between Bučar and Habermas. However, in line with my basic argument, they can perhaps best be explained by examining the differing intellectual contexts these two thinkers were working within. As a West German born in the interwar years, Habermas attributes an "epoch-forming significance to the developments in Nazi Germany (Stirk 2000, 100)." Surveying the physical, moral and political ruin of Germany in 1945 Habermas knew that his homeland would have to change as a result of this tragic experience. Most notably, his desire to "learn from catastrophe" led Habermas to reject nationalism as the primary source of the "bellicose past /that/ entangled all European nations in bloody conflicts (Habermas 2005, 12; Habermas 2001, 26–37)." Habermas's fear of return of fascism and his own experience of the emotional power of nationalism to mobilize state-sponsored atrocities are at the root of his attempt to ground collective action in democratic, rationalistic procedures.

Bučar grew up in a very different context. Unlike Habermas, whose memories of his childhood led him to reject both the nationalism and the totalitarianism of that regime, Bučar's experiences living in communist Yugoslavia – a decidedly anti-nationalist regime that brought together many different "southern Slavs" – taught him rather different lessons. Coming from a context that sought to erase or ignore national differences, Bučar came to see the nation as an important source of cultural and ethical values that could be mobilized against the centralized power of the communist system. He agrees with Count Coundenhove-Kalergi, the founder of the Pan-European Movement, which Bučar helped to reestablish in Slovenia after independence, who argued, "Every nation is a sanctuary – as the hearth and home of culture, as the point of crystallization for morality and progress (Coudenhove-Kalergi 2000, 71)."

These differences point to the power of the broader political and intellectual context to shape a thinker's theoretical positions. Whereas Habermas's memories of Nazism and two World Wars lead him to reject nationalism, Bučar's divergent experience living in a postnational communist regime in Yugoslavia lead him to interpret the nation as a potential source of liberation from the impersonal imperatives of systemic forces. In this sense – and especially in light of my comparison of his intellectual environment to that of Habermas – Bučar's work can be understood as a combination of Eastern praxis with Western critique.

Literature

Bausch, K. C. (1997). The Habermas/Luhmann debate and subsequent Habermasian perspectives on systems theory. *Systems Research and Behavioral Science, 14*(5), 315–330.

Bausch, K. C. (2001). *The emerging consensus in social systems theory.* Boston: Springer.

Bell, D. (1962). *The end of ideology: On the exhaustion of political ideas in the fifties: With "the resumption of history in the new century".* Cambridge: Harvard University Press.

Bernstein, R. J. (2017). The prehistory of the Prague meetings. *Philosophy and Social Criticism, 43*(3), 272–273.

Bučar, F. (1978). Participation of state and political organizations in Enterprise decisions. In J. Obradović & W. N. Dunn (Eds.), *Worker's self-management and organizational power in Yugoslavia* (pp. 416–432). Pittsburgh: University Center for International Studies, University of Pittsburgh.

Bučar, F. (1993). Slovenia in Europe. *Nationalities Papers, 21*(1), 31–41.

Bučar, F. (2003). *Porusena harmonija sveta.* Miš: Dob pri Domžalah.

Bučar, F. (2007). *Rojstvo države.* Radovljica: Didakta.

Chomsky, N., & Cohen, R. S. (1974). The repression at Belgrade University. *The New York Review of Books, 21*(1), 32–33.

Cohen, J., Hazelrigg, L. E., & Pope, W. (1975). De-Parsonizing weber: A critique of Parsons' interpretation of Weber's sociology. *American Sociological Review, 40*(2), 229–241.

Coundenhove-Kalergi, R. N. (2000). *Panevropa.* Ljubljana: Slovensko panevropsko gibanje.

Day, B. (2004). From Frankfurt to Ljubljana: Critical theory from Adorno to Žižek. *Studies in Social and Political Thought, 9*(1), 1–20.

Estrin, S. (1991). Yugoslavia: The case of self-managing market socialism. *Journal of Economic Perspectives, 5*(4), 187–194.

Flaherty, D. (1992). Self-management and the future of socialism: Lessons from Yugoslavia. *Science and Society, 56*(1), 92–108.

Freud, S. (1990). In J. Strachey (Ed.), *Five lectures on psycho-analysis.* New York: Norton.

Gruenwald, O. (1983). *The Yugoslav search for man: Marxist humanism in contemporary Yugoslavia.* South Hadley: J. F. Bergin.

Geuss, R. (1981). *The idea of a critical theory: Habermas and the Frankfurt school.* Cambridge: Cambridge University Press.

Habermas, J. (1971). *Knowledge and human interests.* Boston: Beacon Press.

Habermas, J. (1984/1987). *The theory of communicative action.* Boston: Beacon press.

Habermas, J. (2001). The Postnational constellation and the future of democracy. In J. Habermas (Ed.), *The Postnational constellation: Political essays* (pp. 58–112). Cambridge: MIT Press.

Habermas, J. (2015). *The lure of technocracy*. Cambridge: Polity Press.

Habermas, J., & Luhmann, N. (1971). *Theorie der Gesellschaft oder Sozialtechnologie-was leistet die Systemforschung?* Suhrkamp: Frankfurt am Main.

Habermas, J., & Henrich, D. (1974). *Zwei Reden*. Suhrkamp: Frankfurt am Main.

Habermas, J., & Derrida, J. (2005). February 15, or what binds Europeans together: A plea for a common foreign policy, beginning in the core of Europe. In D. Levy, M. Pensky, J. C. Torpey, & J. Torpey (Eds.), *Old Europe, new Europe, core Europe: Transatlantic relations after the Iraq war* (pp. 3–13). London: Verso.

Howard, M. W. (2001). Market socialism and political pluralism: Theoretical reflections on Yugoslavia. *Studies in East European Thought, 53*(4), 307–328.

Jütten, T. (2013). Habermas and markets. *Constellations, 20*(4), 587–603.

Knodt, E. (1994). Toward a non-foundationalist epistemology: The Habermas/Luhmann controversy revisited. *New German Critique, 21*(1), 77–100.

Kovač, I. (2013). Filozofija Franceta Bučarja znotraj tokov mednarodnih odnosov: "geopolitična etika" in post-pozitivna znanstvena paradigma. *Anthropos, 45*(3–4), 31--55.

Kovač, I. (2014). EU in the struggle for global governance: Geopolitical ethics. *International Journal of Diplomacy and Economy, 2*(1–2), 118–138.

Luhmann, N. (1982). *The differentiation of society*. New York: Columbia University Press.

Luhmann, N. (1990). *Essays on self-reference*. New York: Columbia University Press.

McCarthy, T. (1985). Complexity and democracy, or the seducements of systems theory. *New German Critique, 12*(2), 27–53.

Marković, M. (1976). Marxist philosophy in Yugoslavia: The praxis group. In R. T. De George & J. P. Scanlan (Eds.), *Marxism and religion in Eastern Europe* (pp. 63--89). Boston: D. Reidel Publishing Company.

Marković, M. (1987). Povodom rasmisljanja o filozofije prakse. *Theoria, 30*(3–4), 113–119.

Massey, G. (1991). A final look at the critical perspective of the Yugoslav praxis group. *Humanity and Society, 15*(2), 223–238.

Müller, J. W. (2000). *Another country: German intellectuals, unification, and national identity*. New Haven: Yale University Press.

Müller, J. W. (2007). *Constitutional patriotism*. Princeton: Princeton University Press.

Petrović, G. (1967). La philosophie yougoslave aujourd'hui. *Praxis (International Edition), 3*(2), 313–320.

Rehg, W., & Bohman, J. (2001). *Pluralism and the pragmatic turn: The transformation of critical theory, essays in honor of Thomas McCarthy*. Cambridge: MIT Press.

Sandel, M. J. (2013). *What money can't buy: The moral limits of markets*. New York: Farrar, Straus and Giroux.

Sher, G. S. (1977). *Praxis, Marxist criticism and dissent in socialist Yugoslavia*. Bloomington: Indiana University Press.

Stamm, M. (2005). Konstellationsforshung-Ein Methodenprofil: Motive und Perspektiven. In M. Mulsow & M. Stamm (Eds.), *Konstellationsforschung* (pp. 31–73). Frankfurt am Main: Suhrkamp Taschenbuch Verlag.

Stirk, P. (2000). *Critical theory, politics and society: An introduction*. New York: Continuum.

Šupek, R. (1972). Čemu, uostalom, sada još i ovaj marksizam. *Praxis (Domestic Edition), 8*(3–4), 328–338.

The Prague Conference: Directors, General Themes, Plenaries, Workshops, Papers (1993–2016). (2017). *Philosophy & Social Criticism, 43*(3), 355–372.

Willetts, P. (1978). *The non-aligned movement: The origins of a third world alliance*. New York: Nichols Publishing.

Weber, M. (1958). Politics as a vocation. In H. H. Gerth & W. Mills (Eds.), *From max weber: Essays in sociology* (pp. 129–158). New York: Oxford University Press.

Žižek, S. (2002). *Welcome to the desert of the real!: Five essays on September 11 and related dates*. London: Verso.

Systems Thinking in Politics and Practice – Reflections on France Bučar

Mark Hamilton

The contribution of this chapter is to pull together varied aspects of France Bučar's essays and consider how he employed "systems thinking" in his engagement of politics, economics, and governance.[1] Bučar never discusses formal modeling or reflects directly on a "system dynamics" method. Nonetheless, a unifying theme across his work is that systems matter in shaping individuals' and nations' behavior. For Bučar, the reliance on simplistic solutions – whether driven by ideological, populist, or bureaucratic pursuits – most often lead to folly in policymaking and national governance decisions.

Bučar, of course, was hardly a stranger to political, economic and policy realms. He is widely recognized as one of the founding fathers of Slovenian democracy, a leader in its independence movement, co-author of its constitution, and a leading voice for European integration.[2] The present translation of Bučar's book (e.g., Chap. 2) and his rich life path – bridging roles of academic, activist, politician, and statesman – betrays a deep skepticism with the "power over" knowledge of state bureaucrats, corporate leaders, even charismatic revolutionaries. Practical knowl-

---

[1] I write this chapter as a relative novice on Slovenian history and politics, and any errors or short-comings are likely shaped my background in the Americas and to a lesser extent, South Asia. On "systems thinking", my methodological background is informed by Jay Forrester's classic works in system dynamics literature, which explored industrial (1961), urban (1969) and global political economy (1971) realms. I deepened my understanding of economic cycles and environmental "limits to growth" with Mass (1975) and Meadows, Randers, and Meadows (2004), and much of my own work on violent mobilization and political insurgencies is shaped by Richardson (2005) and his systems engagement of social and political conflict.

[2] For background literature on Bučar's political evolution and his status as one of the founding fathers of democratic Slovenia, see Plut-Pregelj and Rogel (2010) and Mujagić (2014). On Bučar's impact as an intellectual leader for independence, see Cox (2005), Palsan et al. (2011) and Rupel (2005), among others. Finally, as articulator of Pan-European Slovenian nationalism, see Mihelj (2005) and Kirin and Račić (2017).

M. Hamilton (✉)
Inter-American Defense College, Washington, DC, USA
e-mail: mark.hamilton@iadc.edu

© Springer International Publishing AG, part of Springer Nature 2019
I. Kovač (ed.), *At His Crossroad*, https://doi.org/10.1007/978-3-319-78331-4_2

edge for Bučar requires a "big picture" view of systemic relationships and a deep appreciation for the evolving dynamics of social power in a given society.

This chapter continues with a brief primer on "systems thinking" and references system dynamics as a helpful methodological frame of reference. Next, Bučar's emphasis on "systems" is explored by addressing key themes and essays collected in this volume. Finally, a few concluding reflections are offered to synthesize ideas of Bučar and their application to broader systems thinking, modelling and contemporary policymaking.

An Introduction to Systems Thinking

Applying "systems thinking" to a given problem or theme of interest often provides a more comprehensive causal explanation than micro-level views commonly utilized in contemporary social sciences and policy bureaucracies. Systems focus on dynamic interplay among multiple causal mechanisms, considering how dominance shifts over time.[3] Consider the ancient fable chronicling the attempts of several blind men to describe the elephant standing in front of them. According to the fable, each man comments on the reality he feels: an apparent "snake" that is really the trunk, the "spear"-like tusk, the "rope"-like tail. But as in Saxe's poem, "Though each was partly in the right /.../ all were in the wrong (Richardson 2005, 91)!"

In the same way, dependence on a simple ideological explanation, policy response, or isolated causal correlation allows us to see only one part of the "elephant" before us. We are likely to miss the complex, often counterintuitive ways that causal mechanisms interact in a larger social system over time and space. By contrast, a systems view broadens the scope of data analyzed and the diversity of perspectives explored. It tries to tell a "superior story", to adapt the words of historical sociologist Charles Tilly (2002).

System dynamics is a policy-focused research methodology developed by Jay Forrester and his colleagues in the 1960s to examine counter-intuitive effects of decisions in complex systems due to presence of "feedback loops" and time delays. Models can be a useful tool to capture ebbs and flow of behavior in a system's structure over a medium to long time horizon. For system dynamic practitioners, less attention should be paid to linear correlations than to dynamic relationships, tracing how actors are embedded in a larger system, whether this system is political-economic, social, or environmental in nature.[4]

---

[3] "Mechanisms" refer to partial explanations and contingent causal theories that may or may not apply in a given time or place. In a systems view, the behavior of many mechanisms is dependent on "tipping points" (Gladwell 2006) in a competitive struggle between positive and negative "feedback loops" operating within the broader system.

[4] Richardson (2005, 10) stresses that "the structure of a system, that is, the way its elements are inter-connected in cause-effect relationships, is the key to explaining the system's behavior pattern… (and yet) human decisions play an important role in feedback processes."

System dynamics offers a disciplined, yet flexible methodological framework to weave together disparate theories and case observations, operationalizing and testing them as interacting mechanisms. Model results provide insight on system "leverage points",[5] that is, the targeted intervention scenarios in which savvy policymakers might capitalize on system behavior to accomplish alternative outcomes.

Of course, all models feature inherent limits. Per John Sterman (2002, 521), a noted scholar and systems practitioner at the Massachusetts Institute of Technology, "Because all models are wrong we reject the notion that models can be validated in the dictionary definition sense of 'establishing truthfulness', instead focusing on creating models that are useful /…/ and on the continual iteration between experiments with the virtual world of the model and experiments in the real world."[6]

This practical orientation of system dynamics and systems thinking opens the door to its application for a wide array of social, political, and environmental problems. System dynamic scholars often employ "archetypes" as conceptual building blocks. Kim (1993) highlights a few common system archetypes, like "drifting goals" (tracing the gap and time delays between a goal and current realities), "escalation" (mapping the reinforcing threats among conflicting parties), "fixes that fail" (exploring unintended consequences of employing symptom-focused responses to complex problems), and "tragedy of the commons" (reflecting individual pursuits and interests eroding finite pools of "common" resources).

Figure 1 below provides a simplified causal loop diagram that focuses on "new product development", which is another system archetype. The "Word of Mouth" loop is labeled R for reinforcing, which means it drives towards an avalanche-type

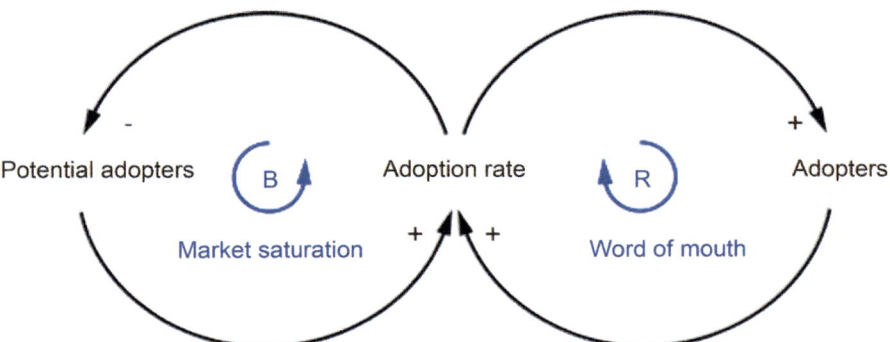

Fig. 1 "New Product Development" Causal loop diagram. (This diagram is drawn from the Wikimedia Commons for open academic publication rights (https://commons.wikimedia.org/wiki/File:Adoption_CLD.svg). However, its original may be found in Sterman 2001, 18)

---

[5] For Meadows (1999, 1), "leverage points" are "places within a complex system (a corporation, an economy, a living body…), where a small shift in one thing can produce big changes in everything". For systems modelers and policymakers, effective interventions are long-term projects that consider how actors, physical properties, and causal mechanisms fit together in a broader system.

[6] Sterman (2002) offers an excellent primer on systems thinking and "business dynamics" in practice.

growth (or decay) effect. The "Market Saturation" loop is labeled B for balancing, which means it shifts the system behavior back towards equilibrium. The plus (+) and minus (−) arrows refer to micro-level causal effects that reinforce (+) or negate (−) the current trajectory.

Over time, rapid growth of any new product, driven by "word of mouth", is likely to give way to "market saturation". A growing segment of the target population ("potential adopters") already has product access and thus the "adoption rate" begins to slow. Adapted applications of this system archetype include models of ideological diffusion, network contagion effects, etc., as discussed by Hamilton (2017), among others.

Systems thinking in general, and system dynamics in particular, offers tools to help policymakers focus on the big picture, to map critical relationships for diverse variables, and to offer a dynamic explanation for the changing system-level behavior across time. Simple causal loop diagrams like those in Fig. 1 can be leveraged as building blocks for more formal, detailed models to test the utility of a given mental model to explain and reproduce (through long-run simulation) the "real-life" behavior observed in the system.

Systems Thinking in Bučar's Writing

System dynamics and formal models are never explored explicitly in Bučar's writing. Nevertheless, ideas related to "systems" and "complexity" appear to be a first order concern for Bučar in the essays included in this volume For example, the word "SYSTEM" is repeated some 130 times, more than terms like "GOVERNMENT" (104), "ECONOMY" (73), "POLITICS" (50), "IDENTITY" (40), "CAPITALISM" (29) and "COMMUNISM" (12).[7] Meanwhile, Bučar's use of the term "COMPLEXITY" is surrounded time and again by systems-relevant terminology like "INTERDEPENDENCE", "SOCIALIZATION", and "ORGANIZATION".

Unlike many contemporary politicians in Slovenia and globally, Bučar's writing is not easily compressed into ideological soundbites or press-worthy tweets. Instead, like many system thinkers, his essays betray a series of inherent tensions. He questions prioritizing "equality" as functional vs. ethical, valuing hierarchy vs. horizontal freedoms, balancing fulfilment of needs (poverty) vs. over-consumption, trusting the wisdom of the expert vs. the population, and valuing governance by individual voters vs. their representatives. Based on Bučar's own political evolution and the modern transitions he observed in his Slovenian nation (and its regional neighbors), Bučar seems skeptical of ideological extremes. He appears interested in achieving a sort of political-economic equilibrium (or a balancing feedback loop, in system dynamics parlance).

---

[7] Other commonly cited themes betray a strong systems orientation in Bučar's worldview. Examples of terms include "society" (repeated 319 times), "state" (268), "democracy" (160), and "equality" (111).

According to Kovač (2014), who serves as this volume's editor, "Bučar's system theory combines quantity and quality approaches and considers both agency and structure." Bučar addresses individuals' roles in system governance, but highlights that "structure shapes not only behaviors but also identities and orientations of agents (Kovač 2014, 122)." This integrative systems framework in Bučar, which values both structure and agency, bucks the reductionist and large-n tendency currently dominating the contemporary social sciences.[8]

Although fairly sparse in his citations of other authors and thinkers in the essays here, Bučar notably references John K. Galbraith multiple times. Galbraith – like Bučar – was an iconoclast, an influential twentieth century economist seeking to bridge micro- and macro-economics. Galbraith looked out for unexpected policy consequences and was skeptical of "expert" knowledge within bureaucracies and corporations.[9]

The present Bučar's text (Chap. 3) joins a hopeful trust in "the common sense of regular people" with the recognition that countries need technocratic expertise. Effective government for Bučar requires a nuanced understanding of popular values and interests as well as sufficient technical expertise to efficiently make system-level decisions: The real solution is a government that enjoys the necessary trust of its voters (Chap. 3).

On economics, Bučar's essays show a generally pragmatic approach, with glimpses of idealism. On the one hand, he is an advocate of economic integration, which is displayed through many years of Pan-European activism. On the other hand, Bučar is quick to cite the ecological, ethical, and socio-political perils of unchecked corporate capitalism. He shares similar concerns to post-World War II political economist Karl Polanyi regarding the popular conflict likely to arise when sociopolitical checks on the "open market" are ignored.[10] In his book – At A New Crossroads –Bučar argues that state should eschew both laissez faire and heavy-handed economic roles in order to be an "important partner" (Chap. 7) in a modern market economy. The optimal goal is to facilitate cooperative relations and a "co-management" framework (Chap. 6) between labor and capital sectors.

Bučar takes an evolutionary and system-focused perspective to politics and the economy. In his essays, norms surrounding "equality" and "democracy" in modern societies are not self-evident but rather embedded in political and economic realities

---

[8] Bučar would find much to critique in the popular research methods text of King, Keohane, and Verba (1994). Bučar's theoretical orientation has been labeled as "post-positivist" (Kovač 2014), but his writing betrays a scientific openness, big picture view, and policy practicality that is reminiscent of (positivist) system dynamics scholars.

[9] Galbraith was comfortable engaging directly with the public and policymakers (including US President Kennedy), often more than fellow economists. The late Donella Meadows (1999), a pioneering figure in the system dynamics field, also cited the ideas of Galbraith (1967) in her oft-republished essay on "Leverage Points."

[10] Polanyi (1944) famously warned of a popular "double movement" based on the embedded social relations of an economy. In systems parlance, we see a shared focus of the two authors on "balancing" factors in search of political-economic equilibrium.

of production and consumption. Bučar is interested in the evolving mechanisms of political-economic system governance at national and global levels.

Applications of Bučar's Ideas to Systems Modelling and Policy Development

As a policy researcher familiar with system dynamics practice and International Relations scholar who studies political-economic, and security decision-making at the highest level, a review of Bučar's writings invites both appreciative and critical reflection.

On a critical note, Bučar's policy optimism implies that optimal approaches will ultimately win out due to superior policy arguments. His ideas merit further engagement of political realism in classical and critical forms. Absent in Bučar's essays is a nuanced appreciation of power, and his otherwise thoughtful ideas on inequality tend to shy away from recognizing the systemic mechanisms of "durable inequality" (Tilly 1998).

On an appreciative note, Bučar's system-level focus, his ethics-steeped reflections on the state, and his long-run approach to governance is a welcome change to most contemporary politicians. It would be very interesting to map Bučar's ideas with feedback loops and adapted archetypes, embedding the complexity of his thoughts and political experience in formalized system dynamic models. His musings on economic philosophy, political evolution, policy goals, and unintended consequences would resonate with many systems thinkers even today.

Conclusion

France Bučar, in his political career and political musings, often explored how systems influence and shape our behavior as individuals, societies, and nations. He was slow to accept simplistic solutions. He challenged his Slovenian compatriots to embrace, or at least consider, a more comprehensive view of political and economic phenomena. In the policy realm, Bučar was an idealist, a committed believer in narratives of progress. Still he always remained skeptical of "big" systems like capitalism and communism.

This chapter offers an overview on "systems thinking" and explores how Bučar's ideas fit in a system dynamics framework. It examines strengths and weaknesses of Bučar's approach to power, inequality, and political-economic governance. It also recognizes the importance of his systematic approach to politics and policymaking in development of the modern Slovenian state and Pan-European movement. Bučar was fascinated with political systems, and ultimately, he achieved a platform to influence change and "leverage points" in his home country and beyond.

Literature

Cox, J. K. (2005). *Slovenia: Evolving loyalties*. London: Routledge.

Forrester, J. W. (1961). *Industrial dynamics*. Cambridge, US: MIT Press.

Forrester, J. W. (1969). *Urban dynamics*. Cambridge, US: MIT Press.

Forrester, J. W. (1971). *World dynamics*. Cambridge, US: Wright-Allen.

Galbraith, J. K. (1967). *The new industrial state*. Boston: Houghton-Mifflin.

Gladwell, M. (2006). *The tipping point: How little things can make a big difference*. Boston: Little, Brown and Company.

Hamilton, M. D. (2017, February). *Why Rebel? Unpacking the Mechanisms of Mobilization from Sri Lanka to Star Wars*. Paper presented at International Studies Association Annual Convention in Baltimore, MD (22–25 February 2017).

Kim, D. H. (1993). *Systems archetypes I: Diagnosing systemic issues and designing high-leverage interventions*. Waltham: Pegasus Communications.

King, G., Keohane, R. O., & Verba, S. (1994). *Designing social inquiry: Scientific inference in qualitative research*. Prinction: Princeton University Press.

Kirin, R. J., & Račić, D. (2017). Claiming and crossing Borders: A view on the Slovene-Croatian border dispute. *Društvena istraživanja, 25*(4), 433–453.

Kovač, I. (2014). EU in the struggle for global governance: Geopolitical ethics. *International Journal of Diplomacy and Economy, 2*(1–2), 118–138.

Mass, N. J. (1975). *Economic cycles: An analysis of underlying causes*. Cambridge: MIT Press.

Meadows, D. (1999). *Leverage points: Places to intervene in a system*. Hartland: The Sustainability Institute.

Meadows, D., Randers, J., & Meadows, D. (2004). *Limits to growth: The 30-year update*. White River Junction: Chelsea Green Publishing.

Mihelj, S. (2005). To be or not to be a part of Europe: Appropriations of the symbolic borders of Europe in Slovenia. *Journal of Borderlands Studies, 20*(2), 109–128.

Mujagić, N. (2014). The European Union as a spectacle: The case of the Slovenian-Croatian dispute over the sea border. In T. Petrović (Ed.), *Mirroring Europe: Ideas of Europe and Europeanization in Balkan societies* (pp. 186–203). Leiden: Brill.

Palsan, C., Casile, C., & Stan, M. (2011). *Avatars of intellectuals under communism (history of communism in Europe) Vol. 2*. Bucharest: Zeta Books.

Plut-Pregelj, L., & Rogel, C. (2010). *The a to Z of Slovenia*. Lanham: Scarecrow Press.

Polanyi, K. (1944). *The great transformation: The political and economic origins of our time*. Boston: Beacon Press.

Richardson, J. M. (2005). *Paradise poisoned: Learning about conflict, terrorism, and development from Sri Lanka's civil wars*. Kandy: International Center for Ethic Studies (ICES).

Rupel, D. (2005). Twenty-five years of democratic development: From Nova Revija to the center-right government of Janez Janša. *Slovene Studies Journal, 27*(1), 45–50.

Sterman, J. D. (2001). System dynamics modeling: Tools for learning in a complex world. *California Management Review, 43*(4), 8–25.

Sterman, J. D. (2002). All models are wrong: Reflections on becoming a systems scientist. *System Dynamics Review, 18*(4), 501–531.

Tilly, C. (1998). *Durable inequality*. Berkeley: University of California Press.

Tilly, C. (2002). *Stories, identities, and political change*. Lanham: Rowman & Littlefield.

Wikimedia Commons. (2018). https://commons.wikimedia.org/wiki/File:Adoption_CLD.svg. Accessed 22 January 2018.

(Non)Enforcement and the Rule of Law, Can Bučar Provide Some Clues?

Urška Velikonja

In 1995, the Russian State Duma adopted the Law on Joint Stock Companies governing Russian corporations.[1] At the time of its adoption, the law was praised as the gold standard for emerging and post-socialist economies, a model to follow (e.g., Black and Kraakman 1996). Over time, however, Russian corporate law became a different kind of model, demonstrating how consequential is enforcement, or lack thereof, for evaluating the quality of a country's legal regime. Although the law on the books changed, the law in action did not. Excellent corporate law on the books notwithstanding, Russian public corporations continue to trade at a substantial discount to similar Western corporations, with the discount estimated to range somewhere between 70% and 99%.

Empirical questions about the enforcement of legal rules permeate the American legal conversation and scholarship but continue to be relegated (for the most part) to non-legal disciplines and politics in continental Europe. The European legal tradition remains wedded to German legal philosophy, most strongly to Hans Kelsen's 'Pure Theory of Law', developed in the mid-twentieth century. Kelsen (1967) understood the law as a hierarchical system of logically-related legal rules that are adopted by a legislator but are otherwise independent from politics and morality. Studying the implementation of legal rules was not within the purview of legal science, which to a large extent remains entirely theoretical.

By contrast, the American legal tradition is much more concerned with how legal rules are implemented and, thus, turns the question about what is the content of the

---

[1] Russian Law on Joint Stock Companies, adopted by the Russian State Duma on November 24th, 1995; the law entered into effect on January 1st, 1996.

U. Velikonja (✉)
Georgetown University Law Center, Washington, DC, USA
e-mail: urska.velikonja@georgetown.edu

© Springer International Publishing AG, part of Springer Nature 2019   23
I. Kovač (ed.), *At His Crossroad*, https://doi.org/10.1007/978-3-319-78331-4_3

law on its head.[2] It begins the research by observing the actions of institutions and individuals and works its way backwards towards legal philosophies that guide courts and other decisionmakers. One cannot appreciate the quality of the law without considering its implementation. As a result, American legal science concerns itself with both, voluntary compliance, and enforcement of legal rules through public or private means.

France Bučar was educated in the 'continental tradition'; as such, his argument is that legal provisions cannot encompass all human actions and activity. Yet, he objects to legal positivism. Moreover, he does not understand legal provisions as an isolated ivory tower. Instead, his system theory studies the interaction of the legal regime with other social sub-systems, including politics and economics. As such, he stresses the role of ethics as a complimentary source of normative action, and more importantly, as the crucial feedback loop for any of the social sub-systems, including legal. He underlines that such a process of internal system diagnostics will necessarily result in a clear mandate for amending any of its integral elements, including the legal sub-system. Thus, since implementing legal rules play an important part in this evaluation process, Bučar hints towards a synthesis of the two legal traditions.

Yet, what would Bučar have to say about laws that are put in place, yet are not enforced? What kind of impetus do such examples present for Bučar's ethics, his system theory and his feedback-loop? As he emphasizes the role of human action, how does he understand (action-motivated) non-action? If the European tradition treats this problem as a political anomaly, how are they treated in the American tradition?

This essay examines the relationship between the rule of law and enforcement, and in particular nonenforcement: decisions not to enforce a valid legal rule. The discussion reveals a considerable legal gap: the law affords law enforcement considerable discretion on whether and how to enforce the law. The only constraints are internal and political. If either prong weakens, so do constraints on enforcement discretion, and so does the rule of law. Laws and policies mean little if they are not vigilantly enforced and interrogated for their efficacy. The essay draws heavily from the American experience, but the observations extend to legal systems overall, differences in the details notwithstanding. My proposals derive from my interpretation of Bučar's theory.

Alternatives for Legal Change

In recent decades, almost every new U.S. Presidential administration has come into office after having made campaign promises to deregulate some area of social or economic activity. Democratic candidates promise to lessen the burdens on those

---

[2] This exaggerates the difference between the European and American traditions. There are many fine legal theorists in the U.S., including normativists, and many excellent empiricists in Europe, just not in law schools.

living in poverty, including by limiting enforcement against law-abiding undocumented immigrants. Republican candidates usually promise to lighten the regulatory burden on business: to pare back laws perceived as excessively costly, to reduce environmental and workplace safety standards, or to deregulate regulated markets.

Deregulation can occur in a variety of ways. First, a President with solid support in Congress can implement a statutory agenda. During his first term in office, President Obama passed the Affordable Case Act on which he campaigned, vastly expanding the availability health insurance for lower-income and middle-class Americans. Second, a President can direct agencies to regulate or deregulate by revoking rules and regulations deemed costly or unfair, and, additionally, can impose roadblocks that make new regulations less likely. Finally, a President can deregulate by appointing department and agency heads who will reduce enforcement of disfavored laws and regulations by directing their enforcement hands to do less.

The three alternatives are substitutes, if imperfect ones. New statutes are difficult to adopt. They usually require the President to enjoy majority support in both houses of Congress – a feat that ordinarily occurs only in the first 2 years of an administration but not after that. They face many layers of review, both inside Congress, in the media, and often in courts. But the advantage of statutory (de)regulation is that statutes are difficult to undo, once adopted. The Affordable Care Act is again a case in point: President Trump and the Republican Congress tried to repeal the statute several times, only to fail each time.

Deregulatory rulemaking faces considerably fewer political challenges and less media scrutiny but is usually no easier to implement than a statute because of significant procedural requirements. All rules and regulations must go through the notice-and-comment process required by the Administrative Procedure Act. The process agencies to justify legal rules, including showing that the social benefits of the proposed rule outweigh its costs. Moreover, interested public have a right to participate in the process and offer comments, to which the agency must respond. In addition, economically significant rules proposed by departments and federal agencies (except for independent agencies that include most financial regulators) must be reviewed by the Office of Information and Regulatory Affairs (OIRA), an agency that is closely associated with the White House and the President of the United States. OIRA often requires substantial amendments to proposed rules, or delays decision on rules it dislikes, effectively vetoing them. Even if a rule survives the many procedural steps, adopted rules are subject to judicial review, where a court may vacate the rule for failure to adequately respond to public comments or for failure to consider valid objections. There is no safe harbor for deregulatory rules or actions to rescind a properly adopted rule; they, too, must jump through all procedural hoops. As a result, repealing rules is just as difficult as adopting new rules, if not more so. An adopted rule had to satisfy many competing factions and demonstrate that the rule provides more benefits than costs. Once that has been established, it is very difficult for an agency to reverse course absent compelling evidence (Revesz and Livermore 2008).[3]

There is a third way to deregulate. In recent decades, U.S. Presidents have often resorted to nonenforcement as the preferred method to deregulate in lieu of legislative or regulatory processes (e.g., Love and Garg 2014, 1217; Deacon 2010; Walters 2016, 1918). The President, and by extension, agency heads, can achieve deregulatory objectives through nonenforcement without significant delays and without any real threat of judicial review[4] – contrary to the very real roadblocks present in statute-making and rule-making. This is because the U.S. Supreme Court afforded agencies considerable enforcement discretion for piecemeal enforcement decisions. As long as a change in enforcement policy is not prospective and categorical, it is immune from judicial review.

Deregulation through nonenforcement may not outlast the administration but has very real consequences nonetheless. In the first year of the Trump administration, agency enforcement has declined across the board. Staffing changes at the Environmental Protection Agency (EPA), the Department of Education (DOE) and the Food and Drug Administration (FDA) have resulted in laxer enforcement against polluters, for-profit colleges, and medical device manufacturers (e.g., Nader 2017). Declines in enforcement have also permeated into the financial regulatory agencies that historically have not faced such cutbacks. The development raises several interesting questions: what are appropriate accountability mechanisms, and whether such swings are good policy? The following sections, explore, in turn, the legal requirements for enforcement, the history of deregulation through nonenforcement, and a discussion of available and appropriate accountability mechanisms.

The Duty to Enforce the Law and Enforcement Discretion

The Take Care Clause of the U.S. Constitution commands the President "to put the laws into effect, or at least to see that they are put into effect, 'without failure' and 'exactly' (Delahunty and Yoo 2012, 799)." The words "faithfully executed" do imply some degree of discretion but most commentators agree that the clause establishes a presumption that Presidents will dutifully follow existing law, in contrast with the older English tradition of the executive suspending or dispensing with enacted laws (Walters 2016, 1919). Thus, the executive does not have the authority to either "prospectively license statutory violations or to categorically suspend enforcement of statutes for policy reasons" (Price 2014, 704). By ignoring the mandate to enforce the laws, agencies can nullify statutes, which is inconsistent with the Take Care Clause and the separation of powers (Andrias 2013, 1114).

---

[3] Explaining that neutrally applied cost-benefit analysis can be pro-regulatory, in particular in environmental, health and safety regulation.

[4] See Heckler v. Cheney, 470 U.S. 821 (1984).

At the same time, most would agree that the President and, by extension, federal agencies have the authority to exercise prosecutorial discretion and decline to enforce the law either because equity considerations or resource constraints prevent full enforcement (e.g., Walters 2016, 1914). Courts routinely dismiss actions challenging the failure to enforce explaining that agencies' individual nonenforcement decisions are not reviewable or that the plaintiff lacks standing. In Heckler v. Chaney,[5] the best-known U.S. Supreme Court decision on nonenforcement, the Court held that "an agency's decision not to take enforcement action should be presumed immune from judicial review under § 701(a)(2).[6]

The two views, the Constitutional duty to enforce the law and the discretion not to enforce, are somewhat in tension because the line between discretionary nonenforcement, which is permitted, and categorical nonenforcement, which is not, is quite blurry in the absence of a clear Presidential or agency directive.[7]

Moreover, enforcement can, to some extent, substitute for regulation; even more so, nonenforcement can substitute for deregulation. An agency that wants to lower the cost of compliance for regulated parties can do so by changing the rule or by not enforcing the rule – the ultimate result is no different. For an administration averse to legal challenges and interested in a quick change, Heckler v. Chaney[8] makes the choice simple: so long as a time-limited change is acceptable, nonenforcement is always better than new rules or statutes. In addition to being quicker, the ultimate result is conservative because nonenforcement decisions receive more lenient scrutiny than affirmative regulatory actions (e.g., Scalia 1983, 868–897).[9]

Yet, that analysis is incomplete (e.g., Biber 2008; Walters 2016, 1929; Bressman 2004; Price 2014). The Supreme Court jurisprudence only immunizes case-by-case discretionary enforcement decisions. But where an agency "'consciously and expressly adopted a general policy' that is so extreme as to amount to an abdication of its statutory responsibilities,"[10] then judicial review is appropriate: such a change is equivalent to a repeal of a legal rule and thus should be treated the same. The line between piecemeal and categorical nonenforcement has not been carefully drawn. The following section reviews the history of nonenforcement, highlighting the different approaches taken by Democratic and Republican administrations, and the different legal consequences.

---

[5] 470 U.S. 821 (1985).

[6] ibid. at 832.

[7] That is, unless only publicly-announced programs of nonenforcement, such as President Obama's Deferred Action for Childhood Arrivals (DACA)/Deferred Action for Parents of Americans and Lawful Permanent Residents (DAPA) programs are prohibited.

[8] 470 U.S. 821 (1985).

[9] Arguing in favor of more relaxed review of nonenforcement than of enforcement.

[10] 470 U.S. at 833 n.4.

The History of Deregulation Through Nonenforcement

U.S. Presidents in recent decades have increasingly resorted to nonenforcement as a substitute to deregulation. Ronald Reagan was elected with a mandate to deregulate. Much of his effort was directed at reducing affirmative regulatory burdens by amending statutes and requiring cost-benefit review for new regulations (e.g., Price 2015).[11] Although President Reagan did not attempt to formally direct enforcement priorities, his administration sought budget reductions in disfavored agencies that limited their capacity to enforce (Andrias 2013, 1059). As a result, enforcement declined at the EPA, the Occupational Safety and Health Administration (OSHA) and the Equal Employment Opportunity Commission (EEOC) by 70% or more (Price 2015, 1126). Republican Presidents that followed, George H. W. Bush and, to an even greater extent, George W. Bush relied more heavily on nonenforcement to further their deregulatory agendas.[12] Like Reagan before them, their efforts focused on disfavored agencies, such as the Department of Labor (DOL), the OSHA, the EPA, the FDA and the Civil Rights Division at the Department of Justice (DOJ) (Andrias 2013, 1061–1063).

President Obama, too, resorted to nonenforcement discretion when his legislative efforts went nowhere in a hostile Congress. Whereas Republican administrations deregulated through nonenforcement by appointing agency heads who were anti-enforcement, President Obama announced a nonenforcement policy by sending a memorandum to enforcement agencies authorized to enforce immigration laws and marijuana laws. Both policies were publicly announced after years of low priority enforcement (Mikos 2011, 1002–1003; Cox and Rodriguez 2015, 104). Both of these categorical declarations followed a "pattern of escalating assurances of nonenforcement (Price 2016, 953–954)." Furthermore, these assurances were announced in a very public fashion.

President Obama's marijuana policy received some support in Congress, in the form of appropriations riders barring the DOJ from using funds to prevent states from implementing their own, laxer marijuana policies.[13] The immigration policy, on the other hand, was challenged in court. Texas and twenty-five other states successfully sued to enjoin the second of the two deferred action programs, Deferred Action for Parents of Americans. The district court, as well as the Court of Appeals held that the program, due to its categorical nature, was not merely an exercise of enforcement discretion but an action, akin to a rule, and thus, should have gone through notice-and-comment review.[14] At least in principle, the Texas v. United

---

[11] Executive Order No. 12,291, 3 C.F.R. 127 (1982).

[12] Kate Andrias, who served on President Obama's White House staff, observed that "Bush exercised more extensive control over enforcement than did many of his predecessors (Andrias 2013, 1061)."

[13] Consolidated Appropriations Act, 2016, Pub. L. No. 114-113, § 542, 129 Stat. 2242, 2332-33 (2015); Consolidated and Further Continuing Appropriations Act, 2015, Pub. L. No. 113-235, § 538, 128 Stat. 2130, 2217 (2014) (including similar restriction).

[14] Texas v. United States, 809 F.3d 134 (5th Cir. 2015), aff'd by an equally divided court, 136 S. Ct. 2271 (2016).

States[15] decision is consistent with the notion that prospective enforcement policies are like rules that apply broadly and should be outside prosecutorial discretion. If not, and to the extent regulation and enforcement are substitutes, the scheme favors enforcement; in particular, if it gives rise to reliance protections (Price 2016).

And President Trump's administration, like his Republican predecessors, has been less willing to enforce laws they perceive as anti-business. This pattern is not new. Between 1948 and 1977, the National Labor Relations Board remedial action decisions in the area of unfair labor were more pro-union during Democratic administrations and more pro-business during Republican administrations (Moe 1982, 208). Unlike his predecessors, Trump's administration has also retreated in enforcement by financial enforcement agencies (Velikonja 2017). Yet, the difference between Trump's approach and Obama's is substantive. If President Obama deregulated through nonenforcement transparently, with a prospective public announcement, then President Trump has done so *sub rosa*, all the while publicly denying that enforcement policy and priorities have changed. This contrast displays a legal challenge in the fact that transparently announced policies have been challenged in court, whereas nontransparent ones have not and, as a general matter, cannot.

Accountability and Nonenforcement

There may be good reasons to treat publicly announced enforcement policies differently from tacitly adopted ones. The most obvious is U.S. Supreme Court precedent. Moreover, an announced enforcement policy is easy to identify. Public announcement may engender reliance that, in turn, can result in significant legal consequences, protected by the due process. For example, an individual brought to the United States as an infant that complied with President Obama's DACA memorandum may be able to stop President Trump's effort to reverse course and remove her legal protections. If so, a nonenforcement declaration really is akin to a new rule and ought to have gone through the same process.

But not every categorical change in enforcement is, or need to be, publicly announced. For example, the U.S. Securities and Exchange Commission (SEC) significantly reduced enforcement against Wall Street financial firms during President Trump's administration. During the second Obama presidency (2013–2016), the SEC prosecuted at least 21 defendants each fiscal year. In the first 6 months of President Trump's administration, the SEC prosecuted six: of those, five were carryover cases from President Obama's administration. The SEC has made no public statement on nonenforcement against large financial firms, but that does not imply that, for example Goldman Sachs or Citigroup, are unaware that there is a new sheriff in town and the sheriff is targeting different villains. The only ones left in the dark about the change is the public. And without a public announcement, no legal

---

[15] Ibid.

challenge to the change in enforcement policy appears possible, even if the rules of the game really have changed for firms like Goldman Sachs or Citigroup.

This essay suggests that the choice between discretionary nonenforcement, which courts cannot touch, and categorical nonenforcement, which they can, is not binary. Enforcement priorities can result in enforcement declines that are substantial, but not down to zero, even in the absence of a public declaration of nonenforcement. Low-priority enforcement such as practiced by the SEC poses a significant accountability challenge. If the availability of judicial review of agency nonenforcement decisions hinges on a public declaration of nonenforcement, the doctrine has a built-in bias in favor of well-heeled, well-connected classes of defendants. In order to change immigration enforcement, President Obama had no choice but to make a public announcement: the targets of his policies were too numerous and not well connected. Similarly, the market of marijuana growers, sellers and users was too large to communicate nonenforcement quietly. By contrast, well-heeled financial firms are few in number and well connected. A public announcement of a nonenforcement policy is neither necessary nor desirable. The only result such announcement would produce is public outrage.

Whatever review is appropriate, there is no reason to treat departures in one direction differently from departures in the other.[16] Enforcement can move in more than one direction: it can increase significantly as the SEC saw in the aftermath of the accounting scandals or the Madoff Ponzi scheme, and decrease precipitously, as evidenced at the SEC under Trump-selected Chair Jay Clayton, and his predecessor, Acting Chair Michael Piwowar. There is no reason in constitutional or administrative law to treat discretionary agency choices differently depending on whether there is an increase or a decrease in enforcement. Both raise similar questions about judicial review, they also raise symmetrical questions about fair notice and due process, and about the separation of powers. It would seem that demanding that agencies give reasons for changes in rules, reason-giving seems appropriate for significant shifts in enforcement, in order to match given reasons with observed enforcement practices, and to subject those reasons to political scrutiny through media coverage and congressional attention, even when judicial review is not available or appropriate.

Bučar on Nonenforcement

A deeper analysis of Bučar's system theory has been provided by other authors in this volume. What is interesting and relevant for my contribution, is Bučar's understanding of power and the interaction of different sub-system in his theory.

Namely, as Bučar displays (e.g., Chap. 2) at several points in his book – At A New Crossroads – he understands power as "power over" others. Putting this in

---

[16] But see Scalia (1983), and Easterbrook (1983) who argues for more lenient review of nonenforcement and inaction, than agency action, on the basis of individual autonomy.

perspective of his system theory, this means that sub-systems interact with one another through multiple different channels – political, economic, legal – in order to get their way. In such a complex relations and system, Bachrach and Baratz (1962) say that power resides also with the actors, who are able to make a non-decision – control the agenda. Bučar warns (Chap. 4) of this power dimension with historical examples, such as: "*Veto Poloniam perdidit*". This does not mean that Bučar opposes or denies this power of non-decision, but that he is cautious of its traps. Bučar normatively prefers human action and decision and consequently also sub-systems' actions and ultimately actions of a system. For him non-action is worse and results in worse situations as a wrong decision or action. Therefore, Bučar understands non-action as a malfunction within a system. As such, it should be corrected through the actions of other sub-systems and multiple feedback-loops.

Thus, my reading of Bučar's argument is that if there is nonenforcement by the legal sub-system, this needs to be and will be addressed by actions of other sub-systems – e.g., political. However, if the nonenforcement resides within the executive branch of the government, it is the other two branches – legislative and judiciary – that will step in and ameliorate the situation.

Therefore, the question regarding the presented American case – should addressing nonenforcement be part of legal, political, or both sub-systems? The primary reason for nonenforcement as described in this essay is to achieve political objectives. For Bučar objectives always have their origins in values (Chap. 2), so the first to address this issue should be the political sub-system, consistent with Bučar's commitment to the European tradition of the separation of legal rules from politics, and morality. Therefore, my recommendations will be political sub-system focused.

What to Do?

Under U.S. federal administrative law, categorical abdications of enforcement are subject to judicial review under Heckler v. Cheney for violations of the Administrative Procedure Act, but case-by-case decisions not to enforce are not. Low-priority enforcement falls in between, in that (1) in the absence of a smoking gun public document one cannot prove that the agency abdicated its responsibility to enforce the law, and thus one cannot show that the agency did so for arbitrary reasons, and (2) a shift to low-priority enforcement may be within agency discretion and thus not subject to judicial review.

Lumping patterns of nonenforcement with nonreviewable case-by-case decisions presents several risks. A change on a large scale in a short amount of time significantly changes the *de facto* legal compliance obligations for a large segment of the financial industry. Under the Trump administration, only "real fraud" is truly prohibited – think Wolf of Wall Street – while more sophisticated types of frauds and other serious violations of securities laws fly under the radar. That change occurred rapidly and largely out of the public eye, even though defendants surely understand the changed landscape.

Whatever the reason for the change, it should not matter from a deterrence perspective or from the separation of powers perspective: a pattern of nonenforcement may be difficult to distinguish from categorical nonenforcement that courts have held is akin to a rule change. If so, it should be evaluated under similar standards. If not, agencies have an incentive to move lawmaking from the more transparent rulemaking to nonenforcement (Deacon 2010), and to move enforcement policies from the more public categorical pronouncements to quiet policy changes. If that is the case, the consequence will be that small, discrete but well-connected minorities will consistently benefit, whereas nonenforcement directed at a more diffuse class will be reviewed under a more stringent standard.

Subjecting patterns of nonenforcement to judicial review would involve difficult line-drawing questions. The district court in Texas v. United States[17] fairly easily classified President Obama's DAPA program as "affirmative action rather than inaction."[18] When is a change in enforcement, without a public declaration, sufficient? Should such changes be reviewed like rules, implying that unless the change went through a notice-and-comment process, it is illegal? Or should enforcement changes be treated like case-by-case agency decisions, which courts reviewed to ensure that the are based on substantial evidence?

Alternately, and perhaps a better approach, one could acknowledge that a change in the patterns of (non)enforcement look less like a rule than a categorical policy of nonenforcement, even if it is quietly communicated to those affected, because it is easier to reverse that a DACA-like program. Since a quiet change in enforcement was never publicly announced, it does not need to be revoked in the court of public opinion and it does not create legally protected reliance expectations. Potential defendants have no legally protected expectations that the law will or will not be enforced with a certain level of intensity, absent a public categorical declaration (Sohoni 2017, 31). The appropriate remedy for excessive crackdowns or gaps in enforcement is not judicial but political. Clear legislative guidelines and mechanisms by which the legislature can police enforcement deviations, and more honest reporting of enforcement activities may be the better approach how to tackle the nonenforcement issue.

Congressional oversight may be of limited effectiveness during periods of unified government, but honest agency reporting has promise. Agencies are already required to report to Congress considerable amounts of information about their activities, including on enforcement.[19] But their incentives are biased. They choose enforcement metrics that they report, and so they use the ones that are more easily manipulated (Velikonja 2016). Rather than disclose reports, disclosing raw data, and outsourcing analysis to the crowd, might be more productive. The SEC, for example, already makes available public company financial disclosures that it

---

[17] 86 F. Supp. 3d 591, 645 (S.D.Tex.) *aff'd*, 809 F.3d 134 (5th Cir. 2015), aff'd by an equally divided court, United States v. Texas, 136 S. Ct. 2271 (2016) (mem.) (per curiam).

[18] 86 F. Supp. 3d 591, 654.

[19] Results Act.

receives. In fact, it requires issuers to tag disclosures, so as to facilitate empirical research. Agencies could do the same with their enforcement data.

Conclusion

Agencies can significantly change enforcement priorities with each change of administration. That is generally as it should be: it keeps courts out of policy choices; it allows for flexibility in setting enforcement priorities that may be necessary in light of a change in circumstances, such as a series of scandals.

At the same time, discretion can swallow the rule of law. Swift and large changes in enforcement policy mean the rule that people face means one thing under one administration, and another under the administration that follows. Worse still, the change occurs quickly, undermining any investments and reliance expectations by those affected.

Although Bučar derives from a different legal tradition, his system theory bears important implications for American legal and political system as well. My proposals derive from my understanding of his system theory, which if applied to the question at hand tells us that there ought to be some constraint on enforcement discretion but as discussed in this essay, the constraint is not and, generally, should not be judicial. Rather, congressional oversight and media scrutiny may be the better avenues for accountability.

Literature

Andrias, K. (2013). The President's enforcement power. *New York University Law Review, 88*(4), 1031–1125.

Bachrach, P., & Baratz, M. S. (1962). Two faces of power. *American Political Science Review, 56*(4), 947–952.

Biber, E. (2008). The importance of resource allocation in administrative law. *Administrative Law Review, 60*(1), 1–63.

Black, B., & Kraakman, R. (1996). A self-enforcing model of corporate law. *Harvard Law Review, 109*(8), 1911–1982.

Bressman, L. S. (2004). Judicial review of agency inaction: An arbitrariness approach. *New York University Law Review, 79*(5), 1657–1718.

Cox, A. B., & Rodríguez, C. M. (2015). The president and immigration law Redux. *Yale Law Journal, 125*(1), 104–225.

Deacon, D. T. (2010). Deregulation through Nonenforcement. *New York University Law Review, 85*(3), 795–828.

Delahunty, R. J., & Yoo, J. C. (2012). Dream on: The Obama Administration's Nonenforcement of immigration Laws, the DREAM act, and the take care clause. *Texas Law Review, 91*(4), 781–857.

Easterbrook, F. H. (1983). On not enforcing the law. *Regulation: AEI Journal on Government and Society, 7*(1), 14–16.

Kelsen, H. (1967). *Pure theory of law*. Berkeley: University of California Press.

Love, J. A., & Garg, A. K. (2014). Presidential inaction and the separation of powers. *Michigan Law Review, 112*(7), 1195–1250.

Mikos, R. A. (2011). Medical marijuana and the political safeguards of federalism. *Denver University Law Review, 89*(4), 997–1009.

Moe, T. M. (1982). Regulatory performance and presidential administration. *American Journal of Political Science, 26*(2), 197–224.

Nader, R. (2017). Trump's anti-consumer agenda hurts his voters. New York Times. https://www.nytimes.com/2017/10/23/opinion/ralph-nader-trump-consumers.html. Accessed 18 Jan 2018.

Price, Z. S. (2014). Enforcement discretion and executive duty. *Vanderbilt Law Review, 67*(3), 671–769.

Price, Z. S. (2015). Politics of Nonenforcement. *Case Western Reserve Law Review, 65*(4), 1119–1149.

Price, Z. S. (2016). Reliance on nonenforcement. *William and Mary Law Review, 58*(3), 937–1027.

Revesz, R. L., & Livermore, M. A. (2008). *Retaking rationality: How cost-benefit analysis can better protect the environment and our health.* Oxford: Oxford University Press.

Scalia, A. (1983). The doctrine of standing as an essential element of the separation of powers. *Suffolk University Law Review, 17*(4), 881–899.

Sohoni, M. (2017). Crackdowns. *Virginia Law Review, 103*(1), 31–105.

Velikonja, U. (2016). Reporting agency performance: Behind the SEC's enforcement statistics. *Cornell Law Review, 101*(4), 901–980.

Velikonja, U. (2017). Behind the Annual SEC Enforcement Report: 2017 and Beyond. https://papers.ssrn.com/sol3/papers.cfm?abstract_id=3074073. Accessed January 18 2018.

Walters, D. E. (2016). The judicial role in constraining presidential Nonenforcement discretion: The virtues of an APA approach. *University of Pennsylvania Law Review, 164*(7), 1911–1948.

Work Task Automation and Artificial Intelligence: Implications for the Role of Government

Matej Drev

We live in an era in which a widespread adoption of artificial intelligence technologies is poised to touch an ever-expanding array of our daily activities. As deployment of sophisticated machine learning algorithms fed by exponentially growing sets of 'training' data becomes increasingly prevalent, 'smart' machines will begin to compete with, and outperform, humans in a variety of work tasks ranging from operating vehicles to analyzing legal documents. According to recent research (e.g., McKinsey Global Institute 2017; Bhalla et al. 2017), up to 30% of all hours worked globally are at risk of being automated by machines in the next 15 years, with the effects of automation being particularly acute in advanced economies such as the members of the Organization for Economic Cooperation and Development (OECD). If the predictions about the near-term impact of artificial intelligence are indeed borne out, labor markets in advanced economies will undergo a transition on a scale that is unlike anything that we have seen since the nascent years of the industrial revolution. In order to successfully navigate what will undoubtedly be a challenging transition period, governments in advanced economies will need to play a leading role that will go beyond the traditional government role of a regulator and warden of a favorable macroeconomic environment, and will necessitate decisive allocation of public investment, long-term policy planning, and deep partnerships with key economic stakeholders. As governments in advanced economies around the world find themselves negotiating the pace of artificial intelligence deployment (e.g., when and in what manner we should allow fully autonomous trucks and cars to drive on public roads), funding and managing massive workforce reskilling and retraining programs (e.g., for fast food workers whose jobs were 'automated away'), and brokering the debate about allocation of technology-fueled productivity gains (e.g., the likely push by affected groups for some form of 'universal basic income'), they will fully embody (and even stretch) the role of modern government as partner so eloquently described by Bučar in the book that this essay accompanies.

M. Drev (✉)
San Francisco, CA, USA

© Springer International Publishing AG, part of Springer Nature 2019   35
I. Kovač (ed.), *At His Crossroad*, https://doi.org/10.1007/978-3-319-78331-4_4

In this essay, I apply Bučar's understanding of state-private enterprise partnership, which he outlines in the present translation (At a New Crossroads) in Chap. 7, onto a contemporary economic problem of artificial intelligence technologies, and present recommendations that flow from this analysis.

Namely, for Bučar private enterprises, guided by profits, and the state, providing public goods (e.g., clean environment, rule of law, and security), are not independent of one another. Both subsystems are connected: in the long run there is no profit without adequate public good provision; reciprocally, public goods cannot be adequately provided if there is no economic surplus generated in the private sector, providing a pool of taxable income for the state. Both entities and their objectives are not mutually exclusive but mutually dependent on each other. As such, common elements or interests emerge between what stereotypically is considered to be two opposed 'logics'. Bučar argues that a new 'economic checks and balance' framework is needed for the future: a system where the logic of profit and the logic of providing public goods will be institutionalized. One such already existing example of a new partnership is economic intelligence (Gaiser 2016): the state by itself nor private business are sufficient for a successful economic intelligence and international business operation. Yet, both are necessary elements of realization of profits and assuring public goods. Moreover, both entities – states and private business – are increasingly aware of these new demands for more associative relations.

The Matrix (Revolution(s))?

The promise and excitement of fast-paced technical progress permeates our world today. In particular, rapid advances in artificial intelligence technologies and their accelerating adoption promise to improve our quality of daily life – bringing us everything from ever smarter home devices and personal gadgets to science-fiction-style autonomous vehicles and hyper-accurate personalized medical treatments – but they also bring along potentially undesirable economic resource reallocation and associated myriad societal challenges. One of such challenges that has the power to materially disrupt the lives of large swaths of the populace is the looming threat of replacement of an ever-expanding array of human work tasks with machines. While the extent and pace of automation will vary across occupations and geographies, estimates suggest that tasks ranging from operating machinery (including vehicles) to preparing fast food, and from paralegal work to accounting, could see rapid near-term adoption of automation technologies fueled by artificial intelligence (e.g., Brynjolfsson and McAfee 2012).[1]

What makes these trends significant is that the occupations most at risk of near-term substitution by machines are also simultaneously those that tend to employ the largest numbers of workers in advanced economics. For example, as shown in the

---

[1] Although an excellent overview of this topic, it is slightly dated.

Table 1 Largest occupations in the United States in 2016

	Denotes significant risk of automation
Retail Salespersons	4.5
Cashiers	3.5
Food Preparation and Serving Workers	3.4
Office Clerks	3.0
Registered Nurses	2.9
Customer Service Representatives	2.7
Laborers and Freight, Stock, and Materials Movers	2.6
Waiters and Waitresses	2.6
Secretaries and Administrative Assistants	2.3
General and Operations Managers	2.2

Data from U.S. Bureau of Labor Statistics, as of May 2016; risk of automation assessed by author based on published research

Table 1, occupations with significant risk of automation such as cashiers, food preparation and serving workers (including fast food workers), office clerks, and freight movers are all among the largest occupations in the United States. If predictions about these occupations being at high risk of automation in the near term are indeed borne out, advanced economies will face an unprecedented transition in the labor market, along with an array of associated economic and societal challenges.

While these predictions are worrisome, it is important to note that while many occupations will likely face a steep decline in demand due to automation, new jobs will likely be concurrently created in the economy. As automation- and artificial-intelligence-fueled productivity gains translate into economic growth tailwinds in advanced economies and meaningful growth continues in emerging economies, labor market demand will rise across the board as a result. Moreover, in advanced economies the aging population will serve as a further key driver of labor market demand as more workers retire and need to be replaced, and as expanded life expectancy leads to stronger demand for occupations in healthcare and personal services. It is thus hard to predict the size and direction of the net overall effect on near- and long-term demand for labor, and this issue is the subject of intense ongoing research by economists across the globe (e.g., Acemoglu and Restrepo 2017). While history suggests that periods of rapid adoption of labor-substituting technologies have always resulted in net long-term labor demand expansion, artificial intelligence is by definition a 'general purpose technology' and its technical limits when it comes to replacing human work tasks are both hard to predict and rapidly evolving.

However, while it is uncertain whether widespread adoption of automation and artificial intelligence technologies will lead to structurally higher near- and long-term unemployment, it is far more certain that large swaths of the workforce will be displaced from their existing occupations, and will thus be forced to find new employment, possibly in occupations that are far removed from their existing field of competence. To illustrate this assertion, we need to look no further than at the ~3.5 million truck and delivery drivers in the United States, for whom the threat of near-term replacement by autonomous vehicles looms particularly large (e.g., Hook and Waters 2017; Dougherty 2017). If we indeed see material commercial adoption of self-driving cars and trucks in the next decade, the demand for human truck driving services could become compressed as a result. According to the American Trucking Associations, the average U.S. truck driver is male, 49 years old, makes approximately $20 per hour, and does not hold a college degree (Driver Solutions 2017). If this group of workers progressively finds its jobs substituted away by machines, they will have to either:

(a) Accept lower-paying jobs with low skill requirements that are less susceptible to automation (e.g., as personal care workers, building and grounds cleaners, or food serving workers),
(b) Retrain to upgrade their skills in order to qualify for well-paying jobs in growing occupations (e.g., in IT, professional services, and healthcare), or
(c) Face protracted underemployment or unemployment.

From a societal standpoint, it is optimal for as many affected workers as possible to reskill and retrain in order to find well-paying jobs in growing occupations; however, research suggests this is a very difficult challenge, especially for older workers and those at lower rungs of the skill and education distribution.[2]

While market forces do tend to allocate economic resources to their most productive uses in the long-run, in the face of large disruptions they can take a long time to 'clear'. Given the demographics and socioeconomic characteristics of truck drivers and many other at-risk occupational groups such as cashiers and fast food workers, it is likely that material swaths of the workforce will face significant challenges in navigating the upcoming labor market transition. In order to smooth the disruptions, governments will need to play a critical role in ensuring that as many displaced workers as possible are able to retrain and gainfully re-enter the labor market without protracted spells of unemployment. However, this will be a truly monumental task as the upcoming labor market transition is poised to be akin in scale to the shift from agriculture- to manufacturing-centered labor markets that occurred in late nineteenth century and early twentieth century North America and Europe, and more recently in China (McKinsey Global Institute 2017). The demands of this task will necessitate that governments actively intervene and use public resources to ensure labor markets 'clear' as quickly and efficiently as possible. This will require timely and targeted investment in large-scale education and retraining

---

[2] For a series of studies on the effects of labor demand decline due to international trade liberalization on American male manufacturing workers, please refer to the following works: Autor et al. (2013, 2018) and Pierce and Schott (2016).

programs, substantial transitional support for displaced occupational groups, and active negotiation of the pace and manner of work task automation across a wide array of use cases.

The Government as the Terminator?

As governments are forced to play a role that goes beyond traditional regulation and ensuring a favorable macroeconomic environment, policy decision-makers will need to show leadership in forming and syndicating long-term public resource allocation decisions, spearhead the public debate about the economic benefits and challenges associated with widespread adoption of automation and artificial intelligence technologies, and, importantly, form meaningful partnerships with affected economic stakeholders (occupational organizations such as trade unions, employer associations such as chambers of commerce, civic society organizations such as NGOs, etc.) as well as successfully broker between their competing incentives in the interest of the long-term public good.

History teaches us that one particularly important pitfall to avoid will be that of falling into the trap of short-termism and protectionism, both of which will become particularly appealing once widespread work task automation begins in earnest. Just as nineteenth century Luddites in England destroyed weaving machinery in protest of adoption of machines in the textile industry, we can easily imagine twenty-first century UPS drivers smashing up autonomous vans in protest of adoption of self-driving technology in the package delivery industry. The push toward 'luddite protectionism' in the pursuit of short-term policy agendas is likely to be strong, and we can already see glimpses of it today (e.g., Ziobro 2018; Plucinska and Posaner 2016). In order that our societies avoid this trap, governments will need to adopt and successfully communicate a long-term policy approach that

(a) Embraces automation and artificial intelligence due to the momentous potential of associated productivity gain all the while simultaneously, and
(b) Ensuring transitional support for displaced worker groups.

When it comes to achieving the latter goal, and if I bring Bučar's ideas to what I believe are their logical conclusions, then we should expect the policy dialogue in some affected economies to be very broad and potentially include considerations of supplementing the existing social contract with new entitlements such as forms of universal basic income. It will be imperative that governments successfully balance this dialogue and steer it in the direction of the two-pronged long-term policy approach outlined above.

Conclusion

A lot is at stake. Artificial intelligence holds the promise to deliver immense productivity gains and potentially drive our societies closer to the Roman ideal of *otium*, but at the expense of significant near-term economics challenges and societal disruptions.[3] How effectively societies navigate this upcoming transition will crucially depend on the role of governments. As Bučar eloquently writes in Chap. 8 that the government is no longer only a bearer of power as it was in the past, but it is becoming a partner whose cooperation with other societal subsystems ensures the conditions of societal survival. The nascent era of work task automation and artificial intelligence adoption will prove this assertion beyond the shadow of a doubt and will serve both as a test of the capacity of our societies to effectively govern ourselves as well as serve to expand the realm of possibilities for modern long-term policy making.

Literature

Acemoglu, D., & Restrepo, P. (2017). Robots and jobs: Evidence from US labor markets. NBER Working Paper #23285.

Autor, D. H., Dorn, D., & Hanson, G. H. (2013). The China syndrome: Local labor market effects of import competition in the United States. *American Economic Review, 103*(6), 2121–2168.

Autor, D. H., Dorn, D., & Hanson, G. (2018). When work disappears: manufacturing decline and the falling marriage-market value of men. NBER Working Paper #23173.

Beard, M. (2015). *SPQR: A history of ancient Rome*. London: Profile Books.

Bhalla, V., Dyrchs, S., & Strack, R. (2017). Twelve forces that will radically change how organizations work. https://www.bcg.com/publications/2017/people-organization-strategy-twelve-forces-radically-change-organizations-work.aspx. Accessed 28 Jan 2018.

Brynjolfsson, E., & McAfee, A. (2012). *The second machine age: Work, progress, and prosperity in a time of brilliant technologies*. New York: WW Norton & Company.

Dougherty, C. (2017). Self-driving trucks may be closer than they appear. The New York Times. https://www.nytimes.com/2017/11/13/business/self-driving-trucks.html. Accessed 28 Jan 2018.

Driver Solutions. (2017). State of trucking. https://greatcdltraining.com/state-of-trucking-2017. Accessed 28 Jan 2018.

Gaiser, L. (2016). *Economic intelligence and world governance: Reinventing states for a new world order*. San Marino: Il Cerchio.

Hook, L. & Waters, R. (2017). Google's Waymo passes milestone in driverless car race. Financial Times. https://www.ft.com/content/dc281ed2-c425-11e7-b2bb-322b2cb39656. Accessed 28 Jan 2018.

---

[3] Beard (2015) explains that live-right, 'otium' referred to a cliché of Roman moralizing that a true gentleman was to be supported by the profits of his estates, not by wage labor, which was inherently dishonorable. Latin vocabulary captured the idea that 'otium' was the desired state of humanity was (a state of 'leisure' or a state of being in control of one's own time) and it stood in contrast to 'negotium', which referred to 'business' of any kind.

McKinsey Global Institute. (2017). Jobs lost, jobs gained: Workforce transitions in a time of automation. https://www.mckinsey.com/~/media/McKinsey/Global%20Themes/Future%20 of%20Organizations/What%20the%20future%20of%20work%20will%20mean%20for%20 jobs%20skills%20and%20wages/MGI-Jobs-Lost-Jobs-Gained-Report-December-6-2017. ashx. Accessed 28 Jan 2018.

Pierce, J. R., & Schott, P. K. (2016). Trade liberalization and mortality: Evidence from US counties. NBER Working Paper #22849.

Plucinska, J., & Posaner, J. (2016). Self-driving cars hit European speed bump. Politico. https:// www.politico.eu/article/uber-volvo-self-driving-cars-eu-regulations/. Accessed 28 Jan 2018.

U.S. Bureau of Labor Statistics. (2016). https://www.bls.gov.

Ziobro, P. (2018). Teamsters tell UPS: No drones or driverless trucks. Wall Street Journal. https://www.wsj.com/articles/teamsters-tell-ups-no-drones-or-driverless-trucks-1516795200. Accessed 28 Jan 2018.

Part II
France Bučar: At a New Crossroads

Introduction

We experience the world in which we live today as obsessed with the desire and need for the fastest possible growth and development. In a word: for progress. This progress—itself an ideological notion—has no clearly defined direction. We speak of progress as creating the highest possible income per capita in order to enable the acquisition of ever more material goods. This might be considered an acceptable goal given that most of the world lives in poverty and deprivation. Even in technologically advanced countries a large share of the population still struggles on the edge of poverty. The problem is that this type of development is distinctly one-sided and internally imbalanced. High income per capita does not necessarily correlate with the greatest possible progress, especially if it confronts us with unresolved issues elsewhere in society, including issues that could potentially threaten our very existence. The current social order and global mentality make it impossible for us to seriously consider these issues.

We are all trapped in an unrelenting race. Higher social income guarantees greater social power, especially political power, along with more material comfort. For the big players, the race to the top is imperative. Smaller and less economically developed players are condemned, as long as they lag behind the more developed players, to constant subservience, including political subservience.

But everyone loses: even the winners. The social cost of such imbalanced development is too high even for them, and they pay it by running a deficit that eventually leads to internal disintegration, particularly with respect to values. For former communist countries, the price is even higher because the era of communism set them behind not only in economic terms, but also in general social terms.

The world needs new answers to today's challenges. The answers that guided the capitalist order in the past no longer suffice. Today's version of capitalism is something completely different from that of the past, and the problems it needs to address are also new. Even the old traditional problems have changed.

Thus it is necessary to subject the current state of affairs to rigorous analysis. If we want development and new growth, we must first know where we are going and what our true goals are. Growth for its own sake, growth without purpose, becomes a cancerous social formation, and moreover a goal is never merely technical—it is always based to one extent or another on values. Where do we want to go? What is our destination? The aim of having more material goods is not enough, and here lies the most significant void in today's society. Responding to this fundamental question is the most difficult task of all as it reaches to the roots of our being. But without a response, we will not be able to continue much longer.

One obstacle is that we keep relying on the old answers and self-evident truths that contemporary neoliberals advocate with increasing desperation. Responses that were correct in conditions that no longer exist, or in conditions that are fundamentally different, are unsuitable and can even be harmful in the new conditions we face today. Such ostensibly self-evident truths prevent us from finding the right responses. The danger lies in the fact that we do not even question their correctness of these truths because they seem self-evident. However, such self-evident answers are particularly dangerous. When we got rid of communism in certain parts of the world, we naturally began looking back to systems before communism, but we kept forgetting that the capitalism of that earlier era was not ideal either. And above all, we forgot that kind of capitalism no longer exists. Today we use the same word to describe two very different economic and social orders.

New responses are urgently needed because we cannot survive without them. However, there are no ready models for producing these responses. We must create them ourselves, mostly from scratch, and the first condition for creating them is to free ourselves from prejudice and self-evident truths.

We need to be just as critical toward the "new" old discoveries offered by the supporters of rapid and limitless—but internally imbalanced—growth. We live in a time of enormous social change and it is hard to get our bearings when we face so many new choices, so many new crossroads. This is why critical thinking is more necessary than ever. But before setting out on a new road, we must first establish where we are.

This endeavor is the aim of this book. It does not offer definitive solutions, let alone proscribe steps to be taken. It only sheds light on where we are, and, above all, it demands that we start thinking for ourselves.

Chapter 1: Prosperity

France Bucar and Igor Kovač

The Transition to Prosperity

In J. K. Galbraith's 1950s book The Affluent Society, the American economist pointed out that the ideas guiding the modern welfare state originated in the conditions of serious poverty that have prevailed since the dawn of man. The failure of society to adapt its underlying ideas to new conditions has caused a range of problems that may jeopardize the prosperity that has been acquired. Poverty and scarcity still exist in much of the world with the exception of a relatively small number of countries inhabited or claimed by Europeans. Until relatively recently, only Western Europe and North America could boast of prosperity. Poor and hungry people have limited choices and few can afford to focus on goals beyond survival. Only the rich face the question of what to do with their wealth. Thus it is more probable that the wealthy will engage in activities that will threaten their very position and prosperity. This is particularly true when the status of affluence came suddenly and represents a radical change from previous conditions.

The question of how to live in affluence was new and challenging for politicians and social scientists in rich countries who found themselves in a situation they had not foreseen. To those of us who lived in scarcity, for example during the economic devastation that prevailed in Yugoslavia after World War II, these challenges seemed absurd and even insulting. Such problems hardly seemed serious or relevant to those of who lived in post-war Slovenia. The question of how to live in affluence could only be articulated by states that enjoyed a surplus: we would certainly know what to do in such a situation! The only question we needed to answer was how to free

F. Bucar (Deceased)

I. Kovač (✉)
Department of Political Science, University of Cincinnati, Cincinnati, OH, USA
e-mail: kovacir@mail.uc.edu

© Springer International Publishing AG, part of Springer Nature 2019   45
I. Kovač (ed.), *At His Crossroad*, https://doi.org/10.1007/978-3-319-78331-4_5

ourselves from poverty. All other questions revealed the boastful arrogance of those who lived in conditions of overabundance.

As it turned out, we would need only a half a century to come to the realization that this and related questions were in fact very relevant. Under communism, we never had the real possibility of catching up to the more developed West. All the same, we could not really talk of scarcity and poverty as they existed in much of the world before World War II. Ignoring the lack of spiritual freedom, our material well-being increased steadily throughout the communist era, and particularly toward its end. Following initial difficulties in the transition to capitalism, prosperity continued to grow in Slovenia after the country declared independence from Yugoslavia in 1991. Slovenia is not in the top tier as measured by various statistical indicators of national income per capita, nor is it among the most technologically advanced countries. Nevertheless it can be considered a prosperous nation because its citizens are able to fulfill their basic existential and housing needs on a level considered reasonable in accordance with generally accepted concepts of human dignity. Some might take issue with this characterization, but it is undeniable that the majority of Slovenians no longer need to deal with hunger, scarcity, and the uncertainty of survival as the primary issues of their lives as was the case in the not-so-distant past.

Consumer Society

That the prosperity Slovenia has achieved still strikes many as too modest—that many people want more, especially more material goods, and better-quality goods than they have now—is an indication that we are living in a new world the problems of which are completely different from the problems that humanity has confronted since time immemorial. Thus the answers we have at our disposal to explain our situation and guide our actions emerged in a world that was different from the one we live in today. We have entered a time that is completely new for humanity and in which we face fundamentally different questions. Even if these questions relate to conditions that on the outside seem similar or even identical to the ones we previously faced, the ready responses we have, although they may have been tested and confirmed by many generations before us, emerged from radically different circumstances, and thus they are inappropriate for today's conditions.

In times of general scarcity and the threat of hunger, the occasional abundance of food represented an opportunity that needed to be used to the fullest. But when the abundance of food is no longer a rare exception that needs to be exploited, this previous response becomes inappropriate. Our attitude toward food can no longer be dictated solely by the survival instinct, which rewards us with a feeling of pleasure when consuming food and satisfaction when we are full, and which functions as the main behavioral regulator in the struggle for existence. This essential instinct helped the human race survive and still serves this function in the rest of the biological world. However, in periods when food is overabundant, this instinct keeps people alive but eventually poses a threat to human health if it is left unchecked. As absurd as it may seem, the modern developed world has a greater problem with an over-abundance than with a shortage of food. Countless magazines and newspapers offer advice on how to lose weight or reduce the excess calories ingested in the large amounts of high-quality and high-fat food that is available. The overabundance of food also is in conflict with new standards of beauty that are growing in importance, having become, now that the burden of immediate survival has been lifted, a concern-inducing secondary need. Obesity was once a sign of affluence and thus an indication of success. Today the slender figure is valued not only aesthetically but also as a sign of control. Sports are not only a means of improving and maintaining health, which is its direct purpose, but also a sign of prosperity. A poor population had no need to engage in sports. On the contrary, the looming threat of hunger meant it was smarter to save energy than to waste it on activities that brought no tangible benefit. The current widespread importance of sports and exercise in society only came with prosperity, as sports was previously limited to the higher social strata. In Ancient Greece, the cradle of athletics, it was reserved exclusively for the free aristocracy. Today obesity has become a health threat for entire generations in many parts of the world. The cost of treating the consequences of obesity are no longer merely a financial burden for households, often exceeding the cost of food itself, but is also becoming a significant burden for national healthcare systems.

And yet in order to acquire more unnecessary goods, including food, we are ready to sacrifice most of our energy, time, limited lifespan, and even personal liberty. In this sense, the economy is paradoxically driven by and subjected to the requirements that governed the past economy of sheer survival.

The overabundance of nutritional and other material goods that once served to satisfy basic bodily needs can have, in addition to physiological strain, severe psychological consequences. The Latin saying plenus venter non studet libenter—a full stomach does not like to study—is a truism. In the past, only the privileged social class that did not need to struggle for daily survival could indulge in the arts and sciences, which elevates a person to a higher spiritual level, while today this possibility is available, with various limitations, to all. The privileged, who enjoyed this option in the past, could choose from a range of other activities to satisfy their needs and did not need to seek pleasure first and foremost in food. As a result, it was easier for them to avoid the dangers of this sort of overabundance.

But for many people, today's prosperity, its abundance of food and other material goods, represents an unexpected situation for which they are not organically or spiritually adapted. It seems to them that the old world in which they were rooted—which provided them with support, values, and meaning to their existence—has collapsed. Stomachs full, they sense a void they cannot fill with values that reflect and give meaning to their new situation. The liberation from the pressure of the threat of scarcity has also liberated people from the value system that used to ensure social integration, while at the same time requiring their abnegation, self-limitation, and observance to a set of rules that regulated behavior. Contrary to expectations, prosperity proved the senselessness of the values according to which people had previously lived. For many, freedom did not manifest itself either in new possibilities or in the revelation of new creative horizons allowed by personal freedom.

Freedom without meaning soon turns into self-denial and falls victim to the pressure of other limitations to which prosperity is linked. This is particularly true in the context of the organization of contemporary society that has enabled such prosperity. Subjugation to this system is a form of modern serfdom, and it is a price modern serfs appear willing to pay in order to fulfill their material needs. Fulfilling material needs has become a method of mental relaxation and a substitute for fulfilling spiritual needs. Most people have never had so many possibilities available to them. The situation is unique in the history of mankind, and yet it has resulted in voluntary subjugation to a new social hierarchy and a declining interest in anything beyond the fulfillment of material needs. This set of conditions is called consumer society.

The Attractions and Traps of Consumer Society

Consumer society leads to a specific understanding of life and a unique hierarchy of values. It results in the abandonment and even rejection of life patterns that have previous ensured survival, creating ambivalence toward them without replacing them with new values or adapting them to new circumstances. Consumer society represents conditions of prosperity that provide survival on a higher material level to a much larger number of people than ever before, but its very existence also puts humanity in greater danger than it has ever been in before.

The fundamental problem and the greatest danger for modern developed civilization lies in consumer society's most significant success—freeing humanity from the direct pressures of nature and the related human instincts that once regulated survival. In the past, those who failed to follow natural instincts providing clear instructions about what to do in particular situations were destined to fail. In contrast, contemporary prosperity allows us to act more independently. In other words, we are allowed to defy our natural instincts, opposing their underlying goals for a short or even longer period, without realizing that there are temporal limits to these negative actions. In times of abundance, conscious actions complement instinctive processes. Since instinctive adaptation has become relatively obsolete in human beings (see Erich Fromm, Man for Himself, p. 40), it is all the more necessary to substitute instincts with reason in order to offset our deficiencies in comparison to the animal world, which is fully governed by natural instinct.

Here humanity is exposed to a series of dangers. Liberation from the direct pressure of instinct leads us to believe that we are in full control of our lives, and that we will come to the right answers on our own without heeding the demands of nature, either internal or external. We first stumble on the issue of adequate knowledge. Prior success, especially successful liberation from the direct pressure of scarcity, often leads us to the conviction that humanity is the master of nature, and that nothing is impossible or unattainable. If this belief becomes a presumption of omniscience and we become too distant from nature, nature will inevitably have its revenge. Nature always has the last say. There is no leeway here. For modern humanity infatuated with science, the seductiveness of omniscience and the lack of modesty vis-à-vis nature pose an extraordinary threat. In a multitude of areas, distancing ourselves from nature and believing we control it has led us to the very precipice of catastrophe.

Furthermore, this apparent omniscience, accompanied by a rejection of the values that governed our behavior in the past, often leads to the false impression that we can fully and freely indulge our impulses, since we will be able to use our knowledge to undo any negative consequences from which our instincts had hitherto guarded us. We fool ourselves, believing that the values and social taboos of the past were only prejudices and have now lost all their worth. We believe we can deliberately act against the laws of nature and our natural instincts, reasoning that we can afford to do so. In the past, this was simply not possible. Functioning in accordance with the rules of nature when we do not necessarily need to—and especially when we expect some transitional short-term pleasure from this—requires a special effort that we are not willing to invest. But the reckoning eventually comes and when it does it is merciless. The bill may be received later but it has a high interest rate, and we somehow think that someone else will pay it.

The Socialization of Production

Despite the success of the developed world in liberating us from the direct pressure of nature, we are not freed from ongoing confrontation with the demands of the world in which we live. It simply means that we have found a way to be more successful in this confrontation than we were in the past. But we are not entirely freed from dealing with quotidian survival because we are still a part of the world, are bound to it and dependent upon it. We need to constantly manage available resources of material and energy in order to ensure a level of production that allows us to maintain the standard of living we have achieved. This calls for a high level of technological skills that need to be constantly enhanced and adapted to the changing environment.

One of the characteristics of this ongoing technological development is an extreme and still expanding division of labor. The division of labor itself calls for integration and coordination at a higher level, and because of the ongoing coordination of this division of labor, purely technical issues extend into the spheres of society and interpersonal communication. This in turn causes a range of secondary consequences that have a crucial impact on modern society and the position of the individual in it.

The most important of these is the socialization of production—something we were warned about in Karl Marx's classic works of economics—which today requires cooperation in the broadest economic context and prohibits former practices of closed economies and protectionism. Because of this, solidarity is necessary and cannot be avoided.

The constantly increasing division of labor and its coordination leads to an increasingly complicated production processes and the interdependency of those who take part in them. The increasing complexity of production demands advanced planning for necessary space and time. This in turn requires the participation of organized society and its various organs, leading to production becoming increasingly socialized. In addition, the high complexity of production leads to higher levels of vulnerability and risk. Humanity has never been as exposed as it is now to natural disasters and on such a scale. The slightest mistake or slip in any vital point of the global economy—and the number of these mistakes is growing—have potentially uncontrollable consequences because of the enormous interdependence caused by the complexity of production.

This means that the responsibility and influence of each individual on the broader environment, which they may not even know or sense, is greater than ever. This is not only true for those who occupy important positions in society or large organizations that are formally authorized to make decisions. The fate of a large number of people may depend on the performance of people in many different positions, even entirely technical ones. One need only consider how the organized engagement of a group of people can directly affect, through their activity or lack of activity, the existence and way of life of much larger numbers of people than that particular group.

It has long been recognized that successful production not only depends on technological skills, but also on the social relationships within an organization. As our interdependence increases, the management of social relationships is becoming an equally important aspect of successful production as technology. But this realization has not penetrated society as a whole. The prevailing view on the relationship between society and the individual has not changed in response to changing conditions.

Prosperity and Freedom

In the past, the availability of means of survival functioned as a limiting factor and ensured a necessary balance among different biological species, and, according to Thomas Malthus, also within human society. Here we are referring to the brutal laws of nature whereby starvation functioned as a regulator to maintain biological balance and therefore as a regulator of human activity. Humanity was directly subordinate to the laws of nature and its fate was determined by its narrow and relentless framework. Within this framework, mankind developed a close relationship with nature, also biologically, because nature governed humanity's actions and attitude to the surrounding environment. There was no other choice. Personal freedom was unnecessary because it served no purpose in this context.

What's more, freedom was not possible. Individuals were unable to survive on their own in conditions that required the constant struggle for survival, and in fact they still cannot today. We have always been bound to coexistence in one sort of community or another, from primitive gangs during periods of low development, to highly hierarchical pre-modern state structures. With such direct dependence on society, there was not much room for individual autonomy or emancipation from social norms. Until recently, the prevailing view on society was holistic, with individuals defined as parts of a uniform social structure, and anything individuals did was considered a function of the society and not of themselves. Individuals did not set the rules but received them from society (i.e. heteronomy). (For more on these issues, see, for example, J. C. Guillebaud's Re-founding the World.)

At the same time, the fate of individuals was entirely bound to the fate of the society in which they lived. Each of us survives only if our society survives. For this reason, societies have mechanisms that bind them together into organisms that are capable of survival and are based on values that reflect this internal interdependence. The first value is solidarity, a value without which no community can survive. Personality is not considered a category independent from the community. An individual's egoism is therefore a foreign body that has no place in the value structure of society. The same is true of competitiveness at the expense of the society. In later and higher stages of societal development, the conceptual link between the internal interdependence of a society and the existing value system becomes very vague— to the point that it has come to be believed that the value system is something that has been imposed from the outside, although it is precisely what allows the society to survive.

With the emergence of the welfare state, the entire system of trained responses and internalized values developed to ensure physical survival, a system on which the behavior of humanity had been based throughout history regardless of particular cultural patterns or religion, lost its foundation in reality and its purpose. The problems that were becoming apparent in the United States and were identified by Galbraith in the 1950s now seem trivial when compared to the extreme consequences that have come with the spread of prosperity to an even larger share of the globe and the tidal wave these consequences have triggered, the full power of which has yet to be revealed.

In some sense, the prosperous welfare state permitted us to be free of the pressure that society itself exerted on our behavior and our direct dependence on society has been considerably diminished. Prosperity has brought the possibility of greater independence of actions for individuals. Only now have we, as individuals, been given a chance to live as truly independent beings and to develop our abilities with an unprecedented level of freedom. Our actions can be almost fully adjusted to our needs, no longer taking into account the social norms that were shaped to suit society as a whole. The contradiction between society and the individual has thus been solved. Nevertheless, even while satisfying their own needs, liberated individuals must still adjust their actions to certain requirements of their social and natural environment because residual dependency remains. If they do not, they undermine the possibilities for their own survival. If individuals within society are not aware of this interdependence and do not behave accordingly, in a way that is to some degree governed by social norms, society itself is in danger of internal disintegration. The greater the divide between possible and actual individual autonomy and the greater the disregard for the needs of society, the more present this danger becomes. Today this divide looms threateningly large.

Prosperity and our Chances of Survival

Liberation from the direct pressure of nature in order to survive has placed the prosperous welfare state in an entirely new position with respect to reproduction. The continuation of the human race had previously been assured by the innate impulses of human nature. Whenever the natural instinct for propagation hit its upward limit in the context of overall survival, nature restored the necessary balance through hunger and disease. Today, humanity's situation has changed in this respect. Advances in biological science have enabled us to decide on the birth of our offspring without the direct pressure of the procreational drive. At the same time, the abundance of means allows us not only to guarantee the survival of our children, but also to prepare them for life at a higher level of human existence. Simply put, we can now decide on and manage the most crucial issues regarding the survival of the species, something that had never been possible before. In this sense, it seems that humanity has truly ascended the throne as the master of life.

Yet due to our insufficient self-awareness and self-control as well as an inadequate understanding of our new role in the world and indeed responsibility for the world, we have proved incapable of replacing the natural instincts that once safeguarded the survival of the species. The problem is not a deficit of knowledge; our knowledge has never been greater. Indeed our knowledge is so developed that we have solved many of the mysteries of the genetic foundations of life. We are even able to clone human beings and alter human nature (both of which may pose further threats to life as we know it). Another issue is that many people are unwilling to sacrifice material comfort and prosperity in order to bear and raise children. It appears that we do not have the will to compel rationality to govern ethical responsibility.

In many of the most developed and affluent countries in the world, declining birthrates already threaten the survival of society despite the unprecedented abundance of the means of survival.

An argument could be made that this represents the most radical break in human history, the most thorough revolution in human existence. All technological discoveries and advances in science that we have viewed as revolutionary breakthroughs in the past—for example, the invention of the wheel—set us on the path that has led to where we are now: this enormous transformation in the situation of human beings (at least in the parts of the world that have reached a certain level of prosperity). What we are experiencing is the transition from circumstances where human actions were predominantly governed by a system of natural impulses to a pattern of behavior that is determined and defined by our cognitive abilities. This moment in human history represents the highest level of liberation humanity has ever achieved. Even globalization, often regarded as the most far-reaching change in the situation of modern man, is merely a side effect of the welfare state and the society of prosperity.

In scientific circles, in the social sciences in general but particularly in political science, a seemingly paradoxical view has become widely accepted: namely that the existence of mankind cannot continue if we persist in the patterns and conceptions that emerged from the scientific revolution and the subsequent transition to the modern era that are the foundation of our current prosperity. New solutions and answers are being suggested for a range of issues extending from environmental protection to the rational use of energy sources. This new mode of thinking includes the realization that we can no longer follow the patterns dictated by an outdated notion of competition among nations and must instead turn to new concepts of supra-national integration. In some ways, the European Union could be considered a frontrunner in this process.

Nevertheless the most important problems remain unaddressed in part because they deal with issues that are largely invisible. These are problems in the realm of the human consciousness that has emerged as a result of new patterns of the possible and relate to necessary questions about how to behave in conditions of freedom. Problems emerging from the consumer society remain almost completely unaddressed, because they are not acknowledged as problems and thus are not clearly defined, which is a precondition for solving them. Problems stemming from the disintegration of the value system that has integrated society up until this point are also not clearly defined and their importance not emphasized. Calls to return to old values as the only possible solution usually represent an escape from reality, reflecting an unproductive and even suspicious moralism without the required social analysis. The relationship between the autonomy of reason as the main factor governing human behavior in conditions of freedom and prosperity, and the heteronomy of ethical rules, is far from a satisfactory response, nor is it grounds for appropriate action. It seems as if the conceptual and ethical challenges posed by the condition of modern liberated humanity surpass our capacity to formulate answers. They leave us in a state of confusion.

These challenges compel us to search for new meaning in life, for new ideals to live by. Thus we come full circle to our initial starting point: the shortage of the basic means of survival reduced our desires and behavioral choices to a relatively narrow frame: namely, what was necessary to protect ourselves from hunger and potentially life threatening external threats. The reaction of human beings who have been liberated from this direct threat is an understandable revenge against historical hunger and deprivation through the consumption of an excess of food and goods that were previously unavailable. The standards that once governed our lives did not emerge from a profound intellectual analysis, but instead were derived from long-term experience responding to direct needs. New responses will come in the same way. The key questions are how long will it take and, taking into account today's rapid development, the complexity of the society, and its internal interdependence, can we afford to delay? These questions are extremely relevant, certainly in terms of social planning as a necessary part of the modern economy. Should modern society at the highest level of development simply persist in patterns of behavior that were developed during past conditions? And by doing so, will we expedite and worsen the crisis resulting from this incompatibility, which is bound to come sooner or later, indeed sooner the more successful society is?

New Values and Concepts

Technological issues related to ensuring the survival of mankind at an extremely high level have essentially been solved, or are solvable with our current level of knowledge. Of course these issues require constant, deliberate, and well-planned attention, which in turn calls for a great deal of energy and creativity. But technical paths are known and there is no lack of will. The principle problem lies elsewhere: in the inappropriateness of the responses and value-related standards that have governed, and continue to govern, social relations, the perception of life, and the position of man in the world. These are so-called new-paradigm issues. However, even with respect to the production of material goods, the success of society—regardless of how questionable and poorly defined this so-called success is, and how dependent it is on the worldview characteristic of the welfare state—increasingly depends not just on technological know-how in production but on a better understanding of social relations.

If we assume the role of architect of our development and imagine the society of the future, the first question we must ask ourselves is what goals we wish to achieve. In the case of Slovenia, for example, the most realistic answer that comes to mind is to achieve the highest possible level of production of goods that will meet the actual or imagined needs of its population. A subsidiary short-term goal would be to catch up with the most technologically developed economies in terms of development and efficiency. From a technological perspective, this subsidiary goal is quite difficult and will consume most of our capacity for some time to come. Nevertheless, as far as so-called realists are concerned, it is the only reasonable goal since anything else would be a fantasy, especially because other goals might extend into a considerably distant future. In any case, it is what people want! Let us not forget that we are a consumer society! And we must make plans that relate to our actual lives and not some idealized distant future.

All of this is true. Nevertheless questions that extend beyond the interests of consumer society are surfacing today. Some of them emerge from a sense of bitterness about the secondary problems that the consumer society has created, many of which threaten the very foundations of the welfare state and the notion of prosperity: to have as much as possible. Numerous problems in areas as diverse as healthcare, social security, social pathology, juvenile delinquency, and crime are changing social priorities, or at least challenging the absolutism of the naked accumulation of material goods.

Even in prosperous welfare states, available goods are not distributed equally. A significant portion of the population remains at or below the poverty line, which itself is a relative concept. Thus we cannot deny the desire of a large number of people to attain greater material prosperity with the reproach that their orientation is consumerist. Modern advertising compels us to buy things we may not need, to satisfy artificial needs. Nevertheless many people, in terms of basic consumption patterns, live well below the average of what is considered a decent standard of living in modern times. The criterion for what is considered an adequate standard of living—during the era of struggling for survival, the criterion was absolutely clear: survival itself—has changed with the advent of the welfare state and consumer society. Even the number of criteria has increased as we have shifted from natural to social standards. This represents an important change. Natural criteria appear negligible, even superfluous, as it has become self-evident that virtually everyone possesses at least the minimum necessary for survival. Vagrancy is a deviation from the norm rather than a standard that is useful for comparison. As a social criterion, appropriate standards or comparisons have shifted to a conceptual plane: ideas such as fairness, human dignity, and the quality of life. Such criteria could only emerge in prosperous welfare states, whereas they previously had no place in our conceptual framework. The criterion of fairness began to play an important role in the Middle Ages (iustum praetium—a fair price) but was mostly related to religion. Its indefinable quality and high level of relativity has no place in the positivist scientific framework that tends to define modern society, particularly in the field of economics.

Even if contemporary economists dismiss fairness and justice as concepts not worthy of considering because they are immeasurable, they have nevertheless become increasingly important social factors: both goals and demands. These concepts, similar to the notion of quality, evade the approaches of positivist science, but this is exactly what makes them important in heralding the transition to a new conceptual framework. Only when the human race is free from the pressure of fighting for base survival can we start dealing with questions that are essential to our humanity. Emancipated people are no longer satisfied with merely formal equality, the first step and indeed a prerequisite for a free and democratic society. We demand as a criterion of comparability not only formal equality, which is measurable and comparable in the legal framework, but also equality in various other social contexts as well. Despite its indefinability, justice, without its previous religious connotations, is one of the most important elements in modern social life, an essential ingredient of social stability and social dynamics.

Equality—not in an intangible absolute sense, but in a relative one—has been a principle impetus and goal of the labor movement since its inception. As a result of the constant progress that has characterized the welfare state, many theoreticians, especially in America, have emphasized that equality as an axiom of labor movements no longer has any purpose. However, in many places, the advent of the prosperous welfare state has ushered in greater social differences than ever before. The general increase in prosperity has ensured that even the lowest-paid worker today makes more than the best-paid worker did a century and a half ago. Even a wealthy capitalist could not afford many of the things that today are available to everyone in the welfare state. However, this argument, even if formally accurate, does not hold up. The comparison is not between the same quantities or concepts. In other words, the quantity of material goods available to people is not the main point: human dignity is. There are no exact measures in this discussion, and perceptions can vary greatly. Nevertheless the issue of social equality is no longer only an ethical question of justice, but an increasingly important economic question. Justice as a social category is also becoming an important pillar of social stability and development.

Full social equality, as the proclaimed goal of communism, proved not only to be utopian, but also an impediment to social, and especially economic, development. As a system, communism suppressed competitiveness and the motivation to be above average. On the other side of the spectrum, the uncontrolled inequality that has resulted from capitalism and an unfettered market economy—a system where the lowest-paid worker cannot earn in several years what the highly paid manager makes in a month—is both an ethical issue and an economic factor. When people see that their hard work and efforts to succeed will not improve their material standing or social status, the general social orientation turns dangerously close to speculations about a society that is successful without any creative work at all. Any path to material success is perceived as better than creative work: such an approach surely leads to society's ruin.

Without much reflection, it might appear realistic and acceptable in our current state of general—albeit still internally imbalanced—prosperity to set the goal that the material prosperity currently only available to some will be available to all. But this goal only appears reasonable, because a condition for reaching such a seemingly simple goal is also greater social justice: this secondary goal is the means to achieve the primary goal.

The High Price of Material Prosperity

Technological development allows us to produce more and better products at lower costs with the same energy input. This sometimes, though not always, increases the general prosperity of society. It allows us to produce more and better goods with a smaller workforce. One consequence of this may be—and indeed this might be considered a general rule—that technological progress leads to higher unemployment. Unemployment in the current system means not participating in the production of society, and this in turn results in greater social inequality and poverty, without doubt one of the most puzzling paradoxes of the current social order.

This phenomenon has other negative ripple effects. As a result of greater selectivity, members of the workforce tend to be the very best while all others are marginalized. The previous competition between labor and capital has thus been transformed into a competition within labor itself, yet another source of social stratification and inequality. Moreover these circumstances require that competitors in the workforce—and indeed the entire workforce is forced into this situation—dedicate all, or at least a substantial part, of their energy and priorities into work.

As a precondition for economic success, defined as a family having a satisfactory living standard and social position, it is almost always necessary for both parents in the family structure to be employed. This has essentially created a situation where family income and material standing have taken priority over family values, which once provided the foundation and legitimacy of the family as the most appropriate organizational entity in which to ensure the continuation of the species and shape the values of children that are an essential part of our existence. Now the family is no longer the primary organizational entity in which one achieves personal happiness and satisfaction. Family has lost its primacy in society and in people's personal lives.

Contemporary society has not been successful in substituting the important social roles of the family. Above all, it has not been able to replace the family in its role of preserving the species. In the most affluent developed countries, where material goods are abundant and there should be the least concern for basic survival, the birth rate has declined to a level where it no longer maintains even a constant population level, let alone growth. In such a situation, economic activities and material prosperity lose their meaning. Progress is defeated by its own logic. It is only a matter of time until such a society meets its own demise. The primary issue can no longer be merely economics because it no longer serves any purpose.

This is the greatest challenge mankind faces today. If the only alternative is the death of society, then we need to act in order to change the core of the social order that has brought us to this point. If constant progress only means getting closer and closer to death, then we are no longer talking about progress, but disease. Humanity shares the biological world's innate tendency to fight for survival as the primary and dominant instinct. Survival is a goal that takes priority over all others. All other goals are just means to that fundamental end: survival. If the production of material goods becomes the primary goal that supplants all others, it means that the society will be unable to replace itself through the biological instinct to survive—having been freed from this imperative through scientific progress—with reason as the main regulator of existence.

Material abundance, which was supposed to free us from the struggle for survival—the most pressing concern since the dawn of man—has for the first time in history created the opportunity for most or even all of humanity to direct its creative capacity into achievements that liberate us from mere animal existence and allow us to ascend to a higher level; one might call it the true level of humanity. Never before have we had such a unique opportunity. Never before have we had the chance to test our actual limits, those that could only be reached and tested in the condition of freedom. And yet maintaining this level of prosperity has become a prerequisite for our continued transition to the so-called realm of freedom, and thus has become the permanent mission of our efforts as a society. Today we remain far from this goal and not only on the global level. Even in societies that have reached a certain level of affluence, prosperity for all remains a distant reality. Increasing the availability of material goods thus remains one of the main concerns for society.

But this is only part of the problem. A larger problem is that the prosperity we have already achieved has not brought freedom but instead a new enslavement to material prosperity. In part, this slavery has its roots in our psychology. Material prosperity has shifted from being a means to being an end in itself, a situation that emerged from low expectations resulting from previously unsatisfied material needs. This is a typical consequence of the consumer society. But it is also clear that the cure for the unacceptable harmful effects of the consumer society will not be located in limiting the production of material goods because, as noted previously, many segments of the population still do not have enough. The roots of the new slavery therefore reside mostly in new production-related social relationships.

Just as the survival instinct previously served as the sole regulator of human behavior in determining responses to challenges from the environment, with progress in science and increasing prosperity merely expanding the possibilities for formulating responses based on reason, so too does economics remain imprisoned by the so-called natural laws of the market. Competition eliminates the weak, favoring those who provide higher quality at a lower cost. On the one hand, the advantage of this kind of economic management is that it leads to constant progress in the production of goods. On the other hand, the system does not necessarily give satisfaction to those whom the production is intended to serve. Indeed, instead of liberation, it has led to a new form of slavery that, as regards its consequences, may be even worse than traditional forms of slavery. To succeed in a company often requires that employees sacrifice not only their spare time but dedicate their entire life cycle to work. Companies often go so far as to formally demand this degree of service. In order to achieve high levels of income, women must often sacrifice not only their free time but also the urges of their biological condition—from motherhood to devoting time to family and bringing up children. People with successful careers often pay with broken marriages, estranged children, and the loss of interpersonal relationships and other activities that give meaning to human existence. The price for what is only ostensibly personal success is a multitude of social pathological phenomena. The biggest losers are children who benefit from the material fruits of this tireless hunt for income and success but are deprived of the care and warmth that only parents and family can provide. As a result, young people often choose the wrong path in life, paying a high of a price for the success of their parents with addiction to drugs among other things.

And, again, all of these costs are sustained despite constant progress in science and technology, which in fact should allow us to have more time at our disposal, time that could be used to enjoy the pleasures of life that were unattainable in the past, to dedicate more time to family, and subsequently reduce the financial costs incurred by the senseless social ills that emerge from the contemporary economic system. Liberating economics from its subordination to the laws of the market and opening it to reasoning dictated by broader social concerns is a condition for the emergence of a truly prosperous society. Thus far we have not succeeded. The failed period of Marxism represents the only serious attempt in this direction. It was neither suitable nor successful, but the issues it addressed remain unsolved, and without a solution the welfare state is nothing but a pipe dream. What's more, without immediate measures to undo the most negative consequences of contemporary consumer society, especially demographic decline, our society, that is the prosperous welfare state, is destined to collapse.

Chapter 2: Contemporary Ethics

France Bucar and Igor Kovač

Of Meaning and Duty

A title like this is a controversial starting point. It alludes to the belief that ethics are not timeless, that they do not exist independently of the particular circumstances of place and time, and, furthermore, that ethics are not innate in human beings, not part of their inalienable being, but rather that they emerge from external, and particularly, social pressures. In other words, the implication is that ethics do not emerge from the individual, but rather from the external environment.

Ethics is a discipline of philosophy that is directly related to the question of meaning. If life does have meaning, then we soon arrive at the question of how we must behave in order to exist in accordance with that meaning. Science does not answer this question because it cannot. Science determines and describes while ethics prescribes. (See Evgenij Spektorski, Zgodovina socialne filozofije I.) Science determines in what form the world manifests itself, but does not ask why, for what reason, or what meaning it has since these questions in general cannot be the subject of scientific inquiry. Moreover science does not evaluate whether the world, as it exists, is ethically good or bad. Such a question can only be posed in the context of our relationship to the world, the meaning we attribute to it, and the actions that flow from these things. And yet the question of the meaning of our existence cannot be avoided because it is part of our being. It is akin to the eternal "why" children ask that can be so annoying to their parents. Many "why" questions cannot be answered, and yet it is through these questions that our humanity is shaped.

F. Bucar (Deceased)

I. Kovač (✉)
Department of Political Science, University of Cincinnati, Cincinnati, OH, USA
e-mail: kovacir@mail.uc.edu

© Springer International Publishing AG, part of Springer Nature 2019   59
I. Kovač (ed.), *At His Crossroad*, https://doi.org/10.1007/978-3-319-78331-4_6

If we cannot avoid questions about the meaning of our existence—perhaps especially when we are older and confronting death—then we also cannot avoid questions about our moral obligations. Each represents both the endeavor and unsolved riddles of philosophy, the essential questions that science cannot answer. Science is not even interested in addressing these issues. Science is interested only in what is, while ethics addresses what should be. Ethics judges and condemns. According to Emmanuel Kant, this school of thought is even more important than theoretical philosophy. Arthur Schopenhauer goes so far as to claim that that all the gods of both eastern and western religious were created in order to answer these fundamental questions. The question of good and evil is essentially only a permutation of questions about meaning and moral duty. If we are unable to distinguish good and evil, then we have no criteria for action.

Community as the Source of Ethical Rules

Human beings are only capable of existence within a community. Only in a community are human beings able to face the challenges of the surrounding environment and acquire the means of survival. In turn, the community dictates how its members must behave. Survival—life or death—depends on whether responses to the challenges of nature and related actions are suitable. The more a community is directly dependent on nature, the more its survival will depend on whether its responses and the related behavior of its members are suitable. The biological world has a code of responses to the demands of the external environment integrated into its genes. Responses to the demands of the environment come instinctively. If the environment to which a species has adapted changes, the species may have no ready responses, and this can lead to its downfall. In comparison to the rest of the biological world, mankind is, on the one hand, in a much worse position, because we are now compelled to formulate many of these responses independently, without relying on the dictates of our instincts. On the other hand, because human beings have critical minds and can learn from experience, humanity has surpassed the rest of the biological world in its ability to generate alternative appropriate responses. Our experience, providing us with information about what responses are suitable in certain situations, is stored as instructions on how to act in similar cases so that we do not need to come up with a new response each time. According to a behaviorist definition, the sum of these responses learned through experience forms human culture as well as the human code of actions—the human code of ethics. Experience and the responses based on it acquire the characteristics of values, and are presented as values in their own right, seemingly independent of the experience from which they originated.

The following is a series of interdependent relationships:

- The more a community depends on the demands of its environment, the greater the need to respect its code of ethics. Indeed the survival of the community may directly depend on respecting these rules. The seriousness of a violation of an ethical rule will be proportional to the rule's importance and the resulting threat to the survival of the community.

• Dependence on the environment is related to the understanding of its laws and the resources a community has at its disposal to deal with the challenges of the environment. The higher the level of technological development, the lower the direct dependence on the environment, and the less important it is to respect the rules that originate from responses to the pressures of the environment. Technological progress alleviates or even substantially eliminates this pressure, and by doing so, it greatly or even fully devalues the code of conduct that developed in order to safeguard the related interests of the community.

Furthermore, the longer a particular rule of conduct was seen as a necessary response to ensure the survival of the community, the higher its place in the mindset of the community—that is, as a value in its own right, detached from the direct experience from which it results.

The Hierarchy of Values

As a basis for required ethical behavior, values are classified in a hierarchical order (higher or lower, that is more or less important whereby lower-ranking values must always be subordinate to higher-ranking ones). This order is created on the basis of underlying experience, the importance of the values for the survival of the community, their permanence, and how firmly their position is fixed in the minds of members of the community.

The highest and most important place is reserved for values and rules of behavior related to the perception and understanding of the humanity's position in the world and the meaning of human existence. These are issues that have puzzled people (and mankind in general) ever since they became aware of themselves and began to question the meaning of existence. Humanity as a species is unable to arrive at completely rational responses—or even the right questions for that matter—because they exceed the limits of rationality, and even today pure rationality fails to provide satisfactory or final answers. People have always related these questions to transcendence and the powers that rule mankind. This general area includes fundamental questions about our behavior, perceptions of good and evil that have emerged in all cultures, and the question of truth. What is the truth? Does it exist? Is it even possible? These are questions that cannot be avoided in the conscious deliberation of human beings. In religion, the truth is not an issue but a fact, not a result of research but the starting point that should be humbly accepted as a given. (Spektorski, ibid.) For science, the problem of truth is solved by finding new facts and the connections between them. But the critical mind poses questions that neither religion nor science can answer. This is why questions about truth, meaning, and ethics will always occupy a high position in the human consciousness: precisely because of our inability to answer them. But we cannot live without asking them, and human beings have always been generating answers to these questions in one form or another. Mostly the form was transcendent: either being religious-based or the complete denial of transcendence. In the end, both sides emerge from the same argument—ignoramus et ignorabimus (we do not know and will not know). These are claims that cannot be validated with scientific evidence. Nevertheless both answers respond to the fundamental ethical questions that we cannot avoid, and that receive more or less the same forms of responses across all cultures.

Values that are derived from rationality or that do not contradict rationality despite their unknown mystical or mythical origin occupy a different and secondary place. These represent ethical commandments that religions substantiate with their divine origin, but that atheists also accept because they are derived from rationality. We do not accept the commandment "thou shall not kill" only because it is a religious instruction, but because reason also confirms it as necessary. According to Kant, rationality is the basis for all ethics.

However, logic strictly applied as the foundation of rationality can lead to different outcomes, and underlying premises can change with new findings. Logical deduction based on premises that represent new findings about the world or humanity may lead to reevaluation and possible shifts in perspectives on issues that had been exclusively or mostly explained through transcendental aspects. This may lead to significant changes in ethical positions. The ongoing development and growth of human knowledge constantly narrows the space of transcendence—including the veneration of natural forces, their deification, and final expression in monotheism—to interpret phenomena that can now be explained by science. A glance at the history of the development of knowledge reveals constant and irrepressible growth, and the related fall in the importance in explanations that had previously been provided by religion. Thus came a growing certainty that science would provide explanations for what had previously been unknown and had once belonged in the exclusive domain of religion. Accordingly a new sense of required behavior ensued, a revision of ethical imperatives, because it seemed that humanity was indeed becoming the ruler of the world. Explanations that relied on the "God hypothesis" were no longer needed—that is, until new findings refuted the seemingly final scientific truths as false assumptions, along with the ethical values that emerged from such false perceptions and the harmful consequences they caused in real life.

The more we descend down the hierarchy of values and find commandments and prohibitions that are essentially practical instructions, the more these values reflect direct conditions and can be identified as responses to specific situations, the more they are affected by time, and the less untouchable and absolute they are. Although they are derived from rationality and direct reason, they must not contradict the higher values in the hierarchy. Nevertheless they have a decisive impact on everyday life. If, because of changes that emerge from technological development changes in the way of life, these values turn out to be inappropriate instructions for actual life, it may happen, because of the interdependence of values and the system of ethic, that the entire system of ethics as the basis for the survival of society will shift.

Ethics and Social Power

One of the greatest historical changes in the understanding of the world and humanity's position in it came with the scientific revolution of the fifteenth and sixteenth centuries and the advent of the modern era. The use of mathematical and geometrical methods ultimately revealed the heliocentric system, which fundamentally changed previous conceptions about the cosmos and humanity's position in it. This initial scientific approach provided the foundation for all subsequent technological development to which we owe then unimaginable advances in all areas of knowledge, not least the discovery of the secrets of the genome and the macro- and microcosm, and the overcoming of many physical obstacles. Indeed virtually all of today's material prosperity is due to the development of the scientific method. Moreover concepts of equality among people and the related notion of democracy as the most appropriate form of the modern social order also rest on this foundation. The seventeenth century philosopher, Baruch Spinoza, used the scientific method to establish a new model of ethics in his work Ethics Demonstrated in Geometrical Order. He rejected all notions of transcendence. Using a continuous string of logical conclusions, he established that nature, which he regarded as a mechanism, was the only legitimate subject of philosophy. For Spinoza, nature equals God. The only difference is the word. To explain the world and the things in it through God's will is to resort to ignorance, and represents the greatest obstacle to scientific development. These same foundations were used as the starting point in the development of modern economics and other new academic fields.

In this sense, Western, that is European, philosophy severed science and religion, and created a formal opposition that lasts to this day. What then should be the measure of the actions of humanity? The dilemmas of the modern world could be perceived as a crisis of ethics.

New scientific findings based on the mathematical method have brought not only a new positivist approach to understanding and exploring the world, but also a new perception of the world. However, the mathematical method can only access the quantitative world, the world that can be measured, weighed, and is open to empirical testing. Likewise the modern equality of people and democracy are, at their core, quantitative categories that have little to do with ethics. Equality among people is necessary as a mathematical unit, and democracy itself can be reduced to mathematical operations. The will of the people is the simple sum of votes, a mathematical majority. Science has no interest in anything that cannot be measured and weighed. This not only closes the door of the positivist worldview to any notion of transcendence, but also to entire spheres of quality (as opposed to quantity) and spirituality. In the field of law, we find the development of legal positivism, creating a division between positive law and justice. Positive law is what the lawmaker has defined as obligatory behavior. It has no relationship to justice other than coincidentally overlapping at times. And the origin of law is not ethics; it is power. Power becomes the focal point of positivism in society, and the final criterion for the legitimacy of actions. Thus power replaces morality.

Along with the discovery and amazing successes of the positivist worldview—which we are still unable to replace with anything more successful—came the growth of humanity's confidence. It is true that we now understand more about how much is still unknown. With each new discovery, the horizon of the unknown expands. But even if most things remain unknown, nothing is considered completely unknowable. Nothing is out of reach of the human mind. The path to infinity lies open, since even mathematics cannot define finiteness. And here we encounter another great problem and paradox of the positivist worldview: the demand for infinity in a world that is by definition finite and limited. This paradox has already come to the forefront in the economy with the demand for constant competition and constant progress with no end. How far can it go? A worldview that does not and cannot accept the finite and believes that everything is attainable necessarily becomes regal and omnipotent, occupies a position that was hitherto reserved only for God. This worldview does not recognize God because it has taken God's place. It recognizes no power from above, and only yields power to something greater than itself. Thus power becomes the driving force of all actions, as well as the main goal in competition with others. This worldview does not question the ethical foundations of the actions it justifies. Superior power simply justifies them. Power has replaced ethics because power is measurable, perhaps not intellectual power itself, but certainly the results it brings. Intellectual power in itself has no exchange value. Nor does truth.

Realpolitik and Social Darwinism

Power as a means of subordinating and controlling the will of others is necessary in all interventions in which people are used as a means to achieve desired goals. We accomplish very few things entirely by ourselves. We are usually compelled to collaborate with and draw on different forms of organization to achieve various goals. In fact, organization is basically a means of compelling individuals to participate in actions that lead to a particular goal. For this reason, we need to have power over various individuals. Obtaining power over others for the purpose of management is the first and most important aim of the activity we call politics. Indeed, without power, management in any field becomes meaningless. Thus politics, as it is usually defined, is not only present in public affairs but in all organized activities, even the smallest economic endeavor.

However, the most important arena of politics is public affairs, particularly in the areas of the government, financial management, and large, especially international, economic organizations. The issue of power in these fields is so essential for management and governance that it has become the top priority and has evolved into an actual science. Machiavelli, the first theoretician in this field, was the quintessential representative of the positivist approach to issues of managing public affairs at a time, the Renaissance, when the first rudimentary signs of the modern concept of statehood were emerging. His views on how a prince should function in pursuing his goals created the foundation of the principle called Machiavellianism: that the use of any means is allowed to obtain power, and that ethics has no place in this endeavor. This principle has become political dogma, even when its practitioners formally invoke ethics, or when ethics are used as a smokescreen for the acquisition of real power. The German First Chancellor Otto von Bismarck formalized the principle with the concept of realpolitik as the rationale and sole acceptable foundation for policy in public affairs, and especially in international relations. He contrasted the principle with Christian ethics in particular: "One cannot govern a state with the Sermon on the Mount." The belief that honesty is not useful in politics and has no exchange value has spread even to those who recognize ethics as a fundamental tenet in social relationships. Honesty in politics is equivalent to naivety. One example from close to home is the fate of the twentieth-century Slovenian writer Edvard Kocbek, whose greatness in the fields of literature and ethics is undisputed by most. However, he was naive in politics, believing in the honesty of the communists (adherents to an ideology that openly claim that power is the highest ethical principle), and is therefore reproached for helping to pave the way for their seizure of power.

Power, rather than ethics, as the driving force behind actions lays the foundation for many theories, and particularly for the practices of not only early but also more mature forms of capitalism. The English social theoretician Herbert Spencer, the father of social Darwinism, argued in favor of merciless economic competition and the survival of the fittest as a legitimate credo. His work is still being reprinted in the Anglo-Saxon world, particularly in the United States. The entire development of capitalism and the social struggles that have emerged from it is characterized by social power as a sheer force uninhibited by ethics.

This "gospel of power" as the driving force of all development is especially prevalent in the international sphere. The principle of Machiavellianism has become the only regulator of relationships between nation states. The past century of nearly ceaseless military conflicts and two devastating world wars does not represent a series of coincidental uncontrolled circumstances, but rather a logical and necessary consequence of a worldview that discarded ethics as being incompatible with positivism, that does not recognize perspectives other than those that view the physical world as subject to quantification and empirical testing.

But questions of ethics have once again become urgent issues in the modern world, as people are becoming aware of not only the advantages but also the extremely devastating consequences of positivism as a worldview and justification for action that excludes all other possible perspectives. The world is seeking new solutions. What is most essential is the creation of a world order that excludes the possibility of military conflict on a global scale because we cannot afford to repeat that. One reaction to this necessity has been—at least in Europe, where both world wars started—an attempt to integrate European countries into a community that, as a united organization with common interests, would preclude new wars. Despite progress on this path, more and more issues are arising that may threaten the entire endeavor. It is becoming clearer that the problem is not merely organizational, but that creating a new European order has meant giving up force as a means of resolving conflicts between peoples and states. This abnegation of force is not only a question of good will. As long as ethics, which have no place in the prevailing worldview, have been replaced by power as the sole regulator in relations, a unified Europe will require more than just a new legal and organizational order. An order that conflicts with the principles that govern our actions—and these principles are comprised of power without ethics—cannot survive because of internal incoherence. The failure of a united Europe reflects the need for a new worldview that will not be based solely on what is quantifiable, but also on quality, one that will also acknowledge the spiritual world and aspects of reality that cannot be empirically measured. Clearly, the fundamental challenge of the future is to bring back ethics as the driving force of our actions.

The Ethical Deficit of Modern Society

The ethical deficit as the primary problem of the modern world is not only the result of the positivist worldview (scientific positivism cannot be renounced entirely) but has other causes independent directly from or indirectly related to this overall worldview. First we must observe the development of the position, role, rights, and emancipation of people. What should be the driving force of individual action? Should people seek an external justification for their actions, and if so where, or should they to find it internally?

People generally do what they believe is good and also beneficial for themselves. This leads to two fundamental questions. Where do we get information about what is good and beneficial for ourselves, and do we have the possibility—or the freedom—to pursue what we believe in? Our independence relies first on how and what we use to fill the reservoir of our knowledge. It is not only an issue of a free social order, which today generally means a democracy where freedom of information is more or less prevalent as opposed to authoritarian states where citizens have limited access to information. But an additional question is where the free and independent media get their information and how they process and transfer it. It is not only that the media deliberately transfer specific information in order to manipulate the perceptions of its recipients in a particular way. It is also about our acceptance of prevalent and generally accepted values, generally accepted concepts, and attitudes about the problems of a given era that also shape the media even if the media is convinced of their own independence. Our era is strongly influenced by the following tenets dictated by the positivist worldview:

- faith in the omnipotence of science and the belief that science sheds light on all mysteries, both of which coincide with a falling interest in transcendence and philosophical questions;
- personal emancipation and autonomy;
- the relativization of ethics and faith into personal success as the sole criterion for individual actions;
- consumerism as the new driving force behind individual decisions and actions.

Science has made it possible for us to overcome the scarcity of the basic means of survival as the fundamental aim of our actions; this used to take priority over all other aims. Science has created a society of relative prosperity, which also promises the further growth of abundance. It offers us a life without hunger, which functions as a sword of Damocles, allowing us to focus on aspects of life that until now only a chosen ruling elite could even conceive of. In the past, all others in society were not even aware of them. Thus life for many is no longer "a vale of tears", but rather a space that can be filled with various pleasures. In other words, life can be enjoyed not merely endured.

All this has been made possible by science, and science keeps promising more of the same. But we must be aware that science, which has created the path to our current prosperity, also denies the transcendental, recognizing power and reason as the sole legitimate principles motivating our actions. Science has no interest in fundamental questions of ethics and meaning. Scientific progress has proved that many of our lower-ranking values, those that provide instructions for our daily life, are irrelevant and even absurd.

The lifestyle required in conditions of general scarcity and struggle for survival is very different from the one where the issue of sheer survival ranks below issues related to the quality of life. Particularly for those who are able for the first time to sit down to a table of food without worrying—and that means most people—this new condition allowed them to turn their interest to other possibilities of material life. These are the psychological roots of today's consumer society of which the material conditions were created by science. And because it was science that gave us this abundance, and not the ethical rules that prevailed during periods of deprivation, an ethical void arose that has been filled with a new faith in science. But because science fails to answer some of the most important questions regarding the meaning of life and ethics, questions that we cannot avoid forever, society is now characterized by superficiality and compliance. When the primary impetus of our behavior is the creation of an abundance of material goods and there is an ethical vacuum, society becomes extremely fragile and is easy prey to forces that have no internal inhibitions in terms of controlling and exploiting that society.

Capital controls the consumer society. Its existence is only possible, with its form and content, within the current capitalist order, which in turn is a result of positivism, is also without ethics, and only recognizes the ethics of power.

A Crisis of Identity

The capitalist market affects our values and perception of ourselves. In the capitalist market economy, the value of goods is not based on their use value but rather on their exchange value. Although the use value may be derived from the exchange value, much more is incorporated in the market or exchange value, particularly demand, which itself depends on factors that also have no direct link to the practical use of the goods. It is also typical in consumer society that a market of personality emerges along with the market for goods, with the same division between the use value and the exchange value. This has had far-reaching consequences for how the mentality and behavior of people in the market are shaped. The market is not based on ethical principles. The market is a segment of the world that recognizes only measurable quantity and acknowledges only rational reasons. Individual actors in the market will likewise only consider rationality, meaning the factors that contribute to their success. Success is the main and exclusive measure to which everything else is subordinate, including ethics, of course, if they conflict with success. There is no mercy or concessions in this competition for success. Use value—which gives an individual a personality and makes him or her an expert in a particular field—has no exchange value if there is no demand for it. Exchange value is determined by a number of circumstances upon which the individual's knowledge and ability have no direct influence: e.g., family background, connections with influential people, membership in a prestigious club or political party, the infamous "old boys' club". One of the main concerns of a supplier on this market is what opinion "potential buyers have about the goods on offer" and not the value of the goods themselves. This doesn't necessarily mean that the goods have to be fashionable, but that the supplier knows what kind of personality is in greatest demand. Being university educated may be a prerequisite for success, but people can learn more about what appearance and performance are needed for success by reading different magazines and advertisements, and by imitating successful entrepreneurs and famous actors. All this has a decisive impact on the perception of the individual as goods for sale.

Our self-respect thus depends on conditions upon which we have no influence. If we are successful, we are worthy; if not we are not successful, we have lower worth. In this system, we are forced to constantly strive for success and every failure shakes our self-respect. If the changeable market reduces our worth, we lose our sense of pride and dignity. All that matters is that we are able to successfully market ourselves. Because we depend on the market, the market's changeability also dictates our identity and our perception of ourselves as independent beings. The sense of I-am-what-I-know-and-do changes into a sense of I-am-what-they-want-me-to-be. In this context, we, as goods on the market, cannot refer to what we are and what we know, but only to the opinion others have of us. Our abilities are thus separated from our being, and our being is defined by the price we can charge for ourselves. Moreover we apply the same standards to others. We evaluate them with respect to their success, which is determined by the market. This measure is completely quantitative. Even equality obtains a new meaning. We are all equal, but because we are all equal, we are also replaceable. Equality means replaceability. Equality as the potential for each of us to develop our capabilities is now perceived as eccentric. The market also creates a special kind of camaraderie. We are all equal, we all strive for success. We all share the same fate, we are all lonely, we all fear failure, we all strive to please. There is no mercy, and no one should expect it.

The orientation of the market determines not only emotions but also how we think. The role of thinking has transformed into rapid understanding of whatever we wish to do successfully. In this context, we need skills in accumulating information. The entire educational system has shifted in this direction. This kind of thinking leads to greater intelligence, but not to wisdom. The surface is important, not the underlying essence. Truth is an outdated concept, not to mention that each of us now has the right to our own truth. Quantity is what is measured, without interest in quality. Thinking and knowledge are seen as a means to success while everything else is useless philosophizing. Thinking that is directed at discovering the truth has no exchange value on the market. (See Erich Fromm, Man for Himself.)

Our moral problem has become our indifference to ourselves. We have become tools for a purpose outside of ourselves, and we experience ourselves as marketable goods. Our potential has alienated us from ourselves. If success is the only measure of value, it is natural that the world of ethics and moral values no longer has a place in our conceptual schema. And human beings, unable to transcend the role of marketable goods, have lost the foundation that gives life meaning and legitimacy. Our problem is how to assert ourselves and our fundamental creative capability and uniqueness. Thus we are confronted with a force that equates our way of life and being with the totalitarianism of the market. This force is stronger than the violence of any totalitarian regime, since it offers the illusion of total freedom and the greatest material wellbeing any society has achieved thus far. Having an independent identity has become even more difficult now than it was under autocratic totalitarian regimes.

This is particularly the case because so-called realists try to convince us that the moral sphere is a thing of the past, arguing that values are culturally defined. Values have always served to protect us and guide us toward particular behaviors necessary for the survival of both society and the individual. The extraordinary technological progress achieved in most of Europe (especially Western Europe) and North America has fundamentally changed material living conditions. Hunger as a Malthusian population regulator has been overcome, and society suddenly finds itself in a condition of overabundance. Many of the values that ensured survival in a society of scarcity no longer make sense. The consumer society has witnessed the collapse of its former structure of values. Because the value-based safeguards that once ensured material survival have become unnecessary, the entire sphere of values is now seen as unnecessary baggage from history, a category that has no place or role in the modern world. Everything is allowed, there are no valid moral principles: the only guideline is benefit.

The Relativity of Truth and Honesty

Denying transcendence as the origin of ethics and something that limits our freedom and autonomy also "solves" another of life's great questions—the question of truth. The truth sets limits to autonomy. The existence of an absolute truth inevitably comes into conflict with absolute autonomy. Because we set the boundaries of our autonomy ourselves, we also define a truth that suits our perceptions of our autonomy. Therefore there can be no absolute truth. Truth has become relative as each of us creates our own truth. There are as many truths as there are people. This relative truth is not and cannot be related to the question of knowledge. If truth is bound to the question of knowledge—conceptually a logical claim—the only acceptable view is faith in an absolute truth. But we do not and cannot know everything. Absolute knowledge is only possible in transcendence, because absoluteness is beyond our cognitive abilities. This is why an absolute truth also demands absolute ethics, which can only have roots in a system where there is a place for an absolute truth. However, the positivist worldview cannot accept such as system, since this would mean giving up the essential underlying thesis that nothing is beyond the reach of the human mind. Thus truth changes as the reach of our knowledge changes. And if there is no absolute truth, there are as many truths as there are bearers of different knowledge and experience. Therefore we cannot accept an absolute truth because of the logical conclusion that we would have to then accept the necessity of a system of absolute ethics. And this in turn would mean the end of our absolute autonomy. We would need to subject ourselves to external commandments that would regulate our behavior, and these would probably conflict with our autonomy. We would need to acknowledge that there is something outside of ourselves to which our own being is subordinate, and this view undermines the entire positivist worldview.

The question of ethics will decide the future of mankind. If there is no system of ethics that binds us all, there is no force that integrates the world, or any broader or narrower social community, into a harmonious whole. As previously established, the survival of the individual depends on the community. Societal integration based only on positivist law has proved to be insufficient. Even the most detailed regulation generated by a state to govern the life of its society cannot provide an answer to the very simple but fundamental question: "Why should I be honest?" Of course it is easy to rationally accept the view that without honesty it is impossible for society to be bound together into a community that is more than the mathematical sum of individuals, in which each forms their own truth and tailors a system of ethics for themselves. Society cannot survive without a generally accepted and respected system of ethics, the credo of which could be summarized as "being honest is also in my own interest". Without belonging to a community, we cannot survive as individuals. Nevertheless our logical reasoning stops at the level of general truths, not penetrating our innermost selves. That is why we must advocate for the general principle of honesty; how will we behave in our own personal sphere where no external force, especially not a state, should interfere. But there are instances when our personal short-term interests may conflict with general ethical principles, and it becomes advantageous to be dishonest. The only obstacle to this behavior may be public opinion because dishonesty harms the public. The state and its regulations, in particular, are supposed to function as an obstacle to our dishonesty. Dishonesty therefore should always be hidden from the public eye, and especially from the state that might impose penalties. Still this brings us no closer to a response to the question of why we should be honest. That question remains unanswered. An ethical issue has merely been reformulated into a question of technical skill at keeping dishonesty hidden from the public and the state. From this perspective, the state is always on the losing side, since the skills and the ingenuity of lawbreakers always remain ahead of rigid state bureaucracy. The state may introduce new regulations to try to close every loophole through which possible lawbreakers may squeeze, but in doing so it only creates additional difficulties for itself. The legal order becomes so complicated and difficult to comprehend that it becomes a form of disorder that the state can no longer control, ushering in additional problems and costs with few benefits.

Absolute respect for ethical principles, and especially state regulations, has never been achieved in any society. Every society has its violators. But the modern society is in a much more difficult situation. A society that derived a system of ethics from transcendence—regardless of how it was perceived—could count on most of its members embracing the system as part of their own value system and regarding violations as dissent from fundamental social values and truths. When the only guidelines for actions come from the relative truth generated by individuals, and thereby relativized ethics based on individual perceptions of good and evil, society loses all access to the internal worlds of its members. Members of society are "honest" according to their own perception of honesty.

In such a society, no external force has access to its members' internal worlds. Society may try to affect this sphere by creating external circumstances that encourage its members to respond in a desired way (e.g., the threat of punishment dissuading people from engaging in socially unacceptable behavior, or the promise of material or spiritual rewards for positive behavior). Nevertheless, even in such cases, actions are first subject to individual judgment. We first decide for ourselves whether it is worth following social norms. "Do I benefit from being honest?" When then is full personal autonomy and truth is relative, we can no longer speak of a categorical imperative.

Methods of informing members of society represent another indirect influence, which have evolved into a powerful force that shape and reshape mentality. Members of society believe they are acting in accordance with their own will, but in fact their minds are to a great extent being controlled the mass media. This force has become so powerful today that people are easier to manipulate than ever, despite the population's relatively high level of education (at least relative to the past), and the presumed emancipation of humanity in most areas of life. People are convinced that they are making their own decisions. As a result, methods of controlling citizens mentally have become much more important for governments than controlling actions through legal regulations. A glance at modern society indicates that personal autonomy in decision-making and general emancipation are illusions. Modern society is much less free than it seems, unless we interpret freedom as complete absolution from general ethical norms.

This brings the relativization of ethics to another level. Those with the greatest influence in shaping mentality, those who shape the perceptions of modern individuals in society and in the world, directly create the conditions in which it is legitimate to ask whether it is worth being honest at all. And yet, even with this mass indoctrination, they have not managed to cross the boundaries into the minds of individuals. The categorical imperative only emerges from full internal autonomy into which only a transcendent force that imposes impassable boundaries has access. This thought was most clearly expressed by the great Russian author Fyodor Dostoyevsky: "If God does not exist, everything is permitted."

The worst problem in modern society is that in principle everything is permitted, that there is no border that cannot be crossed regardless of the circumstances. The rhetorical question of whether it is worth being honest depends on a series of random circumstances that dictate whether a particular society has been successful in creating conditions where there is not too wide a gap between the legal order and its underlying ideology, and the prevailing view on what an appropriate and acceptable material and spiritual condition for members of society is. Being dishonest will always bears a certain amount of risk. But in societies where this gap is large, taking that risk will require less consideration. That is why respect for the rule of law and social rules tends to be less reliable in economically less-developed countries. In countries with a longer tradition of democracy—especially when it stems from a history of material prosperity, often reached on the backs of countries now reproached for a poor sense of legal order and civic integrity—this gap is notably smaller, which leads to a greater inclination to respect social rules. But these are random circumstances that will temporarily enhance the integration of certain societies. The heart of social integration resides in shared identification, which, in its essence, is immaterial. Identification captures an ethical relationship. It means that we accept the value-based principles on which society builds its existence, and that we also acknowledge the limitations that our respect for these values imposes. This means being honest regardless of any gap between ethical demands and our own interests. No society can survive without the social integration of its members. When the integration of its members results mostly or exclusively from the alignment of material interests—a fundamental feature of the consumer society—a society will not be able to pass the test that every society eventually must take. Being honest only because it is beneficial is the beginning of social disintegration. However, a society based on positivist principles cannot acknowledge the need for honesty in the sense of a categorical imperative. This would contradict the demand for absolute autonomy, and acknowledging no boundaries, social or religious, mythological, or philosophical.

Chapter 3: Intolerance

France Bucar and Igor Kovač

Utility and Principle

We evaluate the phenomena that we directly or indirectly encounter in the external world through the lens of our values. Values represent our perception of what is good for us. But what is good or useful for us depends on the role we have been given by certain external environmental factors, whether natural or social. This is so-called objective utility, because we are always influenced by external factors. We do not choose this role ourselves; it is assigned to us from the outside. Because we only come into contact with the outside world indirectly through our consciousness, we perceive our role as independent, and we process the influence of the outside world through our perceptions and conscious selves in accordance with our understanding of it. We function based on our own understanding of our role and our own judgment about the external influences, which is just another expression of how we define our role. We judge for ourselves what is useful for us and what is not. This necessarily results in a difference between objective and subjective utility, which in different situations may be more or less synchronized. If we define values as our perception of what is good for us, then values can also be objective and subjective. We generally operate based on subjective values. The more our personal values correspond with the objective values of the outside world, the more our personal role will fit in with events in that world. The more people in our world act in accordance with our subjective values, the closer these subjective values will be connected to the objective world. But this cannot always be the case because we are dealing with subjective values. The alignment of subjective and objective values determines

F. Bucar (Deceased)

I. Kovač (✉)
Department of Political Science, University of Cincinnati, Cincinnati, OH, USA
e-mail: kovacir@mail.uc.edu

© Springer International Publishing AG, part of Springer Nature 2019   73
I. Kovač (ed.), *At His Crossroad*, https://doi.org/10.1007/978-3-319-78331-4_7

objective utility, and therefore whether our actions are reasonable in a given context. It will also affect the psychological state we call happiness, which is basically our perception of whether our own conditions and actions are in alignment with the objective conditions of the world.

We always judge our own actions—as well as those of others if they affect our value system—from the perspective of their alignment with our own values. For different reasons, our actions—as well as those of others—may diverge from our values. This is especially true because of the internal hierarchy of values. Some values take priority over others, and respecting them is a condition for upholding any lower-ranking value. This hierarchy of values is determined objectively, but at the same time it is internalized through our consciousness and we may perceive it differently from others. In addition, values on the same level often compete with each other. Some can only be upheld, partly or completely, on account of others. Sometimes we are ready to sacrifice higher-ranking values for the sake of certain lower-ranking values.

Upholding certain values may mean different things in different periods of time.

The more we descend the hierarchy of values, the broader the scope of possible actions as a result of the widening range of different situations to which our actions respond. Our options expand, and the interconnections and interdependence among values get blurred, particularly as regards their connection to and dependence on higher-ranking values. Our actions correspond to our own benefit to the extent that our subjective values are in line with objective values. We characterize such behavior as highly ethical and principled, by which we only really mean that it is in agreement with the hierarchy of values. If the subjective world of values of a particular person diverges from the objective system of values so much that they are more or less completely incompatible, we say that this person has no principles and is unethical. Such disharmony—or unprincipled behavior—is necessarily harmful to that particular person, at least in the long run, and also damaging to the broader community. A lack of ethics in an individual is regarded as imprudent, although the individual may be convinced otherwise. We endow such behavior with different labels and evaluations, depending on how we judge its consequences. When the consequences are only harmful for the person in question, they are usually regarded as simply unwise or imprudent, and are treated with scant attention or offense. When the consequences are more serious, but still limited to the individual, the outside environment usually shows a willingness to help restore the lost equilibrium (that is to repair the damage incurred or attempt to change the behavior of the individual).

Tolerance and Privacy

At this point, we already encounter a justification for intervention into the individual sphere and individual rights. It is not theoretically possible to argue that the actions of individuals have no consequences on their surroundings. Individuals, despite their uniqueness, are also the result of the environment. This in turn means that our existence and actions affect our environment. Therefore we cannot maintain absolute inviolability. It is always relative. Personal inviolability is an exceptional value in its own right, particularly in Western Christian civilization. Already at this low level, we see a collision of two fundamental values that are the pillars of every society: the right of individuals to their identity and inviolability, and the right of society to protect the equal rights of all members of society. It is clear that we cannot speak about the absolute quality of rights. Even at the highest level, values can and do conflict with each other. It becomes a matter of judgment as to which value has priority in a particular situation and to what degree. Even helping people, which reflects a high ethical value, means an intervention in their personal sphere and privacy in situations where help is provided without consent. But indifference to the fate of other people is also a violation of the basic value of solidarity, which in turn is a condition for social cohesion.

If we argue that all values are relative, we also claim that all values are absolute in the sense that when they conflict we can never fully sacrifice one value for the sake of another. The situation is always relative. In this respect, tolerance can be defined as the readiness to give up a certain part of a particular value for the sake of another. Although tolerance is often regarded as an important value in its own right, but it has no meaning or role unless it is related to the evaluation of suitability and proportionality. It is about being wise. If values were viewed as absolutely inviolable, tolerance as an ability to adapt and survive would be impossible and meaningless. It would always mean an unacceptable sacrifice of absolute values. Such a view leads to total intolerance, in the sense of total consistency in pursuing values. This is based on the underlying assumption that there are no conflicts between values. However, we can only accept such a comprehension of values if it is static, not as one that can be used in practice. Intolerance leads to perceiving life as static, which is a contradiction with life itself.

Tolerance is not an absolute category that can be established as the antithesis of intolerance. As mentioned above, it represents the wisdom to adapt as a condition for survival. This is why invoking tolerance begs the question of extent, and the question of what we are sacrificing and for what purpose. There will always be concerns about whether we are sacrificing a higher-ranking value for the direct material benefit of a small group of people that have antisocial interests, concerns about whether we are judging the circumstances correctly, whether the stated goals are acceptable, etc. Tolerance could also be defined as the ability to make compromises, and compromises often have a negative connotation precisely because they mean the readiness to sacrifice higher-ranking values for less important (material) benefits. When sacrificing values that are higher in the hierarchical order than the benefits that the sacrifice brings, tolerance can turn into a lack of principle, unsavory compromise, or even the betrayal of values that we should be defending. In contrast, intolerance, although the notion often has a negative connotation, means being consistent and uncompromising with certain values that we abandon under no condition and for which we are ready to sacrifice all others. But under certain circumstances, intolerance can mean the inability to adapt, and this renders coexistence in society impossible.

Tolerance and intolerance are twins, being neither values nor evils, neither positive nor negative categories. They acquire their value function and their place in the sphere of values only in conjunction with other factors that determine our actions and relate to a particular goal, or to an accepted or desired value. From this perspective, they cannot be subject to a priori evaluation. When we want to categorize them in this way, they automatically become political categories, and are used (and abused) for political purposes. Political activity, when it is defined within the formal program of a political party, means taking a position vis-à-vis particular aims in advance, and seeks its own legitimacy through achieving its political aims. That is why notions of tolerance and intolerance are often used to protect specific aims and activities related to them. Whoever disagrees with these aims—especially if an analysis from the opposing side challenges their reasonability or alignment with generally accepted values—will immediately be accused of intolerance, of not being open to argument and persuasion. If it sticks, the reproach of intolerance reduces the weight of the other side's arguments. Opponents are disqualified in advance—not just as people who fail to understand the disputed subject, but also morally for not understanding the problem because of their intolerant—and inconvenient evidence is ignored. Moral disqualification is a burden that often leads to defeat.

Settlement Rights

The reproach of intolerance plays an important role in protecting political aims that are now in the forefront of our political life. In the current period of European unification, the focus of political activity is on processes that lead toward the international integration of and openness among countries, and toward invalidating or at least reducing the role of the elements that have hitherto been pillars of the sovereignty and inviolability of nations. All of these elements, both positive and negative, are defined based on the role that they have played in the past or are supposed to play in the future.

Settlement rights are central among these elements. Thus far these rights have mostly been connected to nation states. Namely, only the citizens of a nation state have the right to settle and have permanent residence on the territory of that state. Nation states will sometimes explicitly grant the exceptional right to settle to others, usually for a limited period of time.

The blueprint for a united Europe—within the framework of the EU and with certain transitional limitations—extends this right to all inhabitants of EU countries. This is one of the foundations of the common market. From the perspective of the common market, it is a logical regulation, the most important requirement of a common market being not only the mobility of goods and capital, but also of people as a principle element in market processes. However, certain aspects of this new order have not been dealt with or have even been intentionally neglected. These aspects and their consequences may call for the revision of some of the foundations of the modern social order, which is based on personal freedom and private property.

Contrary to the market-and-goods capitalist economy of the past, which was based on private property both in production and consumption, it is typical of the current market-and-goods economy that the share of common property is growing and plays an increasingly important role in production and consumption. The concept of property is based on limited goods. Where the availability of goods is unlimited, there is no concept of property, since it is unnecessary and pointless. The role of property is to prevent access to everyone except the owner of property. Today the amount of goods that must be shared is increasing—that is, goods that must be available to everyone in the community if they are to be available to anyone. Common property is still private property, only access is not limited to an individual but to a particular (smaller or larger) group. It still has the same function of limiting access, but in this case with only members of a certain group having access to it.

Today the list of limited goods includes those that in the past were unlimited and thus available to all, such as space, air, and water (although the community distributed these goods according to specific procedures and sometimes required something in exchange). The state or community was the common owner of these goods, but nevertheless they were considered in some sense unlimited. Now they are becoming limited and are increasingly recognized as among of the most important factors not only affecting the quality of life of members of community, but also representing the basic conditions for the survival of the community as a whole.

Today clean air is still unlimited. Water is becoming a resource that must be used economically and prudently, and it is predicted that in the future it will become one of the most strategically important resources. Space is the resource that is absolutely limited, which introduces the possibility of settlement, and at the same time offers the potential for acquiring a number of direct existential needs and for enjoying the environment. Each territory allows only a certain population density that will burden the territory to an acceptable degree and dictate a particular way of life. Each new inhabitant of a national territory becomes a participant in the use of the common goods offered by the territory. With citizenship, we become "shareholders". Citizenship is no longer merely a political right but now also carries certain economic rights. This is not altered by the fact that we are required to pay the community a certain price for using these common goods (space, water, energy, etc.). If these goods are limited, each new inhabitant means an additional burden as both a consumer and as a member of the workforce seeking employment. In certain cases, an increase in the population is needed to balance production and consumption, and in other cases, an increase in the population can be a burden that worsens, or at least changes, the living conditions of the existing population of a particular territory (e.g., less access to community goods, pressure on the way of life caused by the introduction of new or different living patterns).

In all cases, settlement on a national territory represents an intervention in terms of how the existing inhabitants fulfill their needs. This intervention can be perceived by the existing population as desirable or not, depending on an evaluation of how it affects its own benefits. In addition, it also represents intervention in the sphere of self-government, and if we are dealing with a nation state, an intervention in its sovereignty. From this perspective, the right to manage and allow settlement on the territory of a community remains the community's inalienable right as it is needed to protect the living conditions and identity of community members. Demanding that anyone has the right to settle on the territory of any community, with or without the consent of that community, is in fact the same as demanding that the community no longer owns the resources at its disposal and that rather they can be used to benefit some undefined group or humanity as a whole. It also means the abolishment of the protection of private property, as the property of a community is made accessible to all. True, this represents only the undistributed property of this community, but in the current mode of production and consumption, this share is becoming more important, and at the same time directly affects the manner in which private property is used. Thus, free settlement rights would mean a major revision of one of the main tenets of the current constitutional order throughout the democratic world: namely, the inviolability of private property.

From this perspective, it is completely understandable that leftist groups that oppose the institution of private property fight for the right of free settlement on the territory of any community, and label communities that demand sovereignty in deciding who can settle on its territory as xenophobic or hostile to foreigners (xenophobic derives from the Greek word xenos for foreigner). The communist motto "the proletarian has no homeland" is completely consistent with this ideological stance as it denies the concept of homeland and indirectly also the concept of property.

Opposition to the Foreign and Interdependence

Even xenophobia (which carries a pejorative connotation and is thus automatically perceived as a negative value) has a fixed place on the tolerance-intolerance scale. It can be perceived as positive or negative. Its positive aspect is that it performs the defensive role of an immune system. One of the main functions of all living beings is the protection of their identity. The loss of identity equals death. For this reason, all living beings have an innate immune system that defends them from the intrusion of foreign elements. The failure to protect identity would lead to general entropy. Resistance to what is foreign, or xenophobia, therefore is primarily a safeguard against entropy and a necessary component of all living beings. If we transfer this concept to social systems, it does not mean we are equating them with individual organisms. Nevertheless they must also protect themselves from entropy. Therefore resistance to the foreign, or at least caution regarding what is foreign, in order to protect identity is a reasonable and even necessary response. Naturally the immune mechanism in this case is not genetic or physically inherited. Rather conscious judgment is exercised in terms of how and to what extent it should be used. Even the legal institution of private property plays a role in the social immune system, providing protection against general social entropy.

Although one role of private property is to prevent "foreigners" access and to let owners determine who has access, owners are nonetheless compelled to consider the social role of private property. The use of property is subject to ethical rules intended to ensure that it will be beneficial to social cohesion, one of the essential conditions for the survival of both an individual and the community. The use of private property for the exclusive personal benefit of the owner comes under the ethical judgment of egoism, as it denies the social role of the property. Such ethical considerations are included in the legal system, but only partially, since laws cannot cover all situations a private owner might face, not even cases that might be solved with a broader understanding of the demands of the property owner's closest neighbors, or by the concept of welfare. This concept also has limitations: the social role of private property at some point hits the wall of the principle of privacy. If the concept of privacy is transgressed, it will eventually be abolished, and this decision must also be up to the owners—namely, the decision "to dispossess themselves".

Similar arguments can be applied to the common property of a community, and in particular of a nation state. Common property serves the needs of its owners, meaning the community. Just as human beings cannot live in isolation but must live in harmony with the community around them, so too individual communities must coexist with their near and distant surroundings. By tending to the needs of others, the community ensures that its own existential needs will be addressed, because its existence is dependent on others. This interdependence is increasing along with modern technological development. Interdependence is largely defined via contractual relations that provide international legal protection, and yet an increasing number of cases cannot be settled through formal treaties. Even formal treaties cannot be reduced to a directly measurable relationship of exchange. Once again this void must be filled with a code of ethics in order to provide a comprehensive understanding of our interdependence, and also the potential interdependence that may transpire in future situations but are not currently anticipated.

Interdependence is a challenge that communities, and especially nation states, have not faced before or at least not to the extent that they do today. In the development of modern life until this point, individuals needed to integrate into a society that did not fully accept their autonomy. In today's international environment, not even large communities, including nation states, can disregard the needs of the broader surroundings. Even powerful nation states must interact with the international environment. This can prove to be a complex task. As interdependence increases, so too does the evaluation of interdependence become more complex and difficult. For the most part, the modern public is not up to the task because it is burdened by the behavioral patterns of the past. Protection against the intrusion of foreign elements—a function of the immune system—was more appropriate in the past, being a natural response with no necessary analysis of the situation it addressed. The term xenophobia was unknown to the public, and the pressures of the environment were much lower because interdependence was weaker. This does not mean that the natural reflex against the foreign was not strong, or that it was not the predominant impulse governing the responses of the public.

Progressivism and Conservatism

On the one hand, resistance to the foreign has hindered the inclusion of Slovenian society into the so-called progressive currents of social development, and consequently its own development. Because of this, Slovenia, as a community, has politically lagged behind and has often poorly understood the requirements and opportunities arising at milestones in European history, particularly in the last two centuries. On the other hand, precisely this caution regarding the foreign and untested has prevented Slovenian society from taking steps that could have been fatal for it as a nation. Prior to World War I, Slovenians were subject to direct German denationalizing pressures, and it was considered progressive to open up to German cultural, technological, and economic influences, to use the German language in conversations, and thus pave the way toward assimilation. Insisting on domestic Slovenian customs was perceived as sacrificing cultural and technological progress, which in fact did enter Slovenian territory mainly from German circles. Speaking only in Slovenian meant losing access to elite social circles that conversed in German. But the Slovenian defense reflex was strong enough to prevent us from being lured by the sirens of modernity.

And yet demands for "progressiveness" did not end when Slovenia became part of Yugoslavia. The label of progressive was formally attached to those who supported the pro-Yugoslav political side and the declaration of a single united Yugoslav nation as opposed to the conservative label attached to the Slovenian People's Party. But the use of the term progressive in describing demands and policies was even more noteworthy during the communist party's struggle for power, and even during the period after it assumed power. A progressive was essentially anyone who agreed with and consented to whatever the communist authorities said, and those who tried to be independent were labeled reactionary. In retrospect, it is clear where this particular kind of progressiveness led and where it would have continued if it were not stopped. Conservatism is society's defense mechanism against untested interventions into the status quo, and thus serves as a part of the immune system. It is not considered progressive because it defends existing conditions. Existing conditions have already been tested for their suitability otherwise they would not have emerged. From this perspective, conservatism is the only sound foundation for future development, but it does not create new paths because that requires new findings and a readiness to venture into the unknown. Therefore truly balanced social development calls for an internal balance between the conservative and the progressive, whereby caution is exercised before setting out on any progressive path, before trying anything new. The new represents a foreign body as far as the status quo is concerned. In this sense, xenophobia extends beyond resistance to foreigners and becomes resistance to any foreign body, where foreign bodies represent new ideas.

Risk and Adaptation

The terms xenophobia, conservatism, immune system, and protection boil down to the same fundamental meaning. All these terms refer to the defense against the intrusion of the foreign into our own identity. According to systems theory, preserving the identity is essential for both maintaining the diversity of life and nurturing its development, as development depends on variety or differentiation. From this perspective, conservatism represents a condition for progress, although this may sound contradictory. In fact, developments in Europe over the last several decades have confirmed this contradiction. Several countries have achieved substantial change precisely under the leadership of conservative political parties.

Being conservative, or xenophobic—defined as caution regarding what is foreign and untested—has become an extremely difficult choice in the current social dynamic, in part because even conservatism requires some level of adaptation. The status quo cannot be preserved without adapting to changes in the environment, because anything that exists must be in balance with its environment. Indeed the status quo was achieved because it exists in equilibrium with the environment, and this balance was reached in response to the demands of the environment. As the environment changes—and it changes regardless of what we do—it is necessary for the status quo to adapt to changing conditions in the environment in order to maintain equilibrium for its own preservation. In this sense, conservatism is not the default rejection of anything new and the preservation of the old at any price. Even conservatism requires a certain level of dynamics. From this perspective, there is no substantial qualitative difference between conservative and progressive approaches. Both require adaptation to the environment. The difference lies in the quality of the dynamics. Conservative movements emphasize the preservation of values that have proved to be a sound foundation for the current state of affairs, insofar as it is deemed satisfactory. Progressive movements emphasize where the status quo is unsatisfactory compared to current expectations or possibilities for the future. For progressives, adaptation is not just the proportional balancing of our actions to conditions in the environment, but also intervention into the environment so that it will meet our expectations. Current social dynamics make this task much more difficult for both approaches than it was in the past, and calls for a more complex analysis. Both approaches depend on the correct evaluation of the conditions and dynamics of the environment. Conservatives will be unable to preserve what they fight to preserve if they fail to correctly evaluate the conditions in the environment and take appropriate measures to adapt to them. For this reason, their status quo approach is not merely sticking to the safe side as compared to progressives who are perceived as taking risks. Both sides take risks because both depend on assessing the current conditions of themselves and the environment. Any adaptive measure already brings a certain level of risk because it is an intervention in the future, which is indefinable.

Risks taken by progressives will be greater depending on how far into the future they aim, how drastic a change they are striving for, and how extensive the need is to change the current conditions. The higher the stakes, the more courage is needed. But courage is only praised when new facts confirmed that the risks were worthwhile. If the benefits of the goals are not realized, those who took the risks will be called irresponsible—which in some ways they are. In this context, courage is defined as taking responsibility for something we can speculate about but not prove for certain. To create something that is clear and provable from the outset requires no courage, only rationality. Taking excessive risk is generally not described as courageous, but rather as irresponsible and imprudent. Therefore progressiveness is only recognized as prudent and courageous if it does not aim too far into an unpredictable future and stray too far from solid foundations. And yet aiming far into the future is an important characteristic of movements that call themselves progressive. It is because of this that their progressiveness often not only lacks a foundation in reason but is also is based on ideology. The views of which are similar to dogma, that is positions that are believed rather than tested When these movements are connected to political parties, it is typical that the progressive quality of the platform becomes a political selling point and attracts new followers who grant the parties the legitimacy of being socially progressive. This is especially true when they have no achievements with which to substantiate their "progressiveness."

Slovenia, as a nation, tends to be conservative. Slovenians always had to hold firm to the ground on which we stood. This was the only prudent strategy because the Slovenian territory is located at a crossroads and otherwise we would have been swept away. Foreign powers habitually extended their authority into our lands, not always with nationalist intent but generally out of the desire for control (libido dominandi). This continues today, still with a touch of nationalism albeit generally a more covert one. The fear of the new and untested is typical of small nations as they can less afford to take risks. Indeed this is also why thinking and acting big has been uncommon in Slovenian history. Modern liberal ideas do not have deep roots in our nation, because we have never had a social class that was capable of and willing to take big risks and set out into an unknown future.

Caution also proved to be a means of survival for Slovenians when the communists took power in the republic of the former Yugoslavia. The communist party based its legitimacy precisely on proclaiming itself the most progressive political actor, as if it not only had perfect knowledge of the course of history and but could also create a new society comprised of improved social relationships. Naturally it did not merely make pronouncements. In the name of this future society, it demanded immediate change in the social relationships and actions that up until that point had comprised the acceptable foundation for survival. The inevitable downfall of this form of government confirmed and strengthened our society's mistrust of those who peddle the "unsellable goods" of progressiveness. Once again it transpired that we survived and managed to create our own nation state precisely because we did not believe the progressive demands of communism and stuck to the roots from which we had grown. Having our own nation state was not a completely new experience for us because the idea of it, albeit in embryonic and crude form, had been present in our national consciousness for a long time.

Experts and the Public

Today's international social dynamics require a greater level of adaptation than ever before, and a much deeper understanding of the direction and extent of necessary changes. Pursuing the time-tested patterns of the past remains a relatively safe strategy, but it is not sufficient and can even pose risks as it blinds us to new patterns of behavior that might be necessary. When forming responses to new conditions, we depend on analyses that are no longer based on common sense but require a great deal of expertise and information that is not generally accessible and requires extensive processing. Indeed we cannot determine the course of the future development to which we need to adapt without special expert knowledge, which often offers a variety of possible interpretations and responses.

Modern democracy often puts us in contradictory positions, which are not only related to problems with expertise but also to differences in opinion among the participants in democracy. Often these participants do not make judgments based on expert knowledge, but rather on patterns acquired from actions that have proved to be beneficial in the past. This contradiction is revealed in the fact that in the past common sense often provided better answers than knowledge learned from school, but today the better solutions are increasingly coming from experts. How can we address this contradiction? Experts with too much faith in themselves sometimes lack necessary wisdom and are therefore heedless of the views of the general population. There have been cases where the common sense of the ordinary people proved more correct than scientific expertise. If we need to evaluate potential actions in the future, we cannot rely solely on knowledge—knowledge stems from the past—and sometimes common sense is more helpful. In general, ordinary people have more access to common sense than experts who acquired their knowledge from formal education and books. When politicians work exclusively with experts, and neglect or even dismiss the views of ordinary people, tensions inevitably arise. Politicians defend themselves, sometimes even aggressively, with the accusation that ordinary people do not understand the issues and that they should not be in a position to decide such matters. This suggests that referenda on issues where politicians have formed one view and the public another one are not valid and should not be held. Politicians are often open in their condemnation of the public. In Slovenia, the general public as a whole is often accused of being conservative or forming opinions under the influence of various reactionary circles, of being xenophobic and hostile to foreigners. It is often said that xenophobia is one of the negative sides of the Slovenian national character, and that this raises the question of whether the nation state is mature enough to be a member of the EU—the implication being that those who vote against certain proposals are voting against European integration.

When calls for referenda surge as a political method, it is best to resist the mania and look for ways to prevent them. The increasing use of referenda indicates a disagreement regarding specific issues between the views of a majority of the population and the existing political structure, and also that their views differ on fundamental social values. There may be a lack of trust between them, a trust that is a necessary condition for the cooperation that undergirds representative democracy.

The referendum is not the foundation of representative democracy but rather proof of its deficiencies. Excessive demands for referenda reflect a deficit in the people's trust in their representatives. Such demands also arise when the ruling government lacks clear vision about its goals for future development, fears taking risk, and instead passes this risk on to the public. Of course the second example is hypothetical as generally the danger in democracy lies more in excessive government confidence and belief that the government is always right. The ideal solution is a government that enjoys the trust of its voters. This trust should be won through the success of its activities, and proposals that do not diverge significantly from the value-related patterns of the population that entrusted their fate to them.

For the Slovenian public, the most important recent novelty in the public sphere is Slovenia's membership in the EU. This new state of affairs has posed a number of questions that for the most part cannot be answered either by the government that led the EU accession process or by the public that is directly affected by EU membership. But the reproach that the Slovenian public is too conservative or incapable of grasping the importance of this historic shift, or even that its caution can be explained by the small size of the country and its unfavorable history, does not represent proof that the Slovenian public is less "mature" than that of larger Western European nations. The public in these larger countries has also shown its "immaturity" in terms of understanding the significance of creating a new Europe. Polls in many of these countries indicate that more than half of the population views the unification process with mistrust or opposes it altogether. These populations also do not understand the essence of the changes occurring in Europe upon which their own fate directly depends—the constantly increasing global interdependence, which renders impossible the continuation of their privileged position as independent large nation states, along with the fact that previous arrangements led to two catastrophic world wars that must not be repeated because that would mean the end of us all.

Thus all European countries finds themselves in the dilemma of modern democracy, which is founded on the principle of the people, who often cannot decipher the mysteries of their fate because understanding cause and affect increasingly required expertise. Judging by the results of different surveys, the views of politicians and the people continue to diverge. The public remains cautious about new things, especially when it is satisfied with what has already been achieved. If to anyone, xenophobia can be attributed to people from developed Western European countries where it is virtually always related to ignorance about foreigners. The self-absorbed public in these countries tends to know very little about others. I would venture to say: less than we know about them.

The Tendency Toward Uniformity

Caution (more on the part of the public than politicians) emerges from the legitimate fear that integration into a community of different populations and economic power might tend toward uniformity with the prevailing characteristics of bigger and stronger nations. This tendency toward uniformity is natural if no mechanisms are in place to prevent it. Formal equality, on which democracy is based, also leads to a natural leveling out.

Slovenians fought for an independent state precisely because they wanted to determine their own fate. Of course this is not entirely possible in today's conditions of interdependence. Nevertheless the goal of preserving our own identity cannot be questioned under any circumstances, otherwise our statehood and all the efforts invested in it make no sense. But recently our national identity has been threatened as a result of the mentioned right of EU citizens to move freely throughout the EU, and settle on the territory of all member states. For larger countries this is less of a problem because the size of their population and territory makes this intrusion negligible. The same applies to allowing non-citizens to buy land or real estate. But when it comes to the right of a new member of the workforce to make use of the employment opportunities in larger nations states, the latter choose to temporarily suspend the right to the free movement of labor. This represents an acknowledgement that under particular circumstances the free movement of labor can challenge the important interests of nation states, and that, from the perspective of the smaller EU members, this issue may call for special attention.

This issue is of existential importance to Slovenia, and the current arrangement may threaten its identity. The Slovenian territory is relatively small, but it is attractive because it has exceptional potential for tourism and recreation. Because of the saturation of industry and related lifestyle in the economically more developed EU countries, the demand for Slovenia's natural environment will only increase. The notably greater purchasing power of citizens of these countries automatically puts Slovenia at a disadvantage and subjects it to greater danger. Slovenia had to give access to foreigners even before concluding its EU accession negotiations, and was unable to negotiate a postponement, as certain other countries did, in order to develop its defensive capabilities.

Allowing non-Slovenians to buy and own Slovenian territory is at least indirectly related to EU citizens' right to settle. But maintaining the integrity of our statehood related to laws regulating the sale and purchase of real estate. If Slovenian real estate is accessible to all, then free settlement rights directly expose our entire settlement space to the intrusion of non-Slovenian population, which could relatively quickly transform the character of our society. The exposure of Slovenian society to this danger is enormous, and, regardless of a variety of analyses that find otherwise, the Slovenian population senses this on a primal level, and its response is resistance to all government measures as well as economic or political arrangements that may change the conditions and the way of life that accord with the population's perception of itself. For this reason, Slovenian citizens tend to oppose any intrusion of the foreign beyond what they deem tolerable. This threshold is relatively low as a result of historical circumstances and the pressure still exerted on our country by our neighbors, regardless of their actual historical culpability vis-à-vis Slovenians. Although it may strike external observers who come from different conditions as irrational xenophobia, the attitude is completely understandable. The accusation of xenophobia is often used to exonerate the true xenophobes from countries that oppose EU enlargement because of their own national egoism and shift the blame of xenophobia onto others, especially onto those who were victims of xenophobia in the past. The descendants of former Italian Fascists and German Nazis (who participated in genocidal movements against Slovenia) are particularly ardent in levying such accusations. Even segments of the domestic political scene use accusations of xenophobia when fighting political adversaries. Because it carries the mark of conservatism and the inability to understand current events in contemporary Europe, the reproach is a handy tool for disqualifying adversaries by denying them the legitimacy of leadership under current political circumstances.

In contrast, Slovenian politicians tend to refer to xenophobia when countering their critics' claims that they are neglecting national interests and succumbing to pressure during negotiations with the EU and other international partners, in particular neighboring countries. In this case, the accusation of xenophobia is used to defend their own weakness in compromising existential national interests. Politicians who pursue the national interest and are confident of the support of voters should not fear such accusations. If they are self-confident and decipher the accusations correctly, they could even take them as a compliment. Being called narrow-minded and provincial can easily be brushed aside by those whose views are broad and have risen above provinciality.

The preservation of national identity is a touchstone for nearly every political party. The almost unanimous decision of Slovenian voters in the 1990 plebiscite for independence was a surprise for political observers of the time. This surprise still endures and particularly the "most progressive" politicians fail to grasp it, just as the representatives of the officially most progressive political side at the time failed to. Consciousness of Slovenian national identity is one of the steadiest features in the Slovenian national character—maybe because it results from the constant struggle for survival throughout history. Politicians who disregard this fundamental feature of Slovenian national character cannot make inroads into the consciousness of the people. The most damaging thing politicians can do is to neglect and disregard this national feature. Any form of politics that does this will be contradictory. Even to maintain the status quo requires a certain amount of adaptation to the changing environment. One of the tasks of politicians is to maintain, through adaptation, the necessary balance between the current state of affairs and a changing environment. It is to be expected that adaptations will sometimes clash with the value system of citizens. In such cases, politicians can function as intermediaries bringing a new balance through necessary change. Naturally this situation puts such actors under pressure from both sides, that is from the domestic public and the changing environment. Ultimately they must decide whom to represent—their own constituency or the broader environment that itself exerts pressure, and sometimes relieves politicians of the pressures from the domestic public in the short-term. This dilemma can only be resolved by protecting the national interest and adopting changes that will allow the nation to preserve its identity.

Chapter 4: Reality and the Illusion of Democracy

France Bucar and Igor Kovač

It is widely believed that democracy is the best social order for the developed world. The system may have deficiencies, but nevertheless it is considered the best option.

When we review the options, we must first ask ourselves what we want to achieve. Several possible paths lead to the same goals. The paths may differ in effectiveness, efficiency, consistency, speed, and costs, and especially in the values that need to be sacrificed along the way. Moreover the goals themselves may change, and this necessitates a change in method. Goals are not uniform and cannot always be reduced to one common denominator (e.g., the greatest satisfaction for the highest possible share of the population). Even if we agree to such a simplified common goal, it will consist of a series of subordinate or secondary goals, each of them calling for different paths to be taken to achieve them. For these subordinated or secondary goals, democracy at least conceptually may not always be the most appropriate path.

Equality as a Methodological Foundation

One of the essential features and fundamental conditions of democracy is the equality of all members of the community, simply because they are all human beings.

The concept of the equality of human beings did not come from philosophical or ethical considerations. Throughout Antiquity and the Middle Ages, an opposing principle of inequality prevailed. Aristotle mocked equality, claiming that the only

F. Bucar (Deceased)

I. Kovač (✉)
Department of Political Science, University of Cincinnati, Cincinnati, OH, USA
e-mail: kovacir@mail.uc.edu

© Springer International Publishing AG, part of Springer Nature 2019
I. Kovač (ed.), *At His Crossroad*, https://doi.org/10.1007/978-3-319-78331-4_8

thing barbarians have in common with human beings are feet. (See J. C. Guillebaud, Re-Founding The World: A Western Testament.) Porphyry of Tyre, a third-century Neoplatonic philosopher and disciple of Plotinus, expressed scandal at the "novelty" of Christian egalitarian demagogy in his writings against Christianity. A criticism of Christian egalitarianism was articulated a century earlier by a previous Neoplatonic philosopher named Celsus. In his treatise Against the Galileans, the Roman Emperor Julian known as "the Apostate" (331–363 AD) denounced Christianity as a barbaric intellectual sickness after having abandoned the faith. He was especially critical of Christian teachings about equality, claiming that the doctrine was dangerous to society. Moreover he detested monasticism and the cult of martyrs, writing: "What! People were supposed to revere and admire these ignoramuses, who had no education and had not undergone any kind of paideia!" A typical medieval mindset was reflected in his discussion about whether Native Americans have souls or not. The philosopher and theologian Juan Ginés de Sepúlveda (in Valladolid, Spain on April 16, 1550) denied Indians the status of human beings based mostly on the arguments of Aristotle. Even the Encyclopédistes, who formally supported equality (they lived in eighteenth century France after all) still maintained a certain level of elitism, a remnant from the feudal and aristocratic past. (Pierre Charron: "The common people are an untamed beast. Every thought they have is pure vanity; everything they say is false and erroneous; whatever they disapprove of is good; whatever they approve of is bad; whatever they praise is odious; whatever they do and undertake is mere folly.") Social Darwinists, particularly Spencer, continued to reject egalitarian views.

The reason for treating all people as equals—the principle underlying democratic theory—does not lie in a fundamental change in the philosophical perception of human nature. The reason resides in the use of the mathematical-geometrical method as an approach that made it possible for man to penetrate the mysteries of the world. Thus the reason is purely methodological. It was this method that led to the discovery of the heliocentric system at the outset of the scientific revolution in the early modern period, completely overturning the understanding of the universe and humanity's position in it. In order to use the mathematical method to analyze and organize society, we needed a basic unit for calculation that would always be the same and would always represent the same quantity, otherwise the use of the mathematical method is impossible. This basic unit is a human being, an individual, who represents the same quantity in all mathematical operations. Equality is therefore purely methodological and does not even fit any other conception of humanity. Moreover all other conclusions from democratic theory derived from the presumption of the equality of human beings are merely assumptions emerging from this mathematical approach. The most important such assumption is the establishment of the general will of society. The general will is a mathematical sum of a majority of votes by all equal participants expressing their will on a particular issue. Just as the equality of people is merely an assumption that is needed for the sake of the mathematical method, so too is the view that a mathematical majority is proof of general will.

Equality as Part of a New Worldview

The discovery of the new world, and more importantly of the new frontiers of the known world, shook the foundations of the eschatological conceptions of the Middle Ages. In particular, it undermined belief in the hierarchical order of society, and this led to theological disputes, a new schism, and a series of civil wars, peasant revolts and feudal confrontations, that lasted until the mid-seventeenth century and formally ended with the Peace of Westphalia in 1648. A seed of doubt had been sown about all that exists, even about the individual self (Descartes: Cogito ergo sum). A new worldview came into being, and yet despite many attempts to create a comprehensive belief system that goes with that worldview (for example, the positivism of Auguste Comte), none emerged. Because of this, many still question with considerable confidence whether the Middle Ages ended at all, and whether the modern period has truly started. Many elements of medieval mentality are still present today. The medieval worldview was an internally complete belief system based on Christian heritage and culture, and it encompassed everything that human knowledge and premonitions about existence at the time could comprehend, everything that human hope and fear encompassed. Of course the mathematical-geometrical method, which enabled the new findings that shook the foundations of the world, could never become a worldview in itself for the simple reason that it excludes everything that cannot be measured or weighed, everything that eludes empirical methods. A true worldview must be comprehensive: it must provide an answer to any question the human mind generates. The answers do not have to be based in science, and science in any case cannot answer many questions. There have been no uniform responses to philosophical questions about whether our cognition is limited and what a human mind can achieve since Emmanuel Kant.

For the most part, the mathematical-geometrical method, which enthused its pioneers, substantiated their enthusiasm. It only fell short to the degree that it could not explain the spiritual world as scientists of the time hoped, believing that the world and all its phenomena were an integrated mechanism. Baruch Spinoza—author of Ethics Demonstrated in Geometrical Order—was a typical representative of this line of thought, interpreting the world as a giant mechanism that could be fully understood using the scientific method.

As previously stated, the scientific method is the foundation of modern positivist science, which has delivered most of our knowledge about the physical world and promises further breakthroughs into its mysteries, even beyond our home planet. Nevertheless positivism cannot serve as a worldview since it does not deal with anything that cannot be empirically tested. Neither religion nor philosophy provide real knowledge about the world. (See Auguste Comte, Course on Positive Philosophy.) That is why positivism is essentially only a method, alongside which there is an ideological void except when it is filled with the conscious denial of anything beyond empirical perception. For Spinoza, nature equals God: they are two different expressions for the same thing.

Therefore human equality as a basis of democracy has no ethical meaning. Its origin lies only in the method since no proper measurement could take place without a consistent unit. Equality in this sense offers no social program. Christian egalitarianism, which was articulated by Saint Paul and was seen as a real challenge to the hierarchical social structures of the Roman Empire, meant equality before God. This only affected social differentiation by inference and to a limited extent but never directly undermined the hierarchical order of Roman society. Thus even the Roman Emperor could accept this idea. The Church has consistently represented and supported hierarchical order in society. Any attempts at reform aimed at greater equality, or modeled on early Christianity, were met with disapproval including the Vatican's condemnation of Liberation Theology. The common denominator of virtually all attempts at greater equality is social pressure in theological disguise, while in the same way inequality has also used the disguise of Christian solidarity to jeopardize the human dignity and direct survival of the socially most deprived.

Democracy as the Right to Collective Decision-Making

The notion of equality being inherent to human existence and dignity did not emerge with the birth of modern democracy, and in fact has no direct connection to it. Democracy as a form of social order only means the equal entitlement of all those recognized as members of a particular society or community to participate in the governance of the society and other common matters. This membership emerges from various forms of social power permitting membership and was often obtained through the use of power against those opposing inclusion. Democracy in the sense of equal entitlement to manage common affairs does not yet correspond to the notion of modern political democracy. The latter means that all citizens are equally entitled to manage common affairs under the jurisdiction of the state. This jurisdiction also depends on internal power relations in the state, and only on the secondary level is it formalized in legal documents, primarily in the constitution. The democracy of ancient Greece—the historical model of democracy—did not include all of the inhabitants of the city-state but only the elite: namely a minority of free citizens as opposed to the majority of slaves and others without the status of free citizen. Democracy in larger or smaller closed groups of those who exercise power over their social environment—possibly also an entire state—can be seen throughout history, including the explicitly hierarchical feudal society. This implies the equality of the elite within the closed group, which under no conditions granted the same rights to those whom the group governed. From the perspective of social power, it was a balance that was often enforced or acceptable to all but was always inherently fragile, only lasting until the balance of power shifted. Nevertheless the balance had to be in harmony with the general conditions and laws dictated by social and technological developments. A classic example of the opposite that confirmed this rule can be found in the historical Polish parliament, the Sejm, in which any Polish nobleman could veto any (even completely rational) decision on any grounds. Hence the Latin saying Veto Poloniam perdidit, meaning that veto was the downfall of Poland. Thus we come to the following conclusions that are important in understanding democracy:

- Decision-making in any community resides in the hands of those with the necessary power to enforce their will over others. If they do not have absolute power, they must share it with others on whom they thus depend to some degree. This co-dependence leads to the hierarchical composition of government. Democracy is a method of governing a community where no individual member or smaller part of the community can acquire absolute supremacy over others.
- The sharing and distribution of social power is a result and reflection of social and technological development. A society at a lower level of development will have a different distribution of social power than a society at a higher (or the highest) level. If the distribution of social power corresponds to the level of development, the community can make appropriate decisions for its preservation and further development. However, this correspondence is not always ideal and also depends on how it is interpreted by those in power. Substantial divergences are possible and can lead to internal tensions in society.
- Normally, no community enjoys complete internal uniformity, but rather consists of different parts of the community facing a range of challenges from the environment. That is why social power within each community has a unique form of distribution that corresponds to how much individual members or constituent parts are capable of generating appropriate responses to these challenges.

Is Democracy the Best Answer?

Democracy is not always necessarily the best form of government to ensure the most appropriate responses of the community to the challenges of its environment. It is only one of many possible options, and the best only under certain conditions of social and technological development. This introduces the question of systemic conformity. Can the systemic characteristics of one part of the community diverge from the general systemic pattern of the community as a whole? Can the social subsystem of a democratic society use a mode of decision-making that differs, in terms of its internal relations and its responses to the challenges of the environment, or from the democratic pattern of the system as a whole?

Systemic conformity must apply to all decisions made in the system as a whole, otherwise the system will eventually collapse. All decisions of a subsystem must in effect confirm the goals pursued by the whole system and especially not contradict the fundamental values upon which the entire system is based. Nevertheless this does not mean that smaller parts of the system cannot reach decisions in a different hierarchical manner. Democracy is justified by the best possible quality of its decisions. In a number of different areas, social power is hierarchically distributed.

Democratic decision-making conflicts with this distribution and therefore cannot lead to the best decisions. This is particularly true in fields where social power is derived from the capability of those who wield it to find the best possible answers. This is the case in organizations and communities where social power is derived from spiritual or intellectual values.

Democracy is always the result of equally distributed social power. Social power is proportionate to the ability to formulate the most appropriate responses to the challenges of the environment. Even the greatest social power coming from an economic, political, physical, or other foundation is justified in the end only by its capacity to provide the most suitable responses. If those who wield power cannot do this, they will remain in the top decision- making positions for a period of time, but during this time the gap will grow between reality and what the community could have done for its existence and progress but failed to do because of the decision-maker's incompetence—up to the point when the gap becomes so great that the community is no longer capable of surviving and progressing. This means that democracy can only exist in a situation where it is capable of providing the most appropriate solutions, both for itself and for the parts of the community which and in whose name it governs. The premise behind modern democracy is that all citizens are capable of forming appropriate responses for the state as a whole, and it is assumed that the best response is defined by a mathematical majority. This should be substantiated by the success of the community as measured by its capacity to survive and advance. The premise might be accurate but it is difficult to prove, except for certain specific issues, because success only becomes evident over longer periods of time, often exceeding the lifespan of a single generation. That is why the claim that democracy is the best possible order is relative, since modern democracy is still too young to judge whether it is truly the most effective system that delivers the most appropriate responses.

The Modern Concept of Equality

The existence of the modern citizens' democracy rests to a great degree on a supposition that hardly stands up to critical analysis. All decisions are decisions about values. All values are arranged hierarchically, which means that deciding about values on different levels requires a range of capabilities and the ability to manage diverse information. Moreover decisions emerge from different origins, arrangements of social power, interest factors. The structure of values is the foundation for the composition of society. Its binding force is the hierarchical structure of values as all lower-ranking values must be in agreement with higher-ranking ones. Here we are referring to the highest-ranking values that all capable citizens can understand and that pertain to general issues that relate to the direct interests of all community members. These are issues that have to do with the basic concept of human value, the meaning of life, attitudes toward other people, and fundamental ethical principles of duty that enable the existence and survival of the community. The highest level in the hierarchy of values is composed of elements that define actions at lower levels. These issues are timeless and at the same time so general that all community members will confront them at one juncture or another, and will need to come up with their own responses. Nevertheless they are also distinctly social issues because they concern all human beings, and human beings depend on living in a community to survive.

These general issues can and must be decided by each member of the community. Only this gives legitimacy and sense to the democratic order, though this has not always been the case. Throughout history such conditions in communities have been the exception rather than the rule, and have only become more typical in recent times with the advent of the modern state.

Here we need to pose two questions for consideration:

1. What occurs in general social development that leads to all members of a state being given the right to participate in defining the highest-ranking values that affect the life of the community and the individuals in it?
2. How often is this right a reality and not merely a formality?

The answer to the first question lies in the general acceptance of the principle of equality of all people as regards some of the generally recognized characteristics of all human beings (although conceptions still differ: to some, equality only refers to our divine origin and not to equality in real life), and consequently the acceptance of the principle of equal rights. There is of course a fundamental difference between equality and equal rights. However, equal rights cannot exist without a foundation in equality, which legitimizes them in the first place.

Yet this is only a partial response to the first question. How did the notions of equality and equal rights emerge in the first place? The historical development of views on the issue of equality suggests that the opposite should have occurred. It is not possible to find a foundation for equality from the sociological perspective; if it were, we would need to reject social power as the primary regulator of human relations. However, even the rejection of social power would not make it any less real. Accepting human equality means consciously disregarding social power as the fundamental regulator of human relations. Because such a rejection cannot be based on any significant socio-economic interpretations of social power, equality can only have ideologically originated from one of two sources: Kantian rationalization or transcendence.

We could rationally argue for equality by proving that it makes sense, that it is beneficial and even necessary. Such a conclusion might come from a contemplation of social and technological development. The development of capitalism—in which the means of production is owned by the organizer of the production process and the necessary labor is owned by those performing it (i.e. workers)—was only possible with a contractual relationship between these two partners. Theoretically, it is also possible that the stronger partner in this relationship will put the weaker in a subordinate position. This was the case in all social systems before capitalism. Why has this changed? First, more complex production processes, of which capitalism is capable, cannot be achieved with brute physical force, as this would also require ownership of labor, as was the case in slavery or partially the case in feudal systems. Second, the exchange-based market economy, another important feature of capitalism, requires free buyers. In sum, capitalism is impossible without the equality of the contractual parties.

This train of thought reinforces the position that the introduction of the market economy necessitates formal equality in human relations without which the social order could not exist. In this sense, equality has rational grounds, but only as a requirement of the particular pattern of the economic and social order that is generally accepted today. It does not, however, provide sufficient proof that equality is a fundamental component of human identity or that it is absolute. In other words, if the social order based on the market economy changes, the need for equality would diminish and new reasons for it would need to be found in the new system of governance; otherwise the rationale for equality is built on the assumption that the capitalist market economy is eternal and unchangeable. Some perceive it in this way; Francis Fukuyama, for example, came to his conclusion about the end of history on this basis. The current condition of equality is limited to a pattern of exchange relations, which means it is only a matter of formal law. Relations in other areas, especially issues of so-called actual equality, remain outside the reach and interest of the market rationale for equality.

The philosophers of the Enlightenment, the era when the capitalist market economy began to emerge as the prevailing social order, attempted to present equality in a philosophical context as an inalienable feature of human identity. Despite their generally anti-Catholic orientation, they had to resort to reasons that could only be located in transcendence. This was particularly evident in the 1776 Declaration of Independence of the United States of America, which refers to the "Laws of Nature and of Nature's God". The idea of equality as an inalienable feature of human nature articulated in Enlightenment philosophy become dogma in European political theory and practice, and was rearticulated in international documents after World War II, in particular the 1948 Universal Declaration of Human Rights. It is now regarded as an unquestionable axiom. All the same, it cannot be regarded as inalienable on a purely rational basis.

Up until this point, equality only had foundations in Christianity, which was the first theory to introduce the notion of identity previously unknown and inconceivable in European thought. Throughout the development of European philosophy—from the Enlightenment to contemporary aspirations to recognize humanity's emancipation and autonomy—the concept of equality became increasingly important, but the origin of this ascent in the hierarchy of values is the Christian notion of equality before God who created all people equal. Although many strands of philosophy deny the Christian origin of equality, they pronounced it as axiomatic without a satisfactory explanation relying on rationality. In this respect, European culture is different from all other cultures of the world. Even the official doctrine of the nineteenth-century Catholic Church embraced the inequality of people, which stemmed from their different purpose and role in the world, and accepted equality only as equality before God with respect to salvation (a school of thought known as ultramontanism).

The position of the ultramontanes represented a break with the Enlightenment, and the conclusions drawn from this school of thought come very close to the views on equality developed by the ideologists of classical capitalism (Adam Smith and David Ricardo) as well as to those of the nineteenth-century social Darwinists. However, it begs the question of whether the shift from the Enlightenment approach did not merely reflect the actual state of affairs as opposed to representing an ideological return to and the idealization of equality.

Formal Equality as a Vehicle for Actual Inequality

Political democracy is based on formal equality before the law of all citizens or members of a particular community. This creates a foundation from which all citizens can strive to expand their abilities, set goals, and choose the means of achieving them. Here lies the undeniable advantage and even greatness of democracy. And yet this foundation does not yet create the real possibility for all citizens to achieve their goals. Formal equality in the eyes of the law alone does not create equal opportunity. Opportunity is already limited by nature itself, by the advantages it gives to some, and the conditions it imposes. Moreover equal opportunity is limited by existing social conditions and the unequal distribution of social power, allowing the privileged to evolve and develop at the expense of the less privileged that can count only on their own ability to work. Even members of the latter group vary in terms of their abilities to create opportunities in the competition for the same limited goals. Human nature is the most important initial reason for social inequality. Formal equality before the law, which opens the door to everyone to pursue their own goals, is paradoxically one of the biggest reasons for actual inequality. With formally equal opportunity, those wielding greater social power automatically have better possibilities than those with less or no power. This is why democracy, which is based on formal equality before the law, works in the interest of those in an advantageous position in the competition for limited goods. This social power is based mainly on the ownership of property. Democracy is therefore an extremely desirable system for capitalists in particular. Without formal equality, they would be unable to assert their dominance over others who are formally equal but lack the necessary power to effectively compete. At the same time, formal equality gives capitalists the legitimacy to wield their supremacy.

By creating conditions for the establishment of the supremacy of those holding power and at the same time legalizing it, democracy has also become an important tool in the competition that takes place on the international level.

Economically developed countries, which in the eighteenth and nineteenth centuries asserted their dominance mainly through colonialism, no longer have this tool at their disposal and no longer need it. Using their economic supremacy, they achieve the same goals as they previously did through direct colonial aggression, but in an easier and less apparent way. The path to economic subjugation was opened by democracy, which sets the same formal conditions for all but where the weaker get the short end of the stick. Today democracy is the initial condition for breaking into foreign markets and ultimately controlling them. That is why today's imperial powers present democracy to less developed countries as the first and highest value, and also as the condition for faster development. And then they wonder why some of these "recipients" reject this generous gift.

Is the Majority Always Right?

The voters are always right: this is a mantra that is popular in justifying the results of general elections, referenda, and popular votes on questions of general social significance. It is difficult to argue against this statement. Despite reservations about defining the general will of the people mathematically, it is nevertheless controversial to dispute decisions chosen by the majority. We could argue against majority decisions on a rational basis, for example if a majority chooses a solution that clearly conflicts with the positions of science, or if issues of broader international importance or similar issues are at play. After all, the point of democracy is to allow all citizens to independently form their interests and priorities. We do not want to deny the very purpose of democracy—the freedom of choice. This choice is a result of the hierarchy of values that we create and implement for ourselves. Choice is always subjective. Thus it may sometimes seem irrational from the perspective of science or objective reasons. And yet it was precisely the elevation of higher rationality over the 'narrow-mindedness, unsophisticatedness, and lack of understanding of the ignorant and uneducated, or at least people with lack of vision' that brought about modern authoritarian regimes such as Nazism and communism. Democracy includes the inalienable right to do stupid things—which paradoxically have often proved to be the smartest decisions. Plato's vision of the state being run by a philosopher kings necessarily leads to dictatorship. The role the philosopher king is supposedly based on his ability to decide what is most appropriate for his subjects, but this excludes freedom of choice.

Education in Relation to Equality

Democracy is the first system in history to allow society to make use of the capacity hidden in the creativity of its members and to give everyone the right develop and use these skills. Hierarchically organized societies have generally neglected the creative talents of members in the lower social strata who were denied access to higher levels of education, with the transition to higher hierarchical levels of society being limited or even disallowed. Higher levels of education were reserved for the elite, and served as a means of preserving the existing social stratification. However, the hierarchical organization of society with limited possibilities of transition to higher levels also slowed development. In this respect, formal democracy spurred creative dynamics in a way no previous social order did.

But even formal democracy did not actual create those dynamics. It merely did away with the formal obstacles to social flexibility and to the ascension of the hierarchical ladder, sometimes all the way to the top of the social elite. But limitations that were the result of inequality in wealth remained. This is particularly true when we look at access to education. The path of many known talents to higher education, and even more unknown and undiscovered talents, has been cut short by a shortage of material means. Thus, even with democracy, the existing social structure slowed progress and creativity by hindering social flexibility and not allowing people to fully use their intellectual potential. Although formal prohibitions on moving to higher social strata of the society were gone, informal prohibitions remained because of the hierarchy of wealth-based power. These now function as a guardian of the social structure similar to the formalized social hierarchy that performed that role before.

Education means power for those who have received it. In this respect, it creates competition within existing social distribution. Because of this, efforts for the better education of the lower strata do not automatically receive the support of social elites. Limiting social flexibility through access to the highest levels of education has been an important tool for preserving the dominance of the privileged ruling class (or nationality) in multinational states in times of increasing nationalism, particularly in the nineteenth century. This was the fate of the Slovenian people when facing the pressures of German cultural supremacy in the Austrian Empire. Slovenians even had a slogan: "Culture and education—the vengeance of our people!"

However, the existing social elite could not indefinitely maintain its supremacy over the lower strata of society through cultural dominance alone. The reason for this can be found in the nature of capitalism on which their dominance depended. Among the features of capitalism and the market economy is the constant competition for supremacy in the marketplace. This can only be achieved with the production of new higher-quality products at a lower price. This is achieved by harnessing creative potential that can be found anywhere. Therefore it is always in the interest of capitalist entrepreneurs to search for new talent regardless of its origin, and to spend their own resources to develop this talent. For example, initiators and advocates of Slovenian national emancipation in the nineteenth century financially supported students in order to give them university educations. Priests were especially prominent supporters of this program and the main driving force of the national revival of Slovenia in its early stages.

The role of education remains important and perhaps is even increasing in the current, most developed form of capitalism, where competition has moved to the international markets. The economies that lead in newly discovered fields have a competitive advantage. But even top echelons of science depend on the education of the low and mid-level ranks of society. Ensuring that the population is educated has become an important public issue and is mostly the direct task of the state. But education also changes the internal composition of society. Members of society have become much better educated on average than they were in the past. Interest in public affairs that was once the exclusive domain of ruling elites is increasing in other parts of society. Moreover the complexity of the problems modern society confronts is also changing the way society is managed.

Finally, formal democracy, which has spread through society, has also changed its composition and character.

Democracy and the Horizontal Structure of Society

Society is transforming from a vertical to a horizontal structure. All members of society have the right to take part in managing common affairs, to determine what these common affairs are, how to address them, and to define the goals and interests of the community. However, in larger communities such as nation states, this management is only possible through representatives. Modern political democracy comes mostly in the form of representative democracy. But general representation is no longer a direct reflection of the will of those who have the right to decide on common matters, and is therefore by default a deviation from the fundamental principle of self-governance.

Representation cannot be identical to the will of the constituents. If an elected representative could directly express the will of the constituents, the deputy would not be a representative but merely a transmitter of the constituents' decisions. Modern methods of communication open new possibilities in this respect, allowing us to avoid representation and arrive at a direct reflection of the actual will of eligible citizens—whereas we still define the common will as a mathematical majority of votes. Nevertheless we cannot avoid representation in democracy. Contemporary management does not mean deciding individual cases but involves constantly deciding on the comprehensive dynamics of community matters. This requires constant oversight and management. The composition and internal connectedness of contemporary society are so complex and broad that it is not enough to decide on the most pressing individual issues. Representatives must therefore constantly interpret developments in the specific areas of their mandate, while remaining within the framework of their general mandate. But this interpretation is a product of their own processing of the information they receive, their understanding of events, and especially their value systems. Therefore it represents their own understanding of the world and responses to it rather than an actual transmission of the will of the voters who gave them a mandate. This is similar to how the minutes of a meeting are never a literal transcription of every word uttered at the meeting but only a summary. The summary emerges as a product of the mind of the person taking the minutes. This makes the transcription of the minutes an independent creation. Likewise representative government always reflects the representatives' perceptions, understandings, and interpretations of the events for which they have been authorized to decide on behalf of their constituents. This is also the case when the mandate is general and those giving it could not anticipate all the situations for which a decision will be required, situations when they cannot make decisions themselves because they lack the necessary knowledge to understand the challenges of the environment, and when they cannot decide among several possible answers because they cannot identify which choice best fits their interests. The issues faced by modern society are increasingly difficult to grasp and manage because of the growing complexity, interrelatedness, and interdependence of issues. Receiving a mandate to govern is becoming unattainable to average citizens without special expertise, and even elected representatives increasingly rely on information received from experts. Information is never completely original, but is almost always processed by others. This is also true as regards the formulation of responses based on information that has been processed on multiple levels, formulations that inevitably emerge from the value systems of the people preparing the responses.

Formal representatives are compelled to expand and deepen their authorities the more complex the issues become and the more remote from the representatives' fields of expertise. Thus, even the horizontal composition of a democratic society, compared to the previous hierarchy of the feudal and absolutist states, has brought a new vertically structured society, where the hierarchy is based on the hierarchy of rational thought. The justification of the origin of the mandate for managing public affairs is equally questionable in both systems. When justifying their rule, feudal or absolutist rulers referred to its improvable divine origin, while governments in modern democracy rely on the mandate received from voters, which is proved by the results of a democratic election. Yet this proof is merely a formality.

In both cases, the management structure is hierarchical. Along with the divine-origin argument, the feudal order justifies itself mainly with the quality of decision-making, as opposed to formal democracy where the balance leans more toward quantity. The quality of decision-making is supposedly derived from the hierarchy of logical thinking and superior access to information. The hierarchical construction of governance is thus presumed to be a reflection of the logical structure of thinking, which will be reflected in the quality of decisions. Because of the generally lower technological development in authoritarian systems, the relatively simple structure of governance also allowed far greater transparency and clarity of relations as compared to the complex composition of modern democratic society, in particular the greater transparency of the hierarchy itself.

The hierarchical structure is almost completely covert in modern democratic society. The social order is based on formal equality, which suggests a horizontal structure. All political power is derived from the foundation of voters and is built from the bottom up. This is contrary to the process of logical thinking, which always uses hierarchical deduction. At the same time, this contradiction hides the actual structure of the modern democratic society, which on the outside seems explicitly horizontal. But its operations are not defined by the assumption of equality and the formal right of all to participate in the management of public affairs but rather on the method of operations, and this is dependent on the complexity of the issues that must be managed. Decision-making on complex issues calls for a multi-level hierarchy of decisions. We may believe that representatives implement the will of their voters, but the representatives must first translate this will into concrete form, and this is done according to their own views and perceptions.

The Myth of Democracy as the Basic Characteristic
of Modern Society

The actual structure of modern democratic society is not uniform as might be erroneously understood from the term "democratic". It is more like a mosaic set in a uniform democratic frame. Society as a whole decides on matters that are comprehensible to all its members and are also in the interest of all. This pattern of decision-making appears in all subsystems, down to the smallest social cells. Even in the most professionally or intellectually demanding organizations (e.g., scientific and research, or medical institutions), it can be detected in matters that apply to all members of the organization and are comprehensible to all of them, as well as to matters that relate to the organization's existence and survival, and the basic rights of members. All members can decide on these issues, and they have an equal right to do so. However, matters affecting the core activity of the organization are decidedly differently. Such matters cannot be decided by someone who does not perform this core activity outside of the subsystem, even if does not relate to highly specialized knowledge accessible to only certain members. The core activity of an organization always demands expertise rather than general knowledge, otherwise the organization would have no purpose. This pertains to the division of labor based on the logical analysis of a task and how it is understood. This division continues up until the point when an individual member or a group can perform a particular task without further division. Each subordinate level in this division process finds its origin in the directly superior level, and is basically a means with which the directly superior level performs its tasks. Its autonomy thus only refers to the framework set by the directly superior level, and cannot extend beyond it.

Defining these frameworks can differ greatly depending on the character of the organization and its management style, but also on how much its members identify themselves with its goals and the mutual satisfaction that is derived—which in turn relates to the skills and art of management. In any case, here we are not talking about people performing their own work, but rather work assigned by others. Democracy as a right to self-governance can only refer to the way the assigned work is performed, insofar as this is defined in individual cases. Democracy beyond this framework would mean an intervention into the rights of others, by whose authority and for whose benefit the activity is performed in the first place. This is an explicitly hierarchical structure of an organization focused on a particular goal and based on the division of labor, and applies even if we are talking about a democratically structured organization that encourages the greatest possible realization of the creative capacity of its members in various employment positions. Such a "democratic" organization—far from the rigid militaristic organization, or classic serial-structure organization in which adhering to prescribed methods is essential for the organization's success—facilitates greater creativity and identification with the organization. Nevertheless the structure is still hierarchical because it is the product of a logical analysis about how to perform particular tasks and achieve desired goals.

Even a democratic organization does not always produce the best possible solutions, for example when a particular project depends on the highly streamlined cooperation of all participants. There are as many possible forms of organization and management styles as there are goals to achieve, but what they all share is that their core activities are organized hierarchically, and that they are all mosaics of different democratic and hierarchical components within a basic democratic frame. Indeed hierarchy is one of the core activities of all goal-oriented organizations. Furthermore the hierarchical structure of society is an underlying feature of what we call modern democracy, and this is a direct result of the number of people involved and the number of activities related to their interests and self-affirmation.

Hierarchy inevitably means accepting inequality and subordination in the work process, which for most people consumes the largest share of their energy and life. We live in a time that is more hierarchically structured than the pre-modern, authoritarian, and absolutist eras. In those previous eras, there was an almost total absence of liberty in public matters, though this was less total in private areas. A relatively small part of society was in the relationship of hired labor (and the conditions were much worse than they are today). In contrast, virtually everyone is in a hired-labor relationship in today's technologically advanced society, and this necessitates a hierarchical structure.

The pressure for democratization is increasing, in particular because the hierarchical structure of modern democratic society is so obviously disproportionate to the material prosperity of the consumer society. On the one hand, this is the result of technologically advanced modern organizations with extremely hierarchical structures, and, on the other, of the growing demands for personal autonomy. Personal liberation in terms of material prosperity and status combined with the predominantly hierarchical structure of modern organizations is one of the man paradoxes of modern democratic society. The concept of democratization itself is ambiguous and contradictory.

We can conclude from the above discussion that the people (or demos as included in the term democracy) more or less determine who will run society on their behalf, but they have no impact on the actual management because managing the issues of modern society requires a high level of expertise as well as an intensely hierarchical structure. The modern democratic state represents an extremely hierarchical and complex organization.

In commercial enterprises, the owner has the right to make management decisions. Transferring this right to the employed members of a company would require the current owner to be disenfranchised. This of course is not possible because it would mean a reversal of the principle of personal property, which is the basic guarantee of the democratic order and free entrepreneurship. This means that democratization is possible only in goal-oriented organizations. Democratization, but not democracy, where democratization means that as much freedom and creativity as possible are allowed in performing assigned duties in the framework of a hierarchical organization, and that the borders of the assigned tasks are flexible to the extent that the work process allows it. This reduces the sense of subordination among employees, unleashes their creativity, and thus is in the interest of the owner or manager of the work process.

Frameworks of democracy are also much narrower than they appear in public life, where we are limited to the right to freely decide on a representative who will manage public affairs. The actual selection of candidates for public offices takes place mostly out of sight of the public that ostensibly makes the final choice. In most forms of representative democracy, the choice of candidates is in the hands of political parties with the public generally having no direct influence on the procedure. Larger political parties are themselves hierarchically organized, and true political power is concentrated in the leadership of the party. Candidate slates are determined by the elite members of the political party, and are usually a fait accompli for the rest of the party. In this respect, modern political parties are not so different from ruling parties in totalitarian states. The sole difference is the monopoly of the single party in totalitarian systems as compared to the oligopoly of several parties in democracy. Parties also differ with respect to internal democracy, and cases of the dictatorship of a single dominant figure or an elite within a party are not unusual. A classic example of this was the communist party within communist systems, which functioned as a dictatorship governing the entire population. It created the superficial appearance of democracy with general elections, but was in fact a harsh dictatorship with its own hierarchy and a single dictator on top.

Although the determining of candidate lists is a mark of the power of the leading elites in political parties, it is not completely up to them. They must still consider the likely response of the public that will express its views in the polls. Thus, although the public normally has no direct influence on the choice of candidates, it does have the option of not voting for them on election day. Here the power of democracy plays a decisive role, but it can only be manifested in a multi-party system in which parties campaign to persuade voters of the advantages of their political programs and that their candidates are the right people to implement them.

This also reveals the weak point of democracy. The average voter is unable to evaluate the appropriateness and feasibility of political programs, since such judgment often requires a high level of expertise. Voters usually base their vote on their own positions on important domestic issues, and even this emerges mostly from their values. Each political party has a position on important issues on the national level, and voters basically choose the party whose program aligns with their particular interests or value-based judgments. But voters have no direct impact on how the state is actually run or public affairs are managed because public affairs management requires a hierarchical organization structure. Even parliament, as the direct representative of the people and the highest legislator, exerts only an indirect influence on the management of public affairs and has relatively limited oversight into actual government operations. The ruling government, which is the highest body of state administration, has the most direct influence, but in fact it is also an executive tool for the implementation of the policies of the party on whose slate the government came to power. The positions behind the government's most important decisions are not formed in parliament or in the government, but rather in the party leadership. Parliament, in its legislative role, only formally confirms these policies with the required majority, which again is party-based. Finally the direct management of public affairs is not in the hands of political parties, but rather in those of the state bureaucracy on which the public hardly has any influence. Legislation, which requires a legal foundation for all actions of the state bureaucracy, is the main safeguard against arbitrary decision-making, one side effect being that the system becomes rigid and not very adaptable.

Individual Emancipation as Opposed to Social Integration

Democracy as a social order is supposed to determine the position of individuals in society in accordance with their unique personalities while also taking into account their dependence on society. This role is already contradictory. Human nature strives toward liberty and the assertion of individuality. In these efforts, human beings are hindered and limited by the society in which they are compelled to live because they cannot survive on their own without integrating into society. But society is made up of people who have the same tendencies toward liberty and asserting their individuality. Thus democracy provides a response to the position of the individual in society, a middle ground between these two contradictory components of human nature. Different views of democracy have developed along with our self-awareness and the understanding of our position in society.

The most basic human need is for survival. Our perceptions of ourselves and our position in society develop in connection with our capacity for survival. As long as our survival is completely dependent on society, we cannot develop a perception of ourselves as unique or separate from society. Complete dependence on the natural environment is typical of societies in their initial phases of development. Only a compact and internally unified community could prevail in the struggle for survival by making use of what the natural environment had to offer, while at the same time defending itself from threats from that same environment. The community determined the actions of individuals, and few possibilities existed for actions outside of assigned roles. In primitive communities, this social cohesion was so complete that the idea of an individual being unique never developed. Although the emergence of the first technologies and the resulting division of labor gradually relaxed the total dependence of the individual on society and of society on its natural environment, some level of dependence remains an essential feature of the social order. In the so-called developed Western world, the situation only began to change in the last few centuries, while in the technologically less developed world, individuals still significantly depend on society, which determines life roles in accordance with its needs. Even in late Antiquity, the notion of personality was understood as the role of the individual in the community—the Latin term persona and the Greek prosopon initially meant a theater mask, not a person.

The concept of the individual independent from society emerged for the first time in Christianity, not with respect to social integration but rather to the individual's relationship to the new faith. To paraphrase Saint Paul in the Epistles: conversion into Christianity cannot be a decision of the community, but only of the individual. This statement already recognizes the individual as the bearer of free will. At the same time, it recognizes the equality of all human beings in the eyes of God. The concept of the free individual was later developed and elaborated by Saint Augustine whose views served as the foundation for the development of European philosophical thought about the idea and role of the individual.

European philosophical thought later diverged from Christianity, particularly under the influence of the French Enlightenment, but nevertheless ideas about the role and importance of personality are typical of European society and this is a direct result of the Christian understanding of individuality. Indeed European culture, in its understanding of the role and importance of individuality, differs from other world cultures.

Why did this development occur only in Europe when Europe's general development and interdependence was similar to the rest of the world? In many respects, Europe was even less advanced than certain civilizations that developed from different cultural foundations. The answer presumably lies in the way the role of individuality developed in European culture, and in this respect Christianity provided the main impetus. Moreover the development of the role of the individual expedited technological development and the liberation of society from the direct pressure of the natural environment. Advances that spread throughout Europe as a result of the scientific revolution came with the message that, because of science, humanity would no longer depend on nature and would ultimately master it. And it has actually seemed that this might actually be the case, up until now that.

As extraordinary scientific and technological success introduced the belief that humanity was no longer dependent on nature, a parallel process also began: namely, the liberation of the individual from the pressures of society. In this case, this development did not emerge for religious reasons, but because of increasing prosperity. Individuals began to feel free from society, sensing they could determine their own roles and positions in society, define relationships with other individuals as well as their worldview and the meaning of existence and work. Thus human beings became increasingly autonomous vis-à-vis the society in which they lived and gradually also in relationship to the truth.

But the freedom humanity currently enjoys is absolutely dependent on the prosperity generated by society. This is why it is beneficial that society works for the common benefit of all who have the right to participate in the management of society's affairs and decisions that affect their fate. At the same time, all other members of society enjoy the same rights, and the individual must therefore agree with others regarding mutual relationships and common interests.

This position of the individual in society, and also the equal relations among its individual members, is only possible if society has reached a sufficient level of independence from the external environment, specifically a society with a high level of technological development and conditions in the external environment that lead to prosperity. This is what allows the individual to have significant independence from society itself. A society that has not reached this level of prosperity cannot allow the independence of its members. What's more, democracy can even be harmful for a society that has not reached this level of prosperity because it encourages the independence of individuals from society and hinders necessary social cohesion.

This can lead to chaos. It should be noted that independence is not necessarily proportional to technological development. It depends on a range of cultural influences that are not entirely independent of general technological development. Significant personal independence generally comes with a suitable level of general education and other cultural influences that tend toward personal emancipation. Thus we cannot claim that democracy is the only possible or necessary order for a society at a given stage of development.

We also cannot claim that a certain level of technological and cultural development necessarily leads to democracy. However, we could describe democracy as a system where it is generally accepted that society is made up of independent and equal individuals who jointly manage the affairs that bind them together and make them interdependent. The individual comes first, and the society is only secondary, a derivative. Society collectively manages, under the supervision and mandate of its members, the common activities have been transferred to it. Society has nothing original that places it above the individual. It is true that this interpretation of society includes a number of disputable ideological aspects, from the debate about nominalism and realism dating back to the Middle Ages to more recent considerations about the reification of systems.

Democracy cannot be adopted by societies that, based on religious beliefs, derive power directly from God or some other transcendental source. In such societies, we quickly come to the question of what individual is authorized to make decisions that are binding for the entire society. Since religions have a hierarchical order the answer is obvious: the supreme religious leader is also the head of state and basic religious dogmas are the highest laws of the state. Theocracy is the first and oldest social order but has survived to the present day especially in the Islamic world. Democracy is not only an unacceptable social order in theocratic states. Indeed it is a sin because it challenges the divine origin of power. Another sin is personal freedom outside strictly defined religious rules. This is why there can be no trace of religious or social tolerance for personal freedom, not even in inter-state relations.

The same or at least a similar situation can be observed in countries where a secular state order is built on the foundation of an official state religion, and other religions are allowed or tolerated. Rulers in such states can only remain in power only when they function in accordance with the state religion. This was the case in most of Europe during the era of enlightened absolutism. It is interesting, but also logical, that the spread of the principles of human rights and basic democracy in Enlightenment-era France, and particularly as a result of the French Revolution, triggered an open confrontation with the Catholic Church. For a long period of time—until the Second Vatican Council in 1962—the Catholic Church could not accept the principles of modern democracy, because they lead to the secularization of society, and the separation of church and state. The Catholic Church Only could only accept democracy as a legitimate social order, though certainly not an ideal one, when the view prevailed that the individual is free with respect to religion (in some ways a return to the views of early Christianity). Tensions between church and state remain a constant. Modern democracy actually has an inherent anti-religious bias. It stems from the ideas of the scientific revolution and the early modern period, and is based on the assumption that humanity can achieve anything, and that therefore humanity will become the master of the world and does not need God or any other form of transcendence.

The Limits of Contemporary Democracy

Without a doubt, democratic societies have attained rapid progress in science and technology, and have created the great material prosperity. This is certainly because of the freedom, creativity, and potential enjoyed by those who live in democracies. However, equality itself, as a feature of democracy, does not spur creativity or moving past what already been attained toward ever greater achievements. It is more the opposite. It leads to a leveling out, opposing elitism and anything that stands out from the average. This is its conservative side. The average always favors the preservation of the status quo. This also has a positive effect as it ensures social stability, another condition for creativity. And creativity, the nature of which is to endanger the status quo, eventually manages to break through the resistance of the democratic average toward innovation and novelty. The most significant breakthroughs have always posed a danger to existing conditions and were therefore met with resistance. Creativity has a completely different source than equality, the latter being an ideological construct. Creativity grows because of the freedom democracy provides, not because of equality, which serves a completely different purpose in democracy.

Creativity—we can also include entrepreneurship in this category—breeds inequality because it creates social power, and social power only aligns with equality if it is equally distributed among community members. It is precisely creativity that constantly destroys this balance, and introduces a tendency toward hierarchical organization, which conflicts with equality, as it uses people as a means to achieve its goals. Democracy is therefore far from an internally balanced and harmonious social order. It is highly dynamic, with its various features contrasting and conflicting with each other, particularly freedom and equality, stability and dynamics, creativity and tradition, social power, and solidarity, and finally autonomy and heteronomy as the source of decision-making power. That is why we cannot discuss a universal form of democracy. There are as many different democratic orders as there are democratic states.

Above all, democracy is not static. It represents the optimal point or balance where people can behave freely in relationship to society but they are also obligated to abide by certain social norms. This point of balance depends on the knowledge and resources of society for exploiting and overcoming nature, and man-made or other changes in the environment. It is not constant and unchangeable. Democracy vacillates around this point, and is always an approximation. Vacillations take place both as regards social autonomy and the understanding of the pressures of nature on society and methods for exploiting nature.

As far as the individual's relation to society is concerned, contemporary democracy is characterized by extreme personal autonomy developed to a level where the fully emancipated individual no longer recognizes any personal restrictions—religious or mythological, national, or traditional. Emancipated individuals no longer recognize any absolute truth or authority, and create their own truth. The emancipation of the individual from the grip of society is a historical development that has only recently culminated in real personal autonomy. It is a remarkable historic achievement for human beings. Nevertheless freedom is relative. There is no absolute freedom, and as it moves toward absoluteness, it undermines itself by eliminating social cohesion, and, as previously mentioned, an individual cannot survive without society and its norms. The current trajectory toward absolute personal autonomy is reaching the limit where the integration of society has already come under serious threat. Moreover humanity's conception and understanding of its position in the world is changing as well. Extremes often cause reactions in the opposite direction. If the current trajectory—which is already raising great uncertainty about the position of humanity and the meaning of existence—continues, it may happen that humanity will look for solutions by pursuing a completely different direction. In any case, it is fairly certain that the future social order will be considerably different from the present one.

Although humanity has made unimaginable progress in understanding and exploiting nature, it is exactly this progress that has revealed that humanity's goal to be the master of nature is a dream that will never come true. It has revealed that each new discovery leads to unimaginable horizons that stir the human mind, but also set new limits and create new dangers. Mastering limited space and energy resources, breaking the mysteries of the human genome: all will necessarily set new limits on humanity's freedom. Even the contemporary market-based economy does not offer unlimited development potential in our limited world, and will require more social regulation, which will necessarily change the social order. Even contemporary democracy, like everything else in the world, is transitional.

Chapter 5: States in the Hands of Oligarchy

France Bucar and Igor Kovač

Each organization represents a means to achieve a particular set of goals. That is why each organization is structured in a way that, given its understanding of cause and effect, leads to the best possible path toward these goals. As this understanding can change and depends on a number of variables, we cannot assume that a particular organization is the only possible or best structure to achieve these goals.

In terms of states as organizations, it is currently assumed that democracy is the best foundation for their internal arrangement. Moreover, all units within states face the same problem of democracy as the most suitable way to achieve its goals.

But is democracy really the most appropriate method available?

Oligarchy as the New Reality

The issue of organizational structure as a method is addressed by many organizational sciences that specialize in various aspects of the field. The most important organizations for the democratic state are its institutions, which should provide an efficient way for citizens to participate in the management of common social affairs—the so-called democratic element—as well as a suitable way to address issues that society confronts in its natural and social environment.

In developed democratic states, the most common response to the need for a democratic social order is the practice of representation. Details differ as they reflect the particularities of the environment and the historical development of a given

F. Bucar (Deceased)

I. Kovač (✉)
Department of Political Science, University of Cincinnati, Cincinnati, OH, USA
e-mail: kovacir@mail.uc.edu

© Springer International Publishing AG, part of Springer Nature 2019   111
I. Kovač (ed.), *At His Crossroad*, https://doi.org/10.1007/978-3-319-78331-4_9

society, but in general the system is built on the assumption that the representative body best reflects the will of those represented by the state, namely its citizens.

Here the following questions must be asked:

1. How do we arrange the representative body, so it most accurately reflects the will of the citizens, or put another way by what procedure should citizens choose their representatives?
2. What system will allow chosen representatives to implement the will of those who chose them in the most direct way possible?

The best responses to these two questions come in the form of different electoral systems, all of which approach the goal with none meeting it completely. This is because the goal itself is contradictory: first, because the community that elected the representative body is not a uniform body, and its will is to some degree an abstraction, and; second, because representatives are elected in a one-time action, while the opinions and positions of the voters constantly change as time passes and the environment changes. Democratic systems attempt to correct for this by limiting terms in office and holding periodic elections.

In the interim period certain divergences occur that representation cannot bridge. Elected representatives must act without a direct mandate in certain cases. They must respond to problems that are new, not only for the voters but also for them, and the voters, themselves unable to come up or agree on a solution, are usually not consulted in this process. After election day the representational relationship between voters and elected representatives becomes an assumption, and the actual link between them is broken. From that point on elected representatives act independently of their constituents. Having been elected gives them the necessary legitimacy to act independently. It is the legal basis from which they draw power as representatives of their constituents.

But once the polling stations close representative democracy is transformed into an oligarchy until the next election.

The Independence of Deputies as the Foundation of Legitimacy

The election is only the end result of a long process that starts with selecting candidate lists and continues with efforts to win support and persuade voters to choose a particular candidate (the election campaign). The campaigns are generated from a range of programs that reflect the goals that voters wish to achieve by electing the chosen candidates.

Naturally these programs are only general positions or orientations that characterize the personality and identity, and particularly the ideological orientation, of the candidates. The actual programs, which should be the decisive criteria for the election, are unimportant or, more accurately, the least important element of the campaigns. Programs change quickly, and priorities may shift, particularly in the contemporary era, which is marked by rapid development and change. The personal traits of the candidates, the future oligarchs, are more essential. The most important quality for their position is the independence of their individual choices. When elected, the general mandate relationship between themselves and their voters, which endows them with power, is broken. Their position thus loses its legitimacy, though not its legality since formally nothing has changed. Legitimacy is based on the trust of voters in the personal integrity of their representatives: the representative is the person in whom voters entrusted their fate. If elected deputies surrender or lose their independence, they betray the obligations of the representation that has been entrusted to them. The voters choose their deputies based on their personality and identity, but this includes the right to adapt their positions to changing conditions that take place during their term.

Only the personality (and integrity) of the deputy can ensure a stable orientation and act as a constant in changing conditions. This personality was what won the deputy votes to begin with, and this personality (largely) includes the deputy's orientation with respect to values and resulting worldview. In politics, a worldview without values is opportunism in the guise of political ideology, and exists to hide a lack of values and valueless careerism. Personality and identity precede worldview, and it is the identity that "adopts" a worldview. A worldview has no foundations without the underlying power of personality and identity. Its realization cannot be the subject of community decisions; it will always be a matter of a personal decision. Furthermore it cannot be influenced by orders from the political leadership. The orders from the leadership of the former communist regimes that all members of society adopt a communist worldview are proof of this. Most people did not internalize communism as a value orientation, because this led to the disintegration of anyone who adopted it as an ideological orientation out of opportunism or fear. The communist leadership issued orders without any mandate to the society over which they ruled. In such conditions, there was no democratic element. Communism failed because it eroded people's identities.

The Crisis of Identity as a Crisis of Democracy

Identity, which is a characteristic feature and condition of democracy, is at risk in our highly developed modern society. The process of emancipation leading to personal autonomy can in its extreme form lead to a rejection of all authority. This indicates that people find their ultimate justification in themselves. But this is conceptually untenable. For most people, even the effort to reach this state is onerous and unattractive. In the consumer society, the most appealing and easy way to achieve satisfaction is through consumption. For this reason, people without a deep personal foundation in terms of their values are easy prey for political and economic demagogues promising material wellbeing. Indeed voters often choose their representative based on promises of material wellbeing that have no realistic basis or conflict with long-term interests of sustainability and the ongoing survival of the individual and society. In contrast deputies often see their election as simply the next step in their own careers. Can such a "value orientation" lead to greater material prosperity and general development? Is sacrificing one's identity too high a price for such an orientation?

The crisis of identity is one of the most substantial problems in modern society. The personal integrity of deputies is a feature without which the representative system as the foundation of democratic society cannot function. The functioning of the representative system also depends on a number of organizational, material, culture-related and historical conditions, in particular the level of civilizational development. All of these conditions individually and taken together determine whether the institution of representation will function according to its purpose and get close to the goal of democracy at all. But the personal integrity of deputies remains the principle foundation. If deputies lack integral personality, the conditions listed above become irrelevant for the proper functioning of representation.

The notion of the integral personality is an elusive category. It refers to an individual, unique in their genetic circumstances and experience, that responds to external challenges in a unique way. Of course external challenges change with time. The same individual will respond differently in various conditions. There is also a range of mental capacity in terms of how each individual interprets a set of given or changed circumstances in various times and places.

The term integral personality is a pleonasm. A personality is by definition integral, otherwise it is not a personality. Personality is the sum of all the characteristics of a particular person. When we refer to the concept of the integral personality, we are speaking above all about the issue of consistency in terms of generally accepted values. An integral personality is an internally harmonious whole, founded on generally accepted values, whose responses to particular circumstances can be predicted in advance. This is in opposition to a schizophrenic personality where mental illness makes it internally inconsistent.

But we can also think of schizophrenia from the perspective of social pathology. Social circumstances can cause an individual to respond contrary to his or her integral personality: different external factors may throw an individual's internal harmony out of balance, and this may lead to a contradictory response under the influence of new circumstances that challenge the individual's ethics. An individual with an integral personality will always acts as an integrated harmonious whole. The strength to do this can only be drawn from values that individuals identify as an essential part of their personality. Examples of social schizophrenia are common: for example, when people say things like: "Oh, yes, he is an honest person. But you don't need to overdo it with being good. We don't have to be saints." The most common deviation from the integral personality is the relativization of values, which comes from a lack of generally accepted values. But even values are a product of time and circumstances. But the relativists are right to a certain extent. Changes in historical currents do bring different responses to challenges, and these responses are related to values, not in the sense of rejecting values that have provided a solid foundation for the survival of society through history, but rather as adaption to new circumstances. New circumstances may require an emphasis on values that existed in the past but now need to be approached differently. They may call for a different way of implementing values that are taken for granted or neglected. A special case for the relativization of values can be found in politics. It has often been claimed that an honest politician will not get far, and that honesty goes against the nature of politics. Great social shifts in history have always brought with them a seeming crisis of values, and this is a significant feature of our time.

Personal integrity does not mean that there are no differences in how we evaluate certain situations and activities in politics aimed at particular goals. This evaluation of activities is related to our judgment of the causality between means and goals, whereby the latter may refer to the alignment of a series of goals. And with goals, it is always important how they fit into the entire value system. In some cases, we may be talking about issues that require expertise, where assessments can vary greatly. But in other cases, there is less room for differences, although we should not get entrenched and believe that only one particular pattern of behavior is in line with a generally accepted value system. We cannot deny the personal integrity of someone with their own views and positions on the practical goals of a particular policy, or who represents a world-view that is different from the prevailing one, even if the difference is substantial, as long as its broader implementation would not endanger the survival of society. Without such freedom of thought and action, personal integrity as the most important value for the functioning of society and social cohesion becomes irrelevant.

Personal integrity is therefore always related to the courage to persist against a majority that thinks differently. But this is not because courage is a special feature of personal integrity. Courage comes from the internal consistency of the personality and is its logical outcome, otherwise it would contradict itself and no longer reflect personal integrity. An individual who is not ready to consistently manifest his or her personal integrity under any circumstances, someone who lacks the courage to do so, ceases to be a harmonious person. Whoever acts in a contradictory fashion for whatever reason cannot have personal integrity, but is a coward or a careerist. This is why representative deputies must have personal integrity in order to function democratically.

True, deputies are not always elected on the basis of having personal integrity, since voters do not have direct proof of this. This proof may be present for subsequent elections when their personalities have been tested. The first election is usually decided based on party allegiance, and to a lesser degree the worldview of deputies, although the two are often connected. Nevertheless the election of deputies often depends on a number of random circumstances, such as engagement in the interests of the local community, success in sports where success confirms the confidence of the environment identified with the candidate, support for causes that are popular among voters even if they are unrealistic or irrelevant for the general goals of society. It is assumed that success unrelated to the position of deputy proves a certain level of personal integrity, since such success presumably requires personal integrity. But it is also possible that the election of a particular deputy is part of the agenda of those representing special or partial interests that may be only indirectly the same as the general interests of society or may even oppose them. In short deputies are often elected as a result of circumstances that have little or nothing to do with their personal integrity.

Pressures on Deputies

A reasonable question can be raised about whether it is in agreement with the representative role performed by deputies to exert functional or ethical influence on the voters to elect a candidate that suits a particular proponent (e.g., political party) or the particular interests of a group that hopes to benefit through such a deputy (e.g., economic interests). Normally democracies permit, but also regulate, endorsements of candidates. Such endorsements are considered a part of political freedom and are thus in agreement with the principles of democracy.

However, this is mostly appearance, not reality. The appearance emerges from the false assumption that elected deputies maintain a direct link to their constituents throughout their term in office. But in reality this bond is broken once deputies are elected, and from that moment on they function as empowered independent actors and their independence is thus essential for this position. Nevertheless they are subject to influences from the environment, first and foremost from their political party, and then from the direct environment that elected them, particularly interest groups that may have been formed precisely to place pressure on deputies to make decisions in their favor. The personal integrity of deputies serves as the only guarantee that they will continue to work in accordance with the principles and values that shaped their identity.

Pressure on elected deputies to make decisions according to the special interests of different pressure groups, among which political parties are the most important, is legitimate. Political parties are established for the purpose of achieving the goals they pursue. Various economic interests also have the right to attempt, within the framework of the law, to achieve the general conditions on which their success depends. If it brings new information to deputies, such pressure can even be beneficial as it allows them to judge the issue that is being decided from a broader perspective. But new information also exerts a form of pressure on those receiving it. Blocking the inflow of information would mean reducing the possibility of making the best possible decisions. Deputies must therefore expose themselves to the pressure of new information, which it is in their interest to seek in order to make the most appropriate decision in each particular case.

It is a completely different matter when pressures on deputies encroaches on their rights and interests as protected by law, and when the aim is to force deputies to make decisions in accordance with the interests of those exerting such pressure. This may not be illegal; indeed conflicting interests are often legal. Even special rewards for deputies are not necessarily illegal (although they are definitely morally questionable), because deputies do not oblige themselves in advance in terms of how they will vote or define the public interest. Nor can we always ascertain beyond doubt what comprises a bribe. Is it bribery if a deputy is promised a high position in a company that may have become successful based on a decision for which the deputy voted, even when its growth was in the greater interest of the public? Political parties also exert strong pressure on deputies elected on their slates, not only by expelling them if they refuse to toe the party line, but above all by making it impossible for a deputy to pursue a political career in the future.

Any pressure on deputies beyond providing new information means a direct attack on their personal integrity, and is thus unethical and against the purpose of representation, even when it is not illegal. Anything aimed at subjugating deputies to a force outside themselves undermines the institution of representation, and is therefore an assault on the essence of democracy. If this becomes the general rule, decisions are no longer taken in the representative body, but in the centers of power around it. Deputies become a mere voting tool of those actually in power, and the representative body becomes a means to create the illusion of a parliamentary system. Under the illusion of a parliamentary system, interests are pursued that have nothing to do with democracy and the idea of representation. The system of representation may be illusory in any case, but when deputies are excessively or even fully dependent on a particular power center it turns into its own contradiction. In reality the proclaimed state system of representation becomes, without officially changing form, a representative power for centers of power and thus serves as a sort of democratic cover. The most obvious example of such formal representation were parliaments in communist systems where individual deputies would not consider making a decision that differed from what had been ordered by the party. If they did, they would risk more than just their seat in parliament, so they developed a special sense of how to vote even when no specific instructions had been given.

However, total dependence of a parliament on a political party is not limited to communist dictatorships. It is typical of all authoritarian regimes, which rarely have the courage to formally turn parliament into a form of corporatist representation or even abolish it altogether. Although such interventions were, and still are, typical of fascist regimes, they are not restricted to them. In fact, such interventions are the rule rather than the exception in most countries, even in countries where doubts are not openly expressed about whether the society is mature enough for true democracy, and the governing system is described as enlightened absolutism. Elements of enlightened absolutism are common in all ideologically oriented political regimes that wish to use a party majority in parliament to introduce conditions in society that reflect their ideology or create an imagined state of prosperity and quality of life. In short, these regimes pursue goals that would not get the necessary majority in parliament in a free democracy, and they see a shortcut to these goals if deputies are dependent on them for power.

Parliamentary Democracy as a Dictatorship

There is no doubt that parliamentary democracy can also be a form of dictatorship—that is, the dictatorship of the majority over the minority legitimized by the underlying positivist worldview. The party or the coalition of parties that secures the necessary number of votes rules freely—similar to an enlightened absolute ruler although still within the framework of the constitution. The minority may object and invoke the rules of democratic behavior, but it is helpless against the majority as long as it stays formally within the framework of the law. This is particularly true if the majority position of the governing party has helped it to obtain influence over the mass media, financial flows, and the general infrastructure on which the modern economy is increasingly dependent. Such a government is hardly different in terms of content than various forms of totalitarian rule. An intelligent government will not completely neglect the minority because it is not in its interest to do so. Nevertheless it is hard to maintain a clear head with absolute power. Actual parliamentary democracy is a rarity. This is particularly so in countries with an insufficient democratic heritage such as former communist counties. During the transition from a totalitarian system to democracy, the newly formed parliamentary majority often established itself as a new kind of dictatorship. Despite its democratic appearance and being more accessible to the pressure of the newly democratic external environment, these governments became deeply fortified in their ostensibly democratic position. This position can only be successfully defended and maintained through control of the voters. The key to democracy remains in the hands of the voters, and democratic government is controlled by those who control the voters.

Free voters are the foundation of all democracies, and their freedom also gives democracy meaning. Is it compatible with the concept and purpose of democracy if centers of power attempt to control voters? Political parties—and to a lesser degree also different interest groups—that try to influence voters by offering them a persuasive program or the attainment of goals act are for the most part acting in accordance with the law. Voters may also be influenced by other centers of power that act more or less in accordance with the constitution, and whose actions are either permitted or prohibited. But in either case, they cannot be fully controlled, let alone stopped, because they reflect actual power exerted autonomously. Most importantly, these centers of power operate outside the control of the public. Their influence can be substantial but often their origins cannot be located. This is particularly the case when it comes to different forms of economic dependence.

Various centers of power, in particular political parties, normally do not attempt to win support for their programs directly but rather through the selection of candidates. When a political party nominates a candidate in a particular constituency, this puts its political program to the vote since candidates are generally chosen if voters agree with the program. Nominating a candidate usually involves a complicated procedure that can only be carried out by a political party. Moreover the chance of being elected depends on the election campaign, which can usually only be managed organizationally and supported financially by a political party. In this context, organizationally and financially stronger political parties have a significant advantage. The size of a party, especially if it has already been in power, is a force of attraction for voters who are politically unaligned. Voters normally prefer to be on the winning side. They feel safer. For this reason big political parties usually control the political stage.

If a political party has the necessary majority to control the legislation in parliament and also controls the executive branch in the ruling government, it occupies the position of a monarch. This is the political aspiration of all parties. If they cannot achieve it on their own, they seek alliances with other parties that have similar programs. In proportional voting systems, a single party rarely obtains the necessary majority with its own deputies. Normally the relative winner with the highest number of seats in parliament has the opportunity to form a government, but cooperation with other parties must first be negotiated to secure an absolute majority. The party thus forms a ruling coalition. The point of the coalition is to adopt a common program to be implemented during its term in power, with the firm commitment of all participating parties that they will adhere to the agreement, and a distribution of decision-making positions, particularly ministerial posts, among the coalition partners.

The Ruling Coalition

There can be no objection regarding the legality of forming a coalition government since it is based on constitutionally guaranteed freedom of association and private initiatives in pursuit of personal beliefs. It also ensures the desired stability of governance for the state, which is essential particularly in changeable and uncertain circumstances. Nevertheless governing by coalition still changes the foundations of parliamentary democracy. During the period of its term in power, the coalition government becomes a constitutional monarchy while not abandoning the official form of parliamentary democracy. What's more: in a constitutional monarchy the parliament usually has the decisive role in designing legislation and supervising the government. In this situation, the actual "monarch", the ruling political party, controls the government while the parliament participates according to the instructions of the parties in the coalition. The situation is close to enlightened absolutism. The problem of democracy moves from the parliament to the ruling party where all important decisions are made, where the political course of governing the state is set, and where state jobs are assigned.

The ruling political party is, of course, not a copy of the parliament from which it has taken the authority to determine the state's fate. The closest comparison might be to a large corporation. Corporations are governed by the principles of business efficiency and related disciplines as well as the imperative of (material) success, and there is less emphasis on internal democracy or the transparency of activities both of which are important features of democracy. In contrast, the parliament, devoid of content, becomes a mere technical tool that legalizes decisions made outside of parliament in the ruling party. The parliament is no longer the venue for reaching agreements and publicly debating the arguments related to particular decisions. The main goal of parliamentary debates is to inform or convince the public of why a particular decision has been made and to undercut any criticism voiced by the opposition. The latter uses its counterarguments to prepare the ground for the next election but has little influence because it lacks the votes. Whether the ruling majority yields to its perhaps reasonable objections is again a decision taken not by the parliament but by the ruling political party.

Following the party line becomes the priority in parliament rather than the cogency of arguments. Party discipline is the lever used by the ruling party to enforce its policies and defend its positions. If the ruling party does not have the power to ensure obedience in its own ranks and the necessary cooperation within the coalition, it loses its dominant position. Discipline is ensured by strict sanctions as the entire project of the party's policies depends on the cooperation of deputies. In critical cases, disobedience of a single deputy can turn into a major political scandal that can bring down the government or the coalition.

Is it possible to guarantee that the principles of democracy will govern relationships among equals? Is there a state system where these principles can truly be realized? Can they be realized at all? The democratic principle appears to be the most acceptable form of violence: namely the violence of the majority, not violence from a different source. Nevertheless the violence of the majority is violence against the minority. The solution is to test the existence of a majority as often as possible in the context of a constantly changing environment and the new possibilities it brings. The majority can change any time the voters are faced with a new situation that calls for a decision. A new situation does not mean that the majority actually will change but an opportunity must be made to verify it. If we accept that the majority principle is a form of violence, the solution is to verify the majority with each new situation. If one party is to assume the position of the majority for the period of its term in office, the violence is fixed for the entire term. This is no longer democratic rule but feudal rule by the majority party.

Parliament can only function properly as the highest democratic body if its members are free to express their positions independently. The provision in the Slovenian constitution that deputies "are representatives of all the people and shall not be bound by any instructions" (Article 82 of the Constitution of the Republic of Slovenia) carried not only declarative, but also a constitutive, meaning. Without the independence of deputies, there can be no parliament. Is binding deputies to the positions of their party against this constitutional provision, especially when the ruling party obliges deputies to cooperate within the framework of the agreed-upon program for the entire term? Not strictly, because deputies are not obliged to be members of their party and are free to quit it if they do not agree with the party's program or position on a particular issue. But this freedom is only formal. In reality, deputies are not only affiliated with their parties but are dependent on them. They have a moral obligation to their parties since it is mostly due the parties that they are elected. The party put the candidates on the slate and supported them during the election campaign. For deputies who value integrity, this moral obligation is more binding than material ties, although the material aspects are hardly negligible. If the professional lives of deputies are dependent on their position in parliament, they have placed themselves in the control of their party and have bound their personal fate to that of the party. This is particularly the case when deputies have no other sources of income to guarantee their existence. Independence can lead to legal sanctions, although this would not be based on the law, but on the conditions that determine social power.

Democracy in Political Parties: A Condition for Parliamentary Democracy

Formally speaking, even the connection between deputies and their parties' programs does not violate parliamentary independence. But in reality, the commitment of deputies to a pre-defined party program represents a temporary abolishment of parliamentary democracy. The party may not formally violate the freedom of its members in any way with the presentation of its program. After all, this is the reason they became members of the party—to be able to realize their positions on general social issues. If deputies do not agree with the parties' positions, they can choose not to join the party in the first place or subsequently withdraw their membership. But parties themselves should also work to ensure the independence of deputies. Party positions on specific issues cannot be set in advance since the situations that are addressed in parliament change. Deputies should be free to represent their own views within the framework of their parties. It is not necessary for the party to have a uniform position in all cases. Uniform positions are needed for matters pertaining to the foundations of the parties' worldview, or the most important interest-related issues for which parties were established in the first place. But without internal democracy within parties, the parliament will not be democratic.

Democracy within parties depends on general conditions in society. If the atmosphere in society is relaxed and citizens generally hold similar views regarding fundamental social issues, if the society is not too divided on historical issues that have burdened or continue to burden it, and if the society is not troubled by excessive differences in economic and other opportunities, then the competition among political parties will not be so acute that a fall in vigilance or a mistake would change the power relations among them Without this kind of atmosphere, democracy within political parties is unlikely. Similarly, if there is a lack of internal democracy in political parties, then we can expect increased tensions in society.

A governing party cannot allow itself to be lenient. Any decision that runs counter to its principle programs could jeopardize its position in society and the mission it has set for itself. This is especially true if the fundamental mission of the party is to substantially change existing relations in society. In any case, which party governs is critical for society, since parties almost always have a specific ideological orientation. A change in the ruling party not only means a change in attitude toward a number of more or less important concrete issues, but also in ideological orientation and new relations in the distribution of social power, and indirectly on who holds positions running the state. Because of this, it is essential for the party that assumes power to transform its deputies into captives, subjecting them to strict discipline. The engine of the government's majority in parliament must run smoothly. If the party that won the election does not have the necessary majority in parliament, it will need to find allies in related parties. Because the very reason for the existence of different parties lies in their policy differences, they will need to temporarily set aside these differences if they wish to form a coalition government. This may lead to various deals among the parties, and the price is giving up the freedom to vote against the agreements reached in the coalition program. Such coalition agreements guarantee the relative stability of the government and increase the possibility of achieving the goals set by the ruling party, but parliamentary freedom is sacrificed in the process.

Given the conditions of Slovenian society, such a sacrifice is not only inevitable but also necessary in order to break free of the negative legacy of the communist era. But it is often overlooked that this form of governance can cause other problems. It is a vicious circle. A comparison could be made with the reasoning behind rationing food in periods of shortage, for example directly after a war.

A similar fear prevails today regarding the democratization of governance and party discipline in the relationship among parties. Deputies cannot be allowed to escape strict controls on voting the party line. Leniency in this domain could bring down not only the government but also the entire idea and policy orientation of governance. The main point of a governing coalition is to secure the necessary majority of votes, and thereby protect the government and the adopted program. In proportional voting systems, the formation of a multi-party coalition in order to install a ruling government can present an unsolvable problem. Nevertheless coalition deals for forming a government appear to be an inevitable consequence of the proportional system, since a single party rarely secures the necessary majority of votes. Coalitions are necessary particularly in states with greatly divergent views on general social issues, or a state that has gone through a civil war. In such conditions a minority government is inconceivable: it could never be installed.

This is also the general belief in Slovenia. There is no evidence to counter this belief because it has never been tested. The risks would be too high. That is why it can only be established hypothetically, which is certainly a worthwhile exercise.

Minority Government

First we must define more clearly the meaning of majority and minority governments. A majority government is formed by a political party that won enough votes in an election to have a majority in parliament on its own, or by a political party that won a relative majority in an election and has managed to secure the necessary majority based on a joint program with other parties that agree to its program. A minority government is one that was able to secure the majority of votes in parliament necessary to get installed but not the necessary support for its program. Such a government needs to secure a majority for each individual vote.

Let us assume that no party gets an absolute majority in a proportional representation system. This makes it extremely hard to form a minority government and the failure to do so can lead to a new election. A majority is needed to appoint a prime minister in any case. In this situation, a number of parties will need to reach a deal, and the prime minister designate will not necessarily be from the party that won the most seats in parliament. Other parties can also form a coalition, as long as they secure the necessary majority. Such a government can also be called a minority government. The term is a contradiction in itself—democracy only allows governments that have a necessary majority with any other government going against the essence of democracy. With the exception of situations where a single party dominates, a proportional electoral system will always yield this kind of a minority government because no party has a majority on its own. A majority can only be formed through mutual agreement with other parties. In this respect, the situation is quite different in majority electoral systems where the party with the most votes generally receives an absolute majority. In sum, what is defined formally as a minority government is the normal the situation in countries with proportional representation systems.

Minority governments are less durable. They are transitional, being regularly exposed to changes in parliamentary majority but their advantage is that they allow true parliamentary democracy because they are dependent on public opinion.

This type of governance depends on how coalitions are formed every time there is an election. One condition for this type of governance is that society has a uniform view on fundamental values, and there are no substantial differences in views on social integration and general goals. No government that takes the helm will attempt to change these fundamental values. It will not attempt to change the value system of society. Therefore little will change for the ordinary citizen as a result of the ruling government. Parties that deviate from this general pattern are labeled as extreme. Mostly such parties do not make it close to governing or decision-making positions, and this renders them essentially harmless to the established social order, and more an embellishment of the democratic system. Only if an extreme party gains power do they pose a real threat or limiting influence, and this indicates that society is already undergoing processes that herald the possibility of fundamental changes to the existing order.

With respect to fundamental values, there is generally little difference between parties in a democracy, with individual ideological orientations playing an insignificant or no role in governing. Today there is no significant difference on basic social issues between conservative and social democratic parties. Both support fundamental human and citizens' rights, private property, entrepreneurial freedom, the rule of law, and the role of the state as the common service provider for the needs of its citizens, and the only rightful enforcer of limitations to freedom in accordance with commonly agreed-upon rules and goals. Differences mainly reside in their views on what measures will achieve the generally accepted, although not always formalized, goals, and what intermediate goals align with or are necessary to attain the general goals (e.g., general prosperity, universal social security, full employment, equal opportunity). It is a question of degree in social policies that comprise the differences in views between conservatives and social democrats; little divides them in terms of the final goals. As long as they remain within the framework of the basic elements of social cohesion, the differences in worldview and ideological orientation are insignificant to social harmony. Democracy is a tolerant social order precisely because of the broad spectrum of issues that are insignificant to its functioning. This does not mean that worldview and ideological orientation does not indirectly affect attitudes toward fundamental questions of democracy and that they cannot be jeopardized. But there is a high threshold of acceptability. Any meaningful dissent from the fundamental values would mean an end to democracy. This may pose a danger in the case of various theocratic or chiliastic views of the social order.

Parliamentary democracy is only possible if there is general consent on the fundamental value-related elements of democratic society. If such consent exists, the minority form of parliamentary governance is the most appropriate. In contrast, majority rule ensures the stability necessary for realizing long-term plans, particularly if they require a deeper intervention into prevailing views and customs. All such plans will sooner or later conflict with the democratic order. Government intervention is possible only if the citizenry accepts it as being in agreement with their values and interests. For this reason, the majority party or the ruling coalition is always in danger of overstepping the line. There are two sources for this danger. First majority status gives a party absolute power and makes it easy to rule. The ambition to rule as a majority government is very tempting, but it necessarily turns deputies into political tools because the party cannot tolerate their independence that could potentially undermine its majority position. Any vote that dissents from the predefined program of the majority coalition is politically unacceptable. But, of course, this is no longer a democratic parliament.

With minority governments, the situation is completely different, if not the opposite. It is extremely difficult to rule as the government needs to secure the necessary majority for each measure or action that requires a vote in parliament. If it fails to obtain a majority, it means it has lost the confidence of the parliament and must resign. That is why a minority government needs to exercise caution with each of its actions. It cannot simply embark on political adventures. It can only tackle projects for which it has secured majority support in advance, or for which it can justifiably expect such support. Of course, excessive caution reduces the government's reach and decisiveness but it functions well when it has general support. Above all, deputies get to play the role inherent in their position. They can vote according to their beliefs—that is, if they do not become captives of other centers of power. Because the position of deputies is uncertain, deputies will thoroughly weigh their views on important social issues put before parliament. Deputies have the possibility to challenge the government and to take an independent position on issues that are important to society. This greatly increases the transparency of the government's activities. In such circumstances, the government cannot exclude parliament and arbitrarily decide on important issues such as privatization of state property, especially banks. It cannot solely use its own political criteria in staffing important positions in the state, appointing its own political supporters and excluding its opponents. With a minority government, the parliament can directly decide on a range of issues, while in a majority government, the opposition can only force a decision on such issues through a statewide referendum. In fact, a strong majority government has no real opposition because it can always outvote the opposition.

A Return to Previous Patterns of Governance

A number of problems that have become a burden and an obstacle to parliamentary democracy in Slovenia are being addressed through attempts to change the constitution—with opposition parties trying to gain more access to decision-making and majority governments trying to strengthen their supremacy. The constitutional commission is engaged in debating possible amendments to the constitution as the needs and opportunities of each side change. Many of these problems emerge from majority governance with no real opposition and would become irrelevant with a minority government. The pattern of majority rule, which has become prevalent in Slovenia, has led to a situation where we can no longer refer to true parliamentary democracy regardless of which political party manages to form a ruling coalition. This is a restoration of the single-party system as a governance pattern, except that the constitution forces the ruling coalition to undergo a new election each term allowing for the possibility of a different coalition taking the helm. This necessity limits the autocracy of the ruling coalition and prevents it from acting openly as a dictatorship. All the same, its stable position during each term gives it a multitude of possibilities not available to the opposition to secure an advantage in the elections for the next term. The pattern of majority coalitions has permitted virtually all the successors of former communist governments in Central and Eastern Europe to use the democratic system to return to leadership. This pattern, which suited them well as they had experience from the previous system and thus an additional advantage over their adversaries, allowed them to remain in power for a decade or more. The longer they stayed in power, the more their advantage increased and their confidence grew, and the more the old pattern of governance was fixed in place. This led to the impression that the descendants of the former masters— "continuity"—had returned, and that they could not be replaced. For the conditions to change, a new social crisis needed to emerge, which was in any case inevitable under the conditions of single-party rule. Nevertheless change come as a surprise to all, not least the government of "continuity".

Will a New Coalition Repeat the Old Pattern?

Does it have to? Is Slovenia in a position where a change of government radically changes the situation in society? It could occur if society were divided into two fundamentally different segments with divergent views on basic questions of social integration (e.g., communism vs. free enterprise and private property, democracy vs. any form of absolutism, equality vs. corporatism, theocracy vs. secular society). When society is divided in this way, a party or coalition that represents one of the mutually exclusive options for the social order, would, upon assuming power, do everything in its power to prevent its adversaries from realizing the opposing ideas. For this, the pattern of majority coalition rule is necessary.

The public's views on the foundations of social order in Slovenian society are not so divided. On the contrary, when they adopted the constitution, Slovenian citizens unanimously declared themselves in favor of a system that is characteristic of modern, highly-developed societies: namely, democracy and fundamental human rights, the rule of law, private property and free enterprise, a state with a parliamentary system and the separation of powers, and formal equal opportunity for all citizens along with social certain correctives in place. A violent deviation from these foundations would represent a coup, even if the violence took the form of a relative majority coalition.

There is no need for a majority coalition formed in advance, based on a joint program, and backed by disciplined deputies. These constitutional principles, representing a consensus on the foundations of social coexistence, allow a range of options for development and different opportunities that can be achieving using a variety of measures and methods, different approaches, and responses. None of this warrants a fundamental change in the social order. These possibilities are available precisely because of the freedom of decision-making at all levels of the state apparatus, but first and foremost at the top level of the government and parliament. Any limits on the freedom of choice and decision-making reduce these possibilities. If the obedience of deputies is required in advance or forced, it prevents the best possible decision-making at the highest level of government.

Considering the experience of post-communist states, the fear of restoring the single-party system is justified—not in the form of communism, which, in its known form, is a thing of the past, but rather in one of the new forms of authoritarian governance or fascism. Fascism, even not called by its old name, is a danger for democratic states. It means extremely simplified responses to the increasingly complex situations facing developed societies as a result of rapid development, in the sense of an authoritarian government saying to the public: we know everything, we have ready-made responses to everything, and we will implement them. The danger of this new authoritarianism is not limited to political parties on one side of the spectrum, but can come from any party regardless of its program and ideological orientation or its vision of the best direction for society. The danger is the result of the majority governance system, which attempts to ensure the obedience of deputies in advance and thereby eliminate any possibility of different choices and outcomes. Such enforcement of party discipline is formally not a breach of deputies' independence since they freely choose to join a particular party and subject themselves to its discipline. Furthermore, it cannot be proved that deputies are not voting in accordance with their own beliefs that might simply coincide with the program of external centers of power, and in particular their political party. Formal legal interventions cannot solve this problem, because it emerges from power relations. Deputies are only independent to the extent that they are not directly or indirectly under the influence of those who wield power. In Slovenia, political parties are currently the main players that wield power over deputies who depend on the parties for their existence. Freeing deputies from the pressure of their political parties is one of the main conditions for setting up true parliamentary democracy, and this depends on the democracy within political parties themselves. However, parties in Slovenia are still captives of their own histories and the traumas that remained from the civil war that took place in Slovenia during World War II. It could even be said that this civil war still continues—not as a reality but as a farce, and manifested as the fear of an imaginary adversary.

The actual divide that formed an ideological front during the civil war no longer exists. If there is any ideology that has a decisive effect on people's actions in relation to the contemporary world, it is the ideology of consumerism. Indirectly, this means the need to get a job in the public or private sector, which will facilitate survival and bring a degree of social power and greater wealth, and which allows a higher level of consumption and additional social power. The power and influence of the ideology of consumerism define the practical decisions and actions of most people, even when it conflicts with their worldview and values. This ideology often takes priority over affiliation with political parties. In any case, in terms of ideological orientation, there is little difference among the parties, although they proclaim different values and ideals. These proclamations are used as propaganda in the competition with their political rivals when in fact they all the parties pursue the same goals of consumerism. The competition among them is not ideological as they all follow the same consumerist ideology.

Chapter 6: The Grip of Politics Over Production

France Bucar and Igor Kovač

The Decisive Role of Production

The primary social issue of the past was the question of production: how to produce enough material goods to ensure the physical survival of society. Even if the human mind functions on a completely different level, it nevertheless depends on the body. Today the question of production has been at least theoretically solved. True, humanity still produces far less than it needs to meet all of its material requirements. Millions of people in poor countries still die of starvation, which remains the primary Malthusian regulator of the population in certain parts of the world. Poverty has not been completely defeated even in the most developed and affluent countries, and, the production of material goods remains a primary concern. However, although the question of production has not been completely solved in practice, it is solvable from the technical perspective. This is one of the most important milestones in human development and rightly gives us hope for the future.

But solving the riddle of sufficient production does not depend only on technical capabilities. It has become increasingly evident that the issue has shifted from the technical arena to that of social relations and the understanding of our newly created environment. A social order unsuited to the level of technical capabilities will prevent these capabilities from being used to improve the material wellbeing of all members of society. This occurs both on the international level and within a singular technologically developed society. However, the creation of material prosperity introduces new questions about the essence of human nature and the meaning of life that cannot be answered merely by increasing material prosperity.

F. Bucar (Deceased)

I. Kovač (✉)
Department of Political Science, University of Cincinnati, Cincinnati, OH, USA
e-mail: kovacir@mail.uc.edu

© Springer International Publishing AG, part of Springer Nature 2019
I. Kovač (ed.), *At His Crossroad*, https://doi.org/10.1007/978-3-319-78331-4_10

Indeed these questions are raised precisely because mankind has overcome the struggle for survival, which had been its main concern throughout history.

The first question is mostly organizational and sociological, the second is mainly psychological and ethical. These are issues that related to two different levels of human existence. But they are interrelated and interdependent, and at least indirectly form an indivisible whole that needs to be dealt with together while at the same time addressing other important questions about human existence.

Human Beings as a Means of Production

Production, and particularly complex production linked to a high level of division of labor, requires organization. In order to reach this level of division of labor, a form of management that defines people as a means for achieving the goals of the organization is required. In order for the organization to achieve its goals, it is necessary to restrict the freedom of its members to actions that fit patterns that are acceptable for the organization. Managing an organization is not merely technological—comparable to running a piece of machinery—although there is a strong resemblance. The ideal of production management might be to replace workers with machines, but until this can be achieved, the labor of human beings needs to be directed to this end. A condition for success is the dependability and predictability of the activities of an organization's members. This means transforming human activity into something as close as possible to the impersonal performance of a machine, transforming people, at least from the organizational perspective, into instruments. The point of managing any goal-oriented social community is to influence the outside world through people, using human beings as a means of production. Regardless of the principles proclaimed in various human rights documents, it is understandable from the standpoint of goal-oriented organization that its members need to be at least partly transformed from human beings into means. This also contradicts the views of modern psychoanalysis, which posits that people can only fully realize their humanity when they are free—not in the sense of being able to make impulsive decisions or not as the emancipation from the demands of nature, but in the sense of realizing the potential inherent in their humanity. This is a confirmation of the point made in idealized form in the classic works of Marx that the "kingdom of freedom" will only be possible when we transform the management of people into the management of things. Despite extraordinary progress and the advent of information technology and automation, this has not yet come to be. Even if we agree that the technical side of the issue of production has been solved, we cannot confirm that we have solved the problems related to the technology of management. It may be possible to solve these problems in the future, but currently our knowledge does not come close to the essence of the issues. Engaging with questions of production functions prohibitively. For the foreseeable future, questions of organization and management will remain our key problem, on which our success in the area of production will depend. Despite achievements in modern organizational science and the progress of psychology in including people in the work process, the liberation of employees from organizational pressures seems to be increasingly remote.

Freedom as a Condition for More Rapid Social Development

What we have learned from the history of communist states as compared to democratic ones is that the development of material production in democracy is more rapid than in systems with low levels of personal freedom. This is the case even if we take into consideration the fact that democratic states began their development at higher starting points. All the same, the success of communist economies in production cannot be denied either. In the race against capitalist economies, which are based on ostensible through not actual equality and freedom, communist economies failed without exception because of slower development. But this does not mean that they were not capable of development. They only developed at a slower pace and less dynamically. Looked at from a broader historical perspective, there was no need to rush. But in the fight for survival, the advantage is always on the side of those who are better adapted and faster. Thus we can conclude that the odds will always be in the favor of systems that allow individuals a higher level of freedom, and consequently are more adaptable and creative.

The complexity of the problem—that the issue of production can be solved technologically, that a sufficient amount of goods need to be produced to supply all of humanity, and this depends on the arrangement of social relations—presents new dimensions in the relationship between society and the individual that have not come into focus before and have therefore not received adequate attention. The underlying impulse for the rebellion against the communist order emerged from the disparity between what capitalist and communist economies could offer their citizens in the material sense, and far less from the feeling of being deprived of freedom. The latter was a factor for a relatively small circle of intellectuals. If freedom is a condition for greater economic success, it is only apparent indirectly through enabling the greater availability of material goods. For many people in less developed countries, and also in many more developed ones, freedom is still primarily a question of how much a certain level of freedom—and indirectly its influence on public affairs—increases the availability of material goods. Indeed many people are ready to give up some of their personal freedom, and thereby the possibilities of personal development, as long as their desires for material goods are met. This is one of the fundamental contradictions of the consumer society: it endangers both freedom and the perceived need for freedom. Here we touch on the issue of how personal freedom and the potential for developing personal identity affect not only how material needs are met for physical survival, but also the question of the survival of the society, the meaning of life, and a ranger of personal needs that are triggered by the abundance of material goods. It can be said with great certainty that the question of personal freedom and its role in society will become a central social issue on which the questions of material production also indirectly depend. As long as we are hungry, such questions are irrelevant. But once basic material needs are met, a number of new spiritual needs appear because life becomes something more than just eating and being full.

Many questions having to do with the position of the individual in the society are not set in a distant future that is of no interest to us today. Many of these questions, because they remain unsolved, already have a negative effect on the future social order, and finding appropriate responses depends to a great degree on how we meet our contemporary material needs.

Among these questions is the issue of politics as an element of governance.

The Meaning and Contradiction of Politics in Relation to Fundamental Social Issues

Modern developed democratic states accept the principle of freedom and equality of all citizens as the basis of their social order. However, the way society is actually governed mostly denies this status because it is incompatible with the current mode of governance, which is a condition for modern production. This is yet another vicious circle.

The essence of political science is dedicated to the issue of subjugating the will of the individual and aligning it with the goals set by a particular organization. Politics in this sense is not limited to the level of the state or the public administration. Wherever we are dealing with governance and management, we interpret politics as a way of forcing the will of the organization's participants to pursue the organization's goals. This is true even for the smallest organization in any given field.

When we use the term politics, the concept on one hand refer to goals to be achieved, and on other, to strategy used to persuade people to pursue these goals. Both cases represent an intervention into the actions of individuals, in other words an intervention into the kingdom of their freedom. In the case of the former, the aim is to persuade them to adopt the defined goals and actions set by politicians. These goals are not necessarily against the interests and beliefs of the people. In the ideal situation they coincide. Policies that run strongly contrary to the interests and beliefs of those whom they are meant for are destined to fail, at least in the long term. The problem is that they may appear in the short term to be aligned, but are not in the long term, which means that people need to be presented a picture of reality that differs from their own perceptions. This is a challenging task. People act in a certain way because they believe it is right, because it matches their beliefs and interests. The point of all politics is to change how people act, otherwise it would be senseless and unnecessary. In particular, when their direct interests are linked to their perceptions. Significant effort is often needed to make people accept a policy that differs from their existing perceptions. But politics with ambitious goals are ambitious precisely because they represent an extreme intervention into existing conditions, are aimed at thorough change, and extend far into the future. But their weakness lies in the extensive change they require. It is unlikely that the actual achievements of such policies will match the expectations. For this reason, experienced politicians do not present goals and promises that too unrealistic. In general, visionaries are rare. Most politicians are average, and sometimes they attempt to rise above their mediocrity by pronouncing grand ideas about the future that they claim only they can deliver. Indeed it is in the nature of politics to present grand visions and promises. This emerges from its sense of innate mission. But disappointment will inevitably follow if the difference between the visions and promises of policies is too great, if the potential and achievements of policies diverges too much. A range of factors and circumstances that complement or neutralize each other influences the outcomes of any particular policy. The same is true of expectations, which in part depend on the difference between actual and desired outcomes. Many variables make the outcome of a particular policy unpredictable and uncertain, both from the standpoint of the politician and the public the policy affects. Differences between promises and reality are inevitable, but politicians are supposed to emanate great certainty rather than, for example, the attitude of a scientist who doubts everything until doubt is eliminated by solid proof. Because politicians make promises and predictions about the future that require people to act in a certain way and may also require them to sacrifice some of their personal interests, it would be unacceptable and even contradictory for them to reflect skepticism, expressing doubts that what they say will actually happen. Politicians need to appear to have the confidence of experts, not that they merely believe, but know, that what they are promising and fighting for, what they are asking people to make sacrifices for, will actually occur. Otherwise they invalidate their program and sometimes even make a fool of themselves.

In the eyes of serious people with life experience, politicians, with the exception of the odd great politician, are branded from the start as suspicious and unreliable, people who live off promises rather than actual accomplishments, and whose personal integrity should only be trusted if they actually deliver on their promises. But there will always be a difference between politicians' promises and reality, because they build on predictions of the future that by nature is unpredictable. Even politicians who enter the political stage in times of crisis and correctly assess the necessity of change, and as a result receive the support the public, often have to pay for their limited success, eventually losing their reputation among the very people they stood up for. Expectations are almost always greater than achieved results.

Politics in Highly Developed Societies

There is, of course, a difference between what might be called higher politics—politics aimed at changes in the broader social environment and extending into the future—and the politics of smaller organizations, the scope of which is relatively narrow and therefore also easier to implement. If politics and related activities aimed at changing the future is a creative effort, then politics should be considered a future-oriented organized activity. Any creative activity is future-oriented: that is, aimed at changing existing conditions in society or in the external environment in accordance with new perceptions of possibilities and desired conditions. Therefore, there is no creativity without politics—and creativity is an essential element of any goal-oriented activity, not only in art to which the concept is usually restricted. The same can be said of a scientific activity. Every human being is a scientist and an artist. Conceptually, there is no qualitative difference between the highest art or science and the simplest activity of the common worker. Nevertheless, these terms—art, science, politics—are generally used to designate only the highest echelons of mental effort in each respective field. Thus the term politics—often understood as high politics or state politics—is usually only used in connection with the state or other large organizations, especially large international companies. Typically the activities of such organizations cover broad social areas, and they are compelled to contemplate the distant future, which necessitates risky forecasting and predictions. Consequently their reliability drops, and so can their reputation. Because of this, the demands that high politics makes of people increases as the skepticism of the people is at is strongest when it comes to politics. In other words, high state politics faces the greatest mistrust from the public. This is why it becomes aggressive in its pronouncements. It needs to overcome this skepticism in order to succeed.

Responsibility in High Decision-Making Positions

The public's mistrust of high politics is augmented for two additional interrelated and interdependent reasons. The first is that it becomes increasingly difficult to determine the connection between cause and effect the more we move from concrete activities to abstract ones. With direct and particularly physical activities, the causal relationship between the activity and its consequences is immediately clear or possible to determine. That is why responsibility can also be clearly determined. But the further we move from the concrete toward the abstract and the general, the more these causal connections become unclear, and the consequences extend into a less transparent and controllable environment. Moreover the chances of someone being held accountable for such actions decline. This brings us to a contradictory situation: namely, that accountability in high political positions is low while its impact is high. To the contrary, those in relatively low positions in society have the highest accountability and the least impact. This is related to the fact that social power is usually lowest in low positions, and highest in high positions. Due to the social power that comes with these positions, accountability in the highest posts is harder to enforce, even in the exceptional cases where responsibility can be clearly defined. Many scandals involving people in top posts sink into obscurity although responsibility is defined. Often punishing the responsible person through legal proceedings retreats into some hazy future. Thus trust is further degraded. The reduced likelihood of accountability for those occupying the highest political decision-making positions leads to a tendency for them to take even higher risks with potential consequences that the decision-maker will never shoulder.

Instead, the consequences are shouldered by the people in whose name the decision was made but who had no real say in the matter. This is the appeal of political gambles that are aimed at bringing benefits, including greater political power, to political adventurers who place themselves at no personal risk.

The Power and Powerlessness of the Ordinary Citizen

Political decision-making in the highest positions represents a combination of social relations that contradicts the democratic concept of the equality of all citizens. There is no equality among citizens when it comes to responsibility and accountability. Equality is formally embodied in the legal order, but the actual nature of relations among people in different roles in society puts them in unequal positions. Some people in this configuration can get away with more than others. Some are held accountable for every small issue while others bear almost no accountability for actions that have far-reaching consequences. People without access to important social decisions compensate for this inequality psychologically by denying respect and credibility to politicians in high places. These circumstances lead to citizens becoming passive, believing that they have no voice on the most important issues, and that they are unable to discern the direct or indirect effect of issues of high politics on their daily lives. For their part, politicians only care if citizens vote for them during elections because this will return them to decision-making position. Only in this sense do politicians really care about or listen to their constituents. Once the election is over, the interests of ordinary citizens lose importance.

For this reason, voter turnout is an important indicator of a society's connectedness and homogeneity, and the actual state of its democracy (at least under the condition of a minimal level of connection between citizens and the ruling elite). In dictatorships, voter turnout only proves the success of the pressure of the ruling elite (or voter intimidation), which is why it cannot be used to assess the connection between the ruling political elite and general society in authoritarian regimes. In democratic societies, in contrast, voter turnout (and other kinds of public expression on public affairs) is a useful indicator of the quality of this connection. Low voter turnout is not always proof of the organized rejection of a particular political elite, though it gives some indication, and even unorganized voter abstention shows that voters reject the behavior of the political elite or see it as irrelevant to their interests. In both cases, the relationship between the political elite and society is questionable. Democracy is not functioning to a degree that allows voters to achieve a necessary influence in the management of public affairs. They are not subjects in public affairs, but objects. As in any organization, the perception of relative freedom, and the alignment of the interests of its leadership and members, are the key conditions for the organization's successful functioning. The same holds true for a nation state, which is also a kind of organization. A condition of misalignment indicates that the situation is not optimal. If not turning up to vote is the only option voters have to express their dissatisfaction, this means normal paths to influence the management of public affairs are no longer available. Thus lower voter turnout also shows that the mechanism of social institutions, which should ensure the cooperation of citizens, is malfunctioning. Excessively low turnout is proof of a flawed democracy. Low turnout delivers a message from the voters that they do not believe the available options allow them to achieve desired change. In a word, democracy is not working.

Now let us look at the situation from a different perspective. People who are happy with the conditions in society will not give much thought to alternative choices. In this case, low voter turnout could simply mean that voters are satisfied. Satisfied people do not favor change if they see no threat to the status quo. Low turnout could be proof that voters perceive the current situation as unproblematic, unexciting, not requiring a response. Thus they are not interested in elections. The underlying presumption is that the functioning of the state or a particular political elite does not affect their wellbeing or position in society. Or non-voters may be people who are interested in their own affairs, and not in politics. This alone might be evidence of their stability and self-confidence. Such people rely on themselves, not on others, and not on the state. If a particular political elite has low credibility, that it is all the more reason for certain citizens to distance themselves from politics. In such cases, we may prefer to deal with matters that attract respect and esteem, not politics. But doesn't that sound a bit outdated, somehow out of the last century?

Even if we do not wish to be involved with politics, politics will inevitably be involved with us. Wellbeing and prosperity increasingly depend on the activities of the state, and this is not merely an indirect connection. The share of resources directly managed by the state or state-linked organizations is increasing. Even if we only take care of our own needs, we cannot avoid having contact with the state, because state policies affect not only general but also personal prosperity and wellbeing. Avoiding participation in activities that directly or indirectly relate to the content of state politics is to avoid the responsibility that all individuals have both for themselves and, to some extent, for others. Such absenteeism may be an indication of intellectual immaturity, and, in terms of morals, an ethical void and even fearfulness masked as superiority over the "primitiveness" of quotidian politics (in the sense of odi profanum vulgus et arceo – I hate the unholy rabble and stay away from them). This phenomenon is common in Slovenian society, especially among intellectuals, and reflects a lack of national consciousness. It is a consequence of the historical perception that people have no influence on public matters, and if we cannot make a difference, we should stay away. This position was understandable when decisions on the most important matters of public life were made by other states that ruled over our people, but now that Slovenians have their own state, this position is no longer viable. It simply reflects the timidity of small-minded people.

Modern Forms of Subjugation

Politics is not only about setting goals and designing strategies to achieve them. It also is the special skill of obtaining the necessary power to control people, who then are used for achieving certain goals. Without this power, politics and its goals become meaningless. Efforts to gain power over people and turn them into means for achieving defined goals is one of the primary activities of politics. It can only be justified if we accept the defined goal. If we address the question of legitimacy, we may come to the point that every time people are turned into a means to an end, it is a violation of their humanity and fundamental rights. But people cannot be turned into a means without some form of subjugation. Thus the strategy of gaining power over people, although it has no name in formal discourse, is accepted as a given and is omnipresent, not just in politics, but in all organized activities. Owners of small businesses would be surprised if they were told that they engaged in politics, which they often despise. And indeed it is this aspect of politics, gaining power over others, that repulses people the most. If you consent to subjugation, you push it down into your subconscious, persuading yourself that you are acting according to your own will. Any other response would reveal the humiliation and violence that by necessity should be avoided. That is why an agent in any goal-oriented activity— this is most obvious in economic activities—is perceived as someone who by definition encroaches on the humanity of others. Politicians attract suspicion simply because they are politicians. In economic activities, particularly in the past, little attention was paid to the psychological aspect of work disputes and disagreements because the focus was always on wages and the distribution of profit. But the psychological aspect was always present, constituting an important factor that affected not only relations between workers and capitalists but also had an impact on performance. With growing liberation in work relations, this factor has become increasingly important, although it still has no specific name.

It is not surprising that people today want to disguise the conditions of subjugation and supremacy that stem from the nature of management since, although inevitable, they clearly stand in contradiction to proclaimed principles of equality. One solution would be to replace existing power relations with partnership and voluntary participation.

In less developed societies where technology is at a relatively primitive level, the main method of subjugation is physical force, which has a number of weaknesses. The primary weakness of physical violence is that it is visible and cannot always be adapted to the actual needs of society. Worse still, it breeds resistance because inequality is so apparent. Finally it is not very efficient and is only useful for relatively simple activities, being almost entirely ineffective for more complex tasks that require greater responsiveness and a closer identification with the goal. Moreover it resembles slavery in many respects. For these reasons, physical force as a means of subjugation is hardly used in developed countries.

With the Industrial Revolution and the advent of a higher level of technological development, economic subjugation became the method of choice. It has several advantages over physical force. First, it is more efficient. It gives people in a subordinate position a clear choice: obey, or you and your children will go hungry. It requires no direct force, and is thus perceived as a transition to a higher level of human development. No one appears to be forcing others to do something they do not want to do. In the formal sense, those who are subordinate are equal in the position of a contractual partner, and both parties to the contract are subject to the same laws. That is why capitalism appears to be the fairest social order: there is no explicit exploitation, and no physical subjugation is necessary because relations are based on contractual equality. If the contracting parties have different material opportunities, this may be socially relevant, but the situation would need to be addressed on a different level that has no direct connection to labor-capital relations.

Co-Management as Hope

Because of today's emphasis on human rights, management technologies, and politics as a constituent part of these two, the reproach that people at the bottom of the ladder have been transformed into a means managed by those at the top is avoided or hidden as much as possible. These management methods powerfully reduce the sincerity of the lip service paid to human dignity and respect. That is why modern management controls people using methods that conceal undesirable traces of subjugation, and management ostensibly assumes the role of a mere participant. And yet participation and co-management might in fact be a quantum leap into the "kingdom of freedom" to use Marx's terminology once more. It would represent a transformation of the natural and social environment that uses people as means. Participation eliminates this particular kind of exploitation. Both management and employees participate in the process as subjects. But this can only occur if interest among the parties participating in implementing the collective goal is coordinated in advance. The emphasis of organization would then shift to preemptive conflict resolution.

With respect to methods and form, preemptive conflict resolution is the management of so-called false conflicts, where there are no differences in interests. Parties are not pushed into direct clashes of interests resulting from participation in joint projects. Instead, conflict resolution on this level is based on the realization that all participants have common interests and there is no real separation in that respect, and the search for additional information is only intended to clarify the rights and obligations of those involved in the common enterprise, rendering them all true participants. This sort of false conflict resolution eliminates in advance the need to resolve true conflicts, the most common form of conflict resolution in the past. Co-management preemptively eliminates conflicts that were once an inherent result of management using labor as a means. Past disputes between labor and capital were true conflicts, and, by definition, there can be no mutual solution of true conflicts. The side with greater power dictates solutions, which forces its views on the opponent. At the same time, the losing side is left with a feeling of humiliation because it was forced into a solution that went against its interests and self-esteem. This generally means postponing the conflict to a later time when the losing side reassesses its situation and believes it can force its own terms.

Particularly when ambitious goals of general importance are at stake—on the level of a company, a particular industry, or even the entire economy—it has become clear that success is much more likely if the project includes all involved in the entity, that goals cannot be forced on people who do not agree with them and are more efficiently achieved through cooperation. Thus it is desirable to pre-emptively resolve disagreements between labor and capital that emerge from the false perceptions of workers and owners about their actual interests. Large-scale projects of importance for an entire society can only be implemented in today's world with the cooperation of all interested parties. For example, projects related to economic efficiency and stability must be implemented with the support of both capital and trade unions. Such important social goals cannot be achieved by addressing conflicts through power competition, for example, by workers strik-ing against capital, which prevents even the cooperation necessary to meet direct production goals.

The goals of direct production are not achievable without at least a general agree-ment between labor and capital on goals, even if each party agrees for different reasons. Highly complex modern production is only possible when there is coopera-tion between all participants in the process, and this requires that they identify with the goals of the work process to the degree that they also perceive part of their own fulfillment in them. Modern workers (if the term workers, as it is derived from the conception of workers as means of production, is still appropriate at all) are formal parties to their employment contracts, and their relationship with their employer is ended once the contractual obligations have been met. But in reality more is required of them, especially elements that cannot be set down in an employment contract—the attachment to the work they do, and dedication to the goals defined in their work. Indeed only if these elements, which cannot even be clearly defined in an employment contract let alone required, are present can the goals of the organiza-tion be fulfilled. They can be achieved only through full participation. Workers must become coworkers, partners. This can be accomplished in a number of ways, for-mally and informally, with intent or only emotionally. Modern organizations mostly try to foster emotional attachment in employees, because an emotionally unattached worker is useful only for less demanding tasks, and even then these results may be below expectations.

Co-management, as a substitute for managing people as means, might provide a solution to the current situation of social conflict that presents an obstacle to improved production results that technology already allows. Thus it is not only a humanitarian issue but also an economic necessity because it provides the economic means for solving social problems created by technological progress. It is both a hope and a necessity, promising more than merely a new method of management but a change in the entire social composition. Co-management is gaining ground as a concept that reflects a new perspective on future social relations. And yet precisely because it gives hope for a transition to new social relations, it has become both a condition and a result of the social changes that allow for co-management. Nevertheless, with the ongoing and unresolved confrontations between labor and capital, and between social classes, with nation-based exclusion and clashes of interests both on the level of individuals and society, co-management remains more of a hope than a reality.

The Traps and Potential Deviations of Co-Management

Technology creates the conditions for overcoming conflicts of interests in society insofar as it creates the possibility of satisfying material needs at a higher level and thereby eliminating at least one source of conflict: those that stem from deprivation. In particular, it creates the conditions for a population that is better informed, which is the most important quality for resolving potential conflicts that often are generated from ignorance. This potential is somewhat diminished by the fact that technology can be used for the opposite purpose. Modern information technology, in particular, facilitates the use of people as a means to an end. Unlike economic forms of coercion, where despite the formal equality of contracting partners, actual differences in real power and the subjugation of the weaker cannot be disguised (strikes and other forms of industrial action reveal this clearly), contemporary means of informing and transferring information create previously unimagined possibilities of subjugation that were not available to most historical totalitarian regimes that did not shy away from physical violence. These include direct access to people's inner minds, and the omnipresence of these methods creates the possibility of comprehensively transforming the mentality of its victims, who adopt a worldview shaped for them by unknown designers, and treat as their own the goals and interests of those who shape their mentality. They do so even if these goals and interests may be the opposite of their own. Victims of such manipulation do not see themselves as victims at all, and are deeply convinced of their independence, autonomy, and identity. In the past (and today in the less developed world), this was only possible with religious fanaticism, which never achieved the vast reach of the contemporary media or those who control it.

The Nazis were the first to realize the extraordinary opportunity for the subjugation of the masses, and they set up a special ministry of propaganda that was equal to the most important areas of government. Communist regimes did not lag far behind with their fairytales of giving power to the working class. Today, controlling people's minds has reached such proportions that truly independent thinkers are more the exception than the rule, and yet nevertheless pose a challenge to the general state of mind in society. Precisely here lies an unexpected threat to humanity itself. Even if we allowed only idealists to shape the public opinion, we have destroyed the primary capacity of human beings to self-generate their minds, which cannot be replaced by high science or idealism even at their most advanced levels. Science simply cannot know everything, and many hidden corners of the human mind remain unavailable to it. A large share of modern society's problems remains unsolved because the world has become so "advanced" in its techniques of controlling and creating public opinion. Modern psychology theory tells us that only a free person is capable of a full and creative life (Fromm, ibid). Such a person would first ask the almost pathetic question of whether now, having solved the question of production, created a prosperous society, and established a democracy, we can assume that the modern developed world has reached the time for the true liberation of humanity, the opportunity to realize human potential. The answer comes quickly: freedom has been eclipsed by the cloud of dictated public opinion.

Cooperation requires that participants are free, and this freedom must be real. If it is only virtual, we have returned, or rather have remained, with the old forms of management based on subjugation. It could be argued that matters have become even worse. Old forms of subjugation have always been more or less transparent. Modern variants are largely concealed, and furthermore, they reach far beyond the old forms. They govern with the consent of the subjugated, who formally become participants, and at the same time the new forms of subjugation allow the rulers to control the freedom of their subjects.

Partnership on the Level of Society

In recent times, the complexity and interdependence of society has highlighted the need for participation and cooperation not only in the economy but also on the more general level of society. This has brought to the forefront the concept of partnership on the economic and social level in the sense of cooperation among employers, employees, and the state in common social, and particularly economic, endeavors. It has become clear that identified goals cannot be achieved by forcing the views and interests of one side onto the other participants in collective efforts. This means that the highly complex problems of modern society cannot be tackled using old patterns based on subjugation—a pattern that was used particularly in the organization of production. The participants in this cooperation are:

- Employees with no rights but whose expertise gives them social power, and who are not easily replaceable from the proletarian masses even as their role as the most important part of the production is disregarded. An employer cannot compel them to creatively participate without their consent.
- The state, which contributes an increasing share of the elements necessary for economic success in modern production, and can therefore no longer be a mere observer, plays the role of an open or at least covert partner of capital. The state is a partner that must act in an unbiased manner in order to achieve common goals. We can no longer advocate the view that the state should renounce any role in the economy based on the argument that it is a poor manager, with privatization pushing the state out of the sphere of private businesses as much as possible.
- Entrepreneurs, whose position is defined by the position of their employees and the state. Without cooperation with these two partners (and meeting their needs), entrepreneurs cannot pursue their business activities. On the other hand, there is also no economic success without their entrepreneurship and willingness to take risks. This failing was most evident in communist systems in which entrepreneurs were excluded from business processes.

Chapter 7: The State as a Partner

France Bucar and Igor Kovač

The changing role of the state may be the most characteristic sign of the transformation of modern society. The state is no longer the sole bearer of power as it was in the past—it is becoming a partner whose cooperation with other social subsystems ensures general conditions, social conditions, and internal relations for the survival of society. Numerous conditions for the survival of society can only be guaranteed by the state, such as general and legal security, the level of education that must increasing constantly, health protection, environmental protection, and a range of goods and services that are not interesting for private businesses but contribute the social infrastructure necessary for their activities. The state, albeit mostly indirectly, participates in all of these areas regardless of the type and size of the venture.

The New Role of the State in the Economy

The state cannot be excluded from business processes. Naturally the manner and extent of its participation will vary. Normally the state is not a main actor in business interests, because it does not meet the necessary requirements. Business interests are concentrated in entities that are directly affected by the performance of the business, particularly in terms of its profits. The state cannot occupy this role because the possible profits or losses from a particular business activity affect the state budget and not the individuals in the government or the state administration

F. Bucar (Deceased)

I. Kovač (✉)
Department of Political Science, University of Cincinnati, Cincinnati, OH, USA
e-mail: kovacir@mail.uc.edu

© Springer International Publishing AG, part of Springer Nature 2019   143
I. Kovač (ed.), *At His Crossroad*, https://doi.org/10.1007/978-3-319-78331-4_11

directly. Government participants are therefore in a completely different position than the private owners or carriers of business interests. They have no personal connection to the performance of a business as this would conflict with their role of representing the general interests of society. Their sole interest is the trust of the voters who elected them and guarantee their political future. They try to create this trust in other areas, in other ways, and with other means. If the state assumes an entrepreneurial role, it means that the entrepreneurial interest has been excluded from the business activity and thereby also from concern for profitability. Because of this, there is no place for entrepreneurial initiative in social systems where the state directly runs business activities, and profitability, and such systems tends to lag behind performance in market economies.

However, even in market economies, performance is not only reflected in profit or monetary terms. The focus on profit often conflicts with other functions of businesses (e.g., social or environmental), and the state must sometimes intervene for the general benefit of society. A company in the market economy cannot survive if it is unable to prove its performance in the competition against other companies. Companies cannot also be burdened with pursuing the social goals of the economy; that is the state's role. The state can and must demand social responsibility of companies, but financial success is the measure that determines a company's success, and even the state cannot intervene in this area it unless it decides to sacrifice the company to protect the general interests. Merging both functions in an effort to maximize financial performance and the social goals of a company or the state usually hinders both, resulting in the neglect of the social role and financial failure. This recalls the centuries-old revelation of the social sciences that the individual functions of the state must be separated in order to ensure necessary internal balance through a system of checks and balances.

The Role of the Owner and Entrepreneur

An entrepreneur, whose interest is to maximize profitability, is also bound as a member of society to various social goals, and as an individual to a different set of ideals. Naturally, the entrepreneur functions as a person integrating all of these roles. Even in the role of organizing the business process, they are integrated personalities and the managing of the business process represents only one of their social roles. In this role, they are bound by the rules dictated by that role: the goal of maximizing financial performance. They may in this role also seek and realize a certain balance with their values and principles, but the underlying obligation to ensure profitability of the business cannot be sacrificed. Optimal financial performance is also a general social goal of business, but it competes with other social goals not defined by the entrepreneur, but rather by the state as the representative of general social interests. In implementing social goals that work against the entrepreneur, the state maintains an interest in the business's profitability and cannot replace the entrepreneur as owner, nor can it force actions that would threaten the financial survival of the company.

Society ostensibly ensures the conditions for the greatest possible economic development by agreeing to put economic processes in the hands of entrepreneurs who steer companies toward financial success and economic expansion risking their own assets and acting in their own interests. Yet the price for this arrangement of relationships is hardly negligible. Society agrees that the financial fruits of business activities belong to the entrepreneur as the owner, and this opens the path to social inequality, while actual equality and equal opportunity for individual members of society, along with formal equality, remains a condition for the democratic social order.

The state uses tax policies to alleviate the consequences of social inequality resulting from the fact that profits flow to the owners of business processes, but it is only partly successful in this effort. Statistical data for the so-called developed world show that inequality is not decreasing, but is increasing so much that it threatens the stability of society (see, for example, Lester Thurow's The Future of Capitalism.) Increasing inequality particularly undermines the perception of social partnership as the foundation of the contemporary social order.

Does this mean that the price of entrepreneurs being in charge of business activity is too high, or do the other advantages it brings outweigh the disadvantages? Social equality theory emphasizes that while economic development bring inequality, it also brings substantial material benefits that alleviate these effects. As social differences increase due to inequality, even citizens with the lowest social standing have access to material goods that not even the most privileged class could afford in the past. Views diverge greatly in theory and practice on these issues, also because contemporary economic competition leads to the production of consumers good that are unnecessary and may even be harmful, but are foisted on us as needs.

Nevertheless it is a fact that no economy can survive in the international economic system without business interests being in private hands, especially since the global market is not about partnership but about ruthless competition.

Is there an alternative to business interests remaining in the hands of entrepreneurial owners? This is worth considering because management and ownership have long been decoupled in most large companies. Owners normally do not intervene in the running of their companies. They usually lack the necessary knowledge, and the tasks are so demanding that no individual would be able to make all decisions required in managing a modern complex organization. Is ownership then a parasitic institution? (This discussion is limited to large companies where the complexity exceeds the abilities of a single owner to running them individually.) Do owners contribute anything to management at all, or do they only reap the results of other people's labor? Such thinking would suit the political left in certain ways. Until recently it was, despite the new democratic social order, the prevalent mindset in Slovenia. Only when foreign capital appeared in our economy and began to make decisions about on our own market did the role of entrepreneurial capital reach the consciousness of Slovenian politicians. There is no entrepreneurial interest without private property. This interest is an integral part of ownership. In this respect, the point of ownership, which combines a series of functions, is the right of disposal. Owners dispose of the fruit of their ownership, and they also may dispose of their companies. They can move their companies, they can merge them with other organizations, change their line of business, or even liquidate them, all of which has not only economic but social consequences.

The role of ownership went unnoticed when the state was the sole owner in the socialist system of the former Yugoslavia. It was as if ownership did not exist, and theoretical attempts were made to set up the foundations of a society with no possessions, not even common socially owned property. Naturally, property did play an important role even in this order. Although it came through forceful appropriation, which requires the constant presence of physical force, it was the ownership-based right of disposal that became the most important tool for the subjugation of citizens. The most interesting element was how the authorities of the time managed to hide from citizens the manipulations and subjugations of the function of ownership as their basic tool. Because of this, even the generation of leaders who came to power in the new democratic order failed to realize the broad social role of ownership, and saw it merely as an opportunity for personal appropriation. But it soon became clear that ownership was a very important tool for maintaining and increasing political power even in the new system. It took people somewhat longer to understand the relation between ownership and political power, because in the preceding social order state ownership was a given. What was considered important was a place in the state hierarchy, and attention was focused on the distribution of leading top jobs in the state administration, which were distributed through political competition. Because state ownership was taken for granted, focus remained on the secondary phenomenon of management and governance.

This perception, like a syndrome, was carried forward by the new carriers of power. For such a long time, the focus had been on who held leading positions in the state administration that the new leaders failed to understand that losing ownership of the domestic economy could actually threaten their own positions. If they did not have the owner's right of disposal, their fate would be decided by those who did. If domestic companies—private or public, state, or quasi-government organizations—pass fully or partially into foreign ownership, the state's independence is at an end. The most important issues of state will be decided by foreign capital. In the end, this also means the staffing of leading positions. Foreign capital will decide directly in the organizations it owns, while its influence will be indirect in the state administration, which also depends on domestic voters. However, even this indirect influence can be significant. The state mostly relies on taxes and other duties levied on the economy. If the economy is mostly foreign-owned, the state will then also rely economically on foreigners. Our national existence depends primarily on our culture, which is explicitly and specifically ours, and represents the fundamental manifestation of our national identity. But the economy and legal order are becoming increasingly international. This puts our culture in danger, and with it our national identity and existence. Cultural creativity requires material support, and its greatest expansion comes in periods of relative prosperity. For Slovenia, as a small nation, this is all the more relevant because its most important cultural institutions are at least partially funded by the state.

Foreign Capital and Political Independence

Partnership as a condition for economic success is only conceptually possible if mutual interdependence among the partners is established and maintained. If one of the partners falls under the influence of a center of power outside the circle of inter-dependence and its decision can be swayed, then the partnership is over. The clearest example of this is the takeover of an economy by capital based outside the country of the partners. Foreign capital cannot be a defender of other interests than its own.

When any domestic organization, not just an economic one, passes into foreign ownership, the state's independence is diminished in proportion to the importance to the national existence of that particular organization or public asset. Attempting to expand power in relationship to the environment is characteristic of all biological beings, particularly human beings, and human organizations. Thus it is also human nature to attempt to gain power over the environment. The method of doing so depends on the strength and characteristics of the environment. Physical occupation and appropriation prevailed when there was a low level of development of produc-tion resources, and knowledge about others and culture. The main method of coer-cion used to be brute force, the goal being physical subjugation and exploitation or even direct annihilation of foreign inhabitants on a given territory. Some of these forms of subjugation survive to this day.

Because of technological progress, particularly technologies for controlling ter-ritory, and the growing complexity and interdependence of society, the need to con-trol the environment and methods of doing so have changed. With rare exceptions, the physical occupation of a territory has become unnecessary. A technologically highly developed country, or even an individual organization, can control an envi-ronment by increasing its dependence to a level that it will need to accept decisions as its own, or incorporate them as the foundations of its own decisions. A country that is dependent for capital and technology finds itself in the position of a colony without having lost its formal independence. It becomes financially or economically dependent, usually both, which can further accelerate the appropriation of owner-ship of important parts of its economy. Once the country that is more developed in terms of capital and technology owns the economy of the other country, which now depends on its aid, the goal has been achieved. What's more, it is achieved in the most elegant way, in the form of "selfless" aid to the less developed. The new eco-nomic imperialism far exceeds the old political version.

International Cooperation and Neocolonialism

In current conditions, a high level of development, especially technological, is the best protection against the pressures of the environment and the most important method of subjugating it. Interdependence has increased along with the complexity of modern society. Interdependence makes it less possible for a society to isolate itself from the pressures of its environment. Societies that are excluded from the environment have started to lag behind in terms of general development, which in turn makes them incapable of protecting themselves from pressures from the environment. Paradoxically, the position of being less developed serves as fertile ground for the economic penetration of the most developed in their environment. In order not to trail behind, they must open up and allow the entrance of more developed partners into their space. They are forced to accept these would-be conquerors, onto the territory. Their independence is endangered because the advantage in this unequal confrontation will always be on the side of the more developed partners. This is a new form of colonialism that requires no military occupation but is far more aggressive and dangerous than previous forms. Physical violence is not nearly as effective as the power of assimilation through higher cultural development.

The disparity in development is the reason that smaller, less technologically developed nations and their cultures perish, that the power to control the world is moving into a few important centers, and that we are perhaps even witnessing the consolidation of power into a single world center. As a result of globalization, which as a technological phenomenon allows the economic conquest of the global territory, we are facing a new phenomenon that is transforming the existing image of the world: namely, the shift toward global uniformity in patterns of life, customs, clothing, food, entertainment, and even language, and also in ways of responding to the environment. But above all, decision-making power is increasingly concentrating in a single center. This phenomenon undermines the concept of partnership on the national level.

It is hard to assess how this development will benefit the general development of humanity. In the past, development was characterized by great diversity in terms of culture. And this diversity was not a result of advanced development taking place in the broader cultural area, but rather it was the product of relatively closed smaller social communities where the possibility of wider contact was limited by the low level of technological development. That is why these smaller cultures developed independently of each other. Although the old empires controlled vast territories, they were not internally interdependent. For this reason, they disintegrated when they could no longer be held together by military force.

The supporters of today's unified Europe advocate the position that the technological supremacy of Europe over the rest of the world—which has become notable particularly in the last two centuries, and which has dictated political development—is, above all, a consequence of the diversity of the cultures of its nations that has enriched the common European culture. The cultural diversity of European nations has also created technological supremacy and dictated material development in the rest of the world, which has had to adapt to Europe rather than fall to a level of complete backwardness. But the case of Europe is not about the exclusiveness of the cultural development of particular nations, but rather about the internal segmentation, which is characteristic of systemic development. The greater the complexity of the system, the stronger its internal segmentation, which nevertheless reflects the common culture to which the cultures of individual nations give their specific contributions. This framework was introduced first with the Greek and

Jewish cultural heritage, then the unity of Christianity, and finally the common Latin language as a means of communication among intellectuals of most European nations. Also the opportunities for personal contact were not neglected despite the borders of the fragmented feudal territories.

Technological development, a result of this culture, has only created more internal interdependence. This feudal fragmentation did not hold up under the pressure of the struggle for a larger area in which the economy could grow. This expansion is something technological development first requires and then causes. This eventually led to the creation of nation states, which triggered a higher level of economic development and also brought about greater interdependence. Contemporary European integration is not a novelty but a continuation of the same process of development that began with the emergence of the nation state, although it might appear that the importance of the nation state is being diminished. Constant development demands a greater area for further development. At the same time it depends on its own dynamics, the result of internal segmentation and the autonomy of the individual constituent parts in the process. These are two distinct dimensions. A larger area does not necessarily imply unification, but the greater potential for development and for the individual parts of the system to operate beyond the boundaries of their own narrow and closed territories. This applies both to individual nations and to supranational systems.

Brought to its ultimate conclusion, the pressure toward uniformity could culminate in universal entropy on a global scale, which would herald the end of development. This means that the tendency toward uniformity will hit certain obstacles that will stop the process. In other words, the tendency toward growth, which is a natural phenomenon, must be controlled.

We encountered the issue of uniformity when discussing ownership as a means with which the strong and developed expanded the space in which they lived and developed. Controlling a particular space means projecting patterns of behavior onto it in response to the perception of our own interests and the meaning we attribute to existence. This means forcing a particular response on others as the only correct and acceptable option. This reduces the possibility of different arrangements and therefore also of creativity. Progress is based on the diversity that allows individuals to come up with answers autonomously. Autonomy is an essential condition for creativity. We stopped at the conclusion that the transfer of ownership from within the framework of a national economy to foreign owners reduces the independence of the state. Foreign owners do not necessarily represent the interests of other states, and are not necessarily directed against a country's identity. International capital in particular is largely non-national. Nevertheless it is not local and has no stake in local interests. This starts the process by which nationality and culture no longer serve as the factors of differentiation that contribute to the diversity of responses and thereby to progress. Naturally, nationality is not the only possible mechanism with which to formulate answers to the challenges facing humanity. Systemic differentiation is possible through other structures, although this would represent a departure from the pattern that has shaped European development and the identity of its nations thus far. Today—although nationality is a historical and therefore transitional phenomenon—nationality and the nation state, despite common European institutions, are the fundamental criteria for determining interests and defining identity. Nationality is not yet a thing of the past.

The tendency toward uniformity comes not only from the ambition to control the environment as a condition for growth and increasing power. Most technological processes are based on uniform standards, and without these uniform standards modern industrial production would not be possible. Here we come to economies of scale. Production that is technologically possible must also be economically viable. That is why managers push both for uniformity and to increase economies of scale. But their success depends on the ambition of capital to increase its power. Capital is the bearer of aspirations of dominance (in Latin: libido dominandi), not expertise or profession. It cannot be said that capital only aspires to increase wealth, and in this way finding purpose only in itself. The goal of increasing capital is to dominate, and indirectly to eliminate the role of the nation state, its primary rival. The pillar of capital is ownership—it stands or falls on this principle. Capital's goal is to subjugate the state, and the nation state can only exist if it secures control over capital within the framework of the national economy.

The International Perspective of Growth and Partnership

Capital has acquired a bad reputation, as a result of its aspiration for growth, the accumulation of power, and negative social consequences, for making people antisocial, indifferent, greedy, and a range other of pejorative qualities. This is partly true, but these traits are not simply characteristic of those with capital. These traits are inherent in the phenomenon of growth, and growth is a natural aspiration of each biological organism. But growth is only possible at the expense of the surrounding environment, over which the organism must assert its power to achieve this unrelenting growth. Unlimited growth may be a natural aspiration but it is also self-destructive. It destroys the surrounding environment on which the organism lives, and thus undermines its own potential. The destruction of the environment means reducing it to our own needs and creating uniformity. The environment becomes the same as we are, and this ultimately may end our own existence because we cannot survive without the environment. The conclusion is simple: life and development are only possible with diversity. Uncontrolled growth, with uniformity as its inevitable consequence, leads to death. In nature, conditions automatically return to equilibrium. Unbridled growth always weakens on its own and ends up confronting an equal opponent. The same was once true of human society. The ambition for growth and the subjugation of the environment were constant companions throughout human history, and they always ended in a similar way: usually war. These ambitions are still present today and they have expanded to global proportions (see Samuel Huntington, The Clash of Civilizations).

The crucial difference is that solving the situation using past patterns could have apocalyptic consequences, throwing humanity back to the beginning of its existence.

The reason is that human technical capabilities have created the real possibility of self-destruction. We now realize that we can no longer afford uncontrolled growth. Excessive concentration of power in a few hands is also dangerous for humanity. This is the paradox the contemporary world confronts. Growth and progress are the idols that today's leaders worship with unwavering loyalty, not realizing that they have sold their souls in a Faustian bargain and they do not even know to whom. We have also begun to realize that partnership and cooperation are the only way on an international level to prevent interventions into the territory of others and avoid the historical pattern of conflict that would be catastrophic in today's world. In conclusion, controlling growth is necessary and must be tackled deliberately and with intention.

Yet even with a purposeful approach, questions remain about who should grow and how much. Everyone believes they can respond to these questions in their own local area, depending on their power, but this won't get us far. We cannot really talk about controlling growth when growth is the desired goal of all states and communities. We are also talking about how to resolve conflicts peacefully and through agreements, not with violence. But these are all retroactive measures. The core of the dispute is already here. The source lies in the desire for growth. In principle, everyone agrees that growth at the expense of others should be removed from mutual relations. Nevertheless all growth necessarily comes at the expense of the environment, first one's own, and then that of others. An agreement on controlling growth will not be reached because it cannot be reached. The reason is that only the environment can maintain the necessary balance, or restore it, when it has been destroyed. The same rebalance can occurs in human society, but this is the first time that the center of power has been so concentrated in one place, and this has dangerously disrupted equilibrium. A new equilibrium cannot be generated from this center. It can only be ensured by the continued existence of the current configuration of nation states, which guarantees the distribution of social power in its own interest, and thereby the maintenance of political balance in the world. From this perspective, efforts to keep ownership in the hands of national economies are important for maintaining political balance in the world. Ownership is a means that guarantees independence, and independence is the condition for responding to the challenges of the environment.

How much and with what means a nation state keeps ownership within the national economy depends on its policies. It generally cannot take the position of legally prohibiting any foreign ownership. In the case of the EU, for example, such a prohibition would not be possible legally nor would it be rational from the perspective of national interests. An assessment must be made regarding economic and social expedience. For the state, necessary cooperation with the environment mostly pertains to trade. Trade requires the state to allow the foreign environment to acquire certain economic capabilities and to directly intervene in the domestic economy, especially through investments. Cooperation with the environment is always dynamic so rules cannot always be set in advance. With free trade, it is paramount that the state adopts policies that protect its economic interests. It cannot act as if ownership of economic capacity is not important for its existence. This is not only about the resources it owns and has at its direct disposal, but also about the resources in the hands of companies over which the state has no direct right of disposal. This is the essence of the problem. A responsible government will not allow national property to be appropriated irresponsibly and without a long-term economic policy. It will use various measures to dissuade companies from sales of assets that run contrary to the long-term interests of society. Apart from the direct consequences on the market, foreign interventions, and particularly new investments, in the national economy can have long-term consequences that should be subject to economic analysis, also on the theoretical level. But in general it is not the case that foreign investment, and the related inflow of new resources and the creation of new jobs is only beneficial. It can also have detrimental effects.

The Economic Policy of the State

From this perspective, the modern state is a partner in creating the necessary conditions for the functioning of independent companies. Companies directly engage in business activities while the state directs the economy through organizations it has set up for this purpose. Its interventions often have a decisive impact on the performance of independent economic organizations. For this reason, the state must design an economic plan that is more than the sum of the plans of individual companies but an independent project on a different level.

The state does not directly impact the financial performance of individual companies. Rather the state depends on the performance of companies and other economic organizations. Much of the funds covering its expenses come from taxes levied on the economy, collected in the state's budget, and used to finance its obligations. A bankrupt economy means a bankrupt state. Employment and social security policies depend on the performance of the economy. This is true of other policies, particularly science, culture, and healthcare. In sum, politicians depend on the performance of the national economy because the performance of the economy affects state policies in all areas. Thus, although they were elected to achieve the goals set down in their election programs, politicians are handicapped without a successful economy.

On the other hand, the economy can also not be successful if its efforts are not backed by policies that can only be provided by the state or are in the domain of the state: legal security for the functioning of the market and contractual obligations; orderly relations and an open path to international markets for integration into international trade; international financial arrangements that guarantee access to international financial markets; internal financial stability and monetary policy that support profitability in foreign trade; general education appropriate to the demands and level of social development; institutions that provide the capacity for inclusion in complex creative processes; the cultivation of basic science; services crucial for the life of society and the functioning of the economy but that are not necessarily profitable on the market; the basic health conditions of the population, including demographic policy, that guarantees a sufficient workforce, and finally activities that create an awareness of national identity and meaningful existence. Although at first glance, the latter may not seem to have a direct connection to the economy, it is essential for general success in any field.

The benefits of many of these activities cannot be directly measured, especially not in financial terms. Therefore they cannot be included in the economic balance of a particular economic organization, and cannot be the subject of trade relations. That is the reason that the business and management of organizations engaged in these areas are relieved of the pressure of financial rationality typical of the market economy. Above all they are not under threat of liquidation, which hangs like the sword of Damocles over all economic entities that fails to meet the level of financial adequacy.

In Slovenia, the achievement of rational business practices that are comparable with other global economies is the aspiration behind recent attempts at reforming the state administration, all of which have failed. As a result, all these practices are categorized as consumption, although this is not the current methodology of the EU. Thus we arrive at a strange paradox that is in contradiction with the role of the state in creating national income. If this were categorized simply as expenditure, it would be in the interest of the state to cut costs in these areas as much as possible, contributing to the general profitability of the national economy. All state cost-cutting campaigns are therefore first targeted at segments that are not directly related to creating national income, although they may substantially contribute to it: namely, culture, science, and education. The reason for this is easy to understand. National income is financially measurable, while the contribution of these activities is intangible, except as an expenditure on the account of the state budget to which the economy contributes with its taxes. The costs of materials and services paid to create this revenue have already been taken into account in the calculation of the net revenues of companies. In contrast, the value of services provided by the state are not visible on the market exchange, and are evaluated only as a budget expenditure even though they are distributed evenly across the economy.

Because of this, the state is not perceived as an important partner in the national economy but as a wasteful element, the increasing costs of which burden the economy and threaten its survival.

Governments themselves are often guilty for disseminating such views on the role of the state as a result of their inability to quantify and financially evaluate the contributions needed from their activities for the financial success of individual companies and the economy as a whole. Governments mainly present their success through favorable macro-economic indicators. National income is presented exclusively in financial form. International comparisons are primarily made using financial indices. Overall success is expressed as GDP per capita. This serves as the foundation for demands to increase pay and entitlements. The most tangible success is reflected in the budget. Improved financial performance of the economy permits the increase of financial interventions in areas that are treated as expenses in the budget. Understandably governments pay the most attention to the economy, and quite naturally adopt an economic perspective on the problems of the state. A government's economic plan or policy will often be constructed as the combined plans of various companies.

The danger here lies in the government seeing its role as the head of the economy. This was characteristic of governments under socialism where the state was the direct owner of the economy, and the government played the role of the general manager of economic enterprises, which were only economic branches of the government. This principle was known as operative and administrative management. The role of the government in the market economy is completely different, and maintaining the old pattern of state management would prevent companies from behaving in accordance with the laws of the market. The government's economic plan therefore cannot be the passive adoption of projected development as defined by companies, but a new and independent economic projection. It should include both economic forecasts and the goals of state policies. It should include the activities of the state that ensure favorable economic conditions, and goals defined by the government based on its assessment of possible development. Naturally, the government cannot plan its economic policy without the forecasts of companies regarding their own development, but this is only part of the basis for government policy. Similarly, companies cannot plan their development without certain elements provided by the state. Their forecasts are not necessarily the same, and companies do not necessarily depend on government reports except in cases when government forecasts include certain obligations.

In the modern market economy, as mentioned previously, the role of the government in relation to the economy cannot be that of a neutral observer as it was in the age of classical capitalism when the state only enforced the law. Nor can it be that of an operational manager controlling all aspects of business activities, a role that is attractive to politicians because it would allow them to make important decisions and assert themselves with little personal accountability. In neither case is this a partnership. In the first case, the state is excluded, and in the second it is the exclusive master. The state must be a partner in the modern market economy. Without the active cooperation of the state, companies cannot survive and be successful on the market. Just as the national economy cannot be successful without the personal commitment of entrepreneurs and owners of businesses to succeed, the state has become an increasingly important partner in terms of its contributions, and thus the burden of its role also increases. The more society and its segments, including the economy, grow and become more complex, the more it is necessary to address issues on a level where all of the various participating elements intersect.

Chapter 8: The New Position of Hired Labor

France Bucar and Igor Kovač

Wage labor, along with business and the state, is one of the main partners in the economic activities of society. But today labor is faced with so many problems resulting from modern social development that its partnership status is one of the many new questions that require a response, or at least the reconsideration of the solutions that have worked thus far. That is why, although it falls into the same general area, the consideration of wage labor extends beyond our discussion on partnership.

The New Concept of Labor

Notions of "labor" and "working class" evoke many different issues in part because we can no longer speak about labor in the same way as we did in the past, and especially not about manual laborers as the primary component of the working class. In the modern production process, manual labor no longer represents the majority of employees. Unskilled laborers with no specific qualifications represent a negligible proportion of employees, having become in many ways a remnant of the past. Above all, we can no longer refer to the working class as a uniform group with the same common interests. Unity only is relevant insofar as the term encompasses all people who are in a hired-labor relationship to capital (namely, the owners of business entities). In this respect, notions of labor and the working class have expanded as they also include the skilled part of the labor force, which never before considered itself a part of the working class, nor was it seen as such by capital. Its relationship to capital

F. Bucar (Deceased)

I. Kovač (✉)
Department of Political Science, University of Cincinnati, Cincinnati, OH, USA
e-mail: kovacir@mail.uc.edu

© Springer International Publishing AG, part of Springer Nature 2019
I. Kovač (ed.), *At His Crossroad*, https://doi.org/10.1007/978-3-319-78331-4_12

has always been particular. Today this part of the working class makes up the largest share of hired labor. Its share continues to grow steadily, and it is quickly becoming the majority of hired workers. This has increased its self-awareness, and changed the perception of its role and mission from that of the historical working class.

This represents a change in the relationship with capital. Because of its rising numerical size, the perception of hired labor as special is falling. A class that is so massive and diffuse can hardly be seen as special. Yet many of the demands and views that were once typical of the working class are returning, even among the elite that was not traditionally part of the working class and now has become its most important members. This is due to the fact that the elite are in the position of hired labor and are thus dependent on capital. This dependence on capital—and on the state in the case of public servants and those employed in subsystems financed from the state budget where orders come from the state, a segment which is also increasing—connects all members of the hired labor force through common interests that were once represented in trade union activities. The role of trade unions is to bring together workers who would have little or no power as individuals into a joint organized force, the unification of which enables them to act as a partner in negotiations with the state and capital.

Historically, elite experts did not draw their social power from unions but rather from their own expertise. That is why this segment of society has generally not been interested in unionization since they had no need of it. On the contrary, unionization would reduce their status. Today such an elevated position can only be claimed by those experts upon whom the organizations employing their services directly depend. This dependence gives them a special status and the possibility of stepping outside the hired-labor relationship and acting as independent partners selling their services. Formally this represents a shift to the entrepreneurial aspect of the relationship.

This is more the exception than the rule. Most experts—even those with the highest level of expertise—have the status of hired labor. In comparison to their former status as the working elite, this is a degradation, and many of them have difficulty reconciling psychologically with this perception of themselves, and this causes them difficulties adapting to new conditions. The shift, coming in less than a generation, was too sudden.

A change has also taken place in the conception of workers' solidarity. The power of the working class as a social partner is derived from solidarity—only through unity can it acquire power as a negotiator. Previously there was no exception to this rule, but today solidarity is largely a thing of the past, especially in the most technologically advanced areas or industries. These fields no longer employ a uniform, more or less undifferentiated mass of replaceable workers. The labor force is highly structured and covers diverse fields of expertise as well as different levels of expertise within individual areas. Companies can only take the lead by being the best, or among the best, in all aspects of their particular fields. They attempt to achieve this by employing the top experts in their fields, continuing in the path of the differentiation already achieved and causing even greater competition. Only the best survive; only the best can hope for promotion. This fits with the kind of progress we have seen in the contemporary era, which automatically expels all that is subprime, and also delivers social consequences that the working class did not have to face in the past. The concept of competition has replaced that of solidarity among workers. Those who connect their career success to the companies for which they work, have also connected their own personal success to the performance of these companies. The performance and survival of these companies are much more important to them than unionization. This already represents a chink in the ostensibly insuperable barrier between labor and capital. Workers identify themselves with the companies for which they work. Capital intentionally promotes this identification, not least through different forms of employee participation in ownership. This is another example of new forms of relationships that were not previously known or recognized in the accepted understanding of the position of labor. This also redefines the role of trade unions, providing a completely different sort of legitimacy than before.

The Conflict Between Labor and Capital

When we speak of labor as a partner, we are not referring to its technical role. From the perspective of technology, it is paradoxical that labor would only now become a partner as production has always depended on workers. There could be no production without labor. But now we are reconsidering the social relationship. In this regard, labor has not been given (and is still not given) the role of partner. It has been perceived as a labor force, bought and sold on the market, and not as an equal participant in the economic process. The working class never even vied for such a position. It believed it had been pushed out of the economic process, was estranged from it, and even an adversary of it. This response is understandable to a certain extent. If labor and the owners of capital are in a sale-and-purchase relationship, the buyer and the seller are on opposite sides of the transaction as regards their interests. The buyer wants to obtain goods as cheaply as possible, while the seller would like to sell them as dearly as possible. From this perspective, there can be no cooperation between them, more likely the opposite.

We will not debate the point of whether the labor force can really be perceived as goods to be bought and sold, or whether such an interpretation is ethically acceptable. Formally, rejecting this view would negate the existing legal order, particularly the function of private property as the fundamental basis of the legal order.

Recognizing the right of labor to participate in business would be the same as dispossessing the owner, and would mean a rejection of the absolute rights of ownership. This is a revolutionary demand, and has been seen as such by both the working class and capital. That is why neither private capitalism nor Soviet state capitalism ever adopted it. In this sense, the Soviet system did not reform the position of labor in the production process. The only innovation was that a single capitalist, the state, replaced a multitude of owners. The state became the sole employer and created a monopolistic relationship toward the worker not previously known by the capitalism of the time, and this resulted in the position of labor deteriorating even further. In any case, the demand for workers' participation in the business process is the same as a demand for the partial dispossession of existing owners, which would benefit the workers. This would represent a revolution in the previous relationship of power between them.

Labor has no real social power until it confronts capital as an organized force. Individual workers have no power in relationship to capital, because other workers can replace them at any time. But as an organized whole, the labor force becomes a factor that capital must consider. Nevertheless labor remains passive in the role of an expense in the process, not unlike other expenses that owners must manage such as raw materials and energy. Unionization allowed labor to set a higher price for itself and take a place at the negotiating table.

However, the relationship between labor and capital has never been an impersonal relationship between buyer and seller on the labor market that can be observed in other buyer-seller relationships—if you do not like the price, you simply decide not to buy or sell. In the case of organized labor, we have a confrontation of two monopolies whose existence depends on reaching an acceptable price in negotiations. Not finding an agreed upon price means economic death or the loss of physical survival by one side or the other. Although labor and capital are pulling the same wagon, their interests are diametrically opposed. Overcoming this framework can only be implemented through a radical transformation in the foundations of social relations. This transformation moves us close to the edge of a deep social chasm that carries an emotional name: social revolution. Whenever capital felt the confrontation with labor threatened the core of its interests, it would turn to the state and its armed forces for help. At such times, the atmosphere in society reached a state of emergency, and there was a feeling of danger, almost the question of life and death, to be or not to be. In short, labor and capital have never viewed each other as partners but rather as adversaries with contradictory interests. That is why they engage in what appears to be negotiations but in fact is a class struggle in which pressure is applied to achieve a more or less sustainable balance. In times of equilibrium, it is in the interest of capital, in order to maximize profit and maintain competitiveness, to keep labor costs at the lowest level still acceptable for labor. The main weapon labor has in this struggle is direct rebellion: strikes in which strikebreakers had the same status as deserters from armed combat.

The goals of organized labor never extended beyond the desire for a higher price for work.

Under such conditions, the concept of a partnership between labor and capital had no chance of being accepted on either side, not even as a visionary idea worthy of serious consideration. In terms of the ideology of labor, the belief in the irreconcilable contradiction between labor and capital only grew over time. The only possible solution was for labor to take ownership of capital, which would require an upheaval in the social order, nothing less than a social revolution. Thus state capitalism was established. This also changed the nature of capitalism itself from market to monopoly capitalism, with no clear vision of what the implications of this would be. Capitalists could only be dispossessed of their property by force, which meant that the new state capitalism had to be created through violence, a revolution that included the abolishment of democracy and a takeover of the entire state structure.

Although this discussion describes the system that was actually implemented and failed in the Soviet bloc, the topic is not merely historical but continues to have relevance today. Modern capitalism is still caught in the throes of these unresolved issues, and a number of economically and technologically less developed countries face similar problems as the former communist countries did prior to the beginning of this experiment. What was the fundamental mistake that allowed this historical intervention to take place at all? The fact is that this system was established in a country where the social situation was extremely complex, and it seemed that the accumulated contradictions in society could not be solved in any other way. But as in similar cases that followed, the general societal distress was only multiplied by the strife that engulfed these countries. Communist revolution succeeded only in conditions of war, not because of the war itself, but because war brought social conditions to a point where there seemed to be no other way out. In such situations, sound reasoning yields to the necessities of survival. Yet the history of these regimes has clearly shown that no social problem can be solved through violence. Violence breeds violence, which prevents reasonable solutions and leads to new forms of extremism. The persistence of an unjust society is also a form of violence. The roots of contemporary violence around the world lie in the injustice of the social order, both globally and in individual countries.

The Emergence of Social Democracy

The state plays an important role in the relationship between labor and capital, not as an unaffected observer but as an involved participant, this despite the fact that it appears neutral, unbiased, and above both camps. In fact, the state has always been the protector of capital, simply for the reason that it has to serve as the guardian of the legal order, and this order is based on the principle of private property as a foundation of the social system. If the state performs its role, it must side with owners of capital against the demands of labor when tensions between the two escalate. Marx was correct in his claim that the bourgeois government plays the role of an executive board for capitalists. This claim may sound extreme, but the role of the bourgeois government was in fact to protect capital, and this remains its role today in any legal order that is based on the principle of private property. Owners will always have a closer relationship to the state, the role of which is to protect private property, than those who have no property. Most of the working class remains in the latter position, which is why a certain mistrust persists between the state and labor despite the many changes in the relationship ushered in by modern developments.

The understanding of the state's role as a mediator between labor and capital led to the belief that the conflict between labor and capital could be resolved if labor seized legislative power in the state by participating and winning enough votes in parliamentary competition. From this position of power, labor could enact laws that would favor workers' demands in relation to capital. This could potentially overcome the seemingly irreconcilable hostility between labor and capital, and peaceful coexistence could be achieved through parliamentary procedures. This does not necessarily mean that a consensus or common views would have to be found. Diverging views could remain but would be resolved by both sides using the means of power available against the other side. The confrontation would take place in parliament, using parliamentary methods. In this sense, social democracy not only accepted the democratic method of conflict resolution, but also cemented democracy as the foundation of its existence. Without parliamentary democracy, there can be no social democracy.

As such, social democracy is one of the most important factors in the development of modern democracy, democratic pluralism, and particularly human rights, because it has expanded these principles to cover the social component as well as the political one. Moreover, contrary to the Bolshevik doctrine that the state was dying, social democracy emphasizes the role of the state as a means to resolve social tensions and conflicts. What is perhaps more important is that social democracy accepts private property as the foundation of the social order. This also created the conditions for including labor issues in the ideologies that have shaped the European identity, the understanding of identity and worldview, and interpretations of the meaning of human existence. Bolshevism could not achieve this, because its basic positions were directed against elements of European culture and the values underlying human civilization in general. This, more than economic failure, was the biggest cause of its downfall.

Social democracy represented a turning point in the relationship between labor and capital. This was mostly the consequence of the spiritual development of modern society, which resulted from the socio-economic development. New technological discoveries and inventions drastically changed life style and conditions for satisfying material needs, increasing the possibility of attaining a previously unimaginable standard of living. Progress in understanding human nature and the functioning of human society brought individual consciousness (and awareness of self) to a new level, and also changed levels of expectations that increasingly began to depend not only on personal activities but also on interconnectedness and interdependence with others. This interdependence ushered in a number of new concepts regarding the rights and obligations of individuals in society, and this in turn led to the establishment of institutions and mechanisms to ensure the survival and continued functioning of society. Society has become a highly complex and internally interlinked system. Natural laws can no longer be relied on to automatically solve internal contradictions without sacrificing the achievements of modern civilization. The ongoing existence and development of society needs to be guided and adjusted, and the state plays the central role in this endeavor.

Nevertheless social democracy—even when it is at the helm of society in the form of a well-organized party—still faces the question of how to resolve the contradictions between labor and capital. In principle, social democracy recognizes private property, and with it all the ownership-based rights of capital that are the primary source of the confrontation between labor and capital. As long as capital acts as the buyer of labor and labor is the seller, the conflict will persist because it stems from the opposing interests of buyer and seller. The only solution to the conflict would be a change in ownership. Nationalization is not a good option because it means a return to the communist solution, which is in direct opposition to social democracy. Even a partial change to the ownership-based right of disposal would represent an intervention in the absolute primacy of ownership. In Slovenia, the principle of private property has already lost its absolute inviolability with the constitutional principle that private property must also serve a social role. This new principle opens the way to partial reform of the right of disposal. However, the question remains: how far can we go down this road without abolishing the principle of private property completely? The abolishment of the principle of private property would bring down the entire structure that is the foundation of the current market system and democratic order.

The situation has not been resolved in countries where social democratic or any other democratic party has come to power. The contradictions remain, the only difference being that the improvement in wellbeing, the recognition and protection of human rights, and the general atmosphere of greater humanity have alleviated the consequences. This has been accomplished with social legislative measures that, among others, relate to work safety, unemployment benefits, pension, and insurance plans. These developments have not occurred in all countries, and even where they have, they go only a certain distance. Workers' strikes, which address residual conflicts between labor and capital and the absence of true belief in the partnership, offer the most vivid proof of this.

The Myth of Co-Management

Slovenia has attempted to take a further step. The Slovenian constitution formally recognizes the right of workers in so-called co-management. Since the right to co-management means an intervention in the constitutionally guaranteed right to private property, we cannot deny a certain contradiction in the Slovenian constitution itself—unless we consider the right to co-management as part of the social function that private property must perform. But even with this proviso, we hit a bump that all social-democratically oriented forms of government do regardless of their formal affiliation. Social legislation, which improves the conditions of workers compared to those that prevailed during the brutal capitalism of old, means concessions to labor but in no way touches the essence of capitalism or changes it. For this reason, the constitutional right to co-management in Slovenia caused no real change in the position of labor as compared to democracies in which this right is not guaranteed, and the country continues to face the same contradictions between labor and capital as it did before.

The right to co-management should not be confused with the right to self-management. Self-management means all of the rights of owner are transferred to workers, and in effect is the same as completely dispossessing current owners of capital for the benefit of labor. Not surprisingly, this never truly happened in Yugoslav socialism because it would have meant dispossessing those in power at the time, namely the communist nomenklatura. Dispossession of owners was reduced to the formal right of workers to participate in the operation and management of companies. Operative management does not concern ownership itself, as even capitalist owners often relegate management to professionals whom they hire and dismiss at will. Giving workers the right to participate in management is giving them something that even capitalist owners have relinquished, and it is a specialized activity for which they may not be qualified. In reality, the right to self-management was reduced to a situation that leant legitimacy to decisions made by professional management as representative of the true owners, the party elite. Indeed workers' self-management turned out to be one of the best psychological tools for subjugating labor. It far surpassed all other psychological methods used in the capitalist system to persuade workers to pursue the goals of capital.

Workers' co-management, in contrast, remains ambiguous. It would bring about the partial dispossession of the owner of capital for the benefit of workers, but it remains unclear what this would actually involve. Would it give workers the right to veto owners' decisions that interfere with their benefits? This would still not bring true partnership since it is in essence opposed to the interest of business. It would only prevent entrepreneurs from taking measures that disregarded the workers' benefits. In any case, workers' rights are already taken into consideration being protected by law. But workers' benefits cannot be protected without determining what they are in each individual case. Rights are a subject of social legislation and oblige owners regardless of whether the right of workers to co-management is formally enacted or not. The interests of labor and capital remain in conflict since the interests of labor still represent costs for capital. The greater the rights of labor, the lower the yield of capital. Unless there is a more fundamental change and congruence, labor and capital remain in the same contradictory situation. The conflict therefore remains a standoff between opposing sides, and the right to co-management is revealed as an empty psychological slogan.

The only relevant measure would be social legislation establishing the right of labor to define the additional obligations of owners toward workers. Labor did not achieve these rights from co-management in companies but rather as a partner at the level of the national economy. On this level, it is the government that represents the general interests of society, integrating the specific interests of labor in the context of general interests. Here, specific interests acquire a concrete definition when confronted with other interests. In this way, the problems of labor are not resolved through the confrontation of labor and capital but on the level of society as a whole. Issues affecting labor and the role of labor are the concerns not only of the working class but also of the entire society.

The Social Role of the State

Society as a whole is not interested only in the rights of workers but also in the success of the entire economy. There is no definitive solution for the conflict of interest between labor and capital because the final defeat of one or the other would represent the downfall of society. Labor and capital are interdependent, and the fate of the entire society rests on the relationship between the two. There can never be a final resolution in this classic confrontation, only temporary truces. Only when the state intervenes with social legislation do the positions of the two sides come closer, although the contradictions are never fully overcome because they are embedded in the core dynamics of the relationship. General societal transformations along with growing complexity and interdependence have integrated society to a point where even the smallest disruption in its functioning can endanger the whole. Parties to this conflict cannot afford a class struggle in the traditional sense of the term. Capital cannot do without a relatively satisfied labor force, and is thus compelled to seek compromise. Labor also has an interest in the success of capital. Successful businesses objectively have increased potential to serve the interests of labor. That is why the demands of labor should not jeopardize the performance, much less the existence, of a company because this would endanger its own situation. Disputes still arise, yet conflicts are not resolved with the use of violence and power, but are approached as so-called false conflicts, emerging from the assumption that the parties in conflict have common interests, and that differences reside in how they wish to achieve their shared goals. The common goal is clearly the success of the company. Misunderstandings result from a lack of satisfactory information on one side or the other. Negotiations are therefore comprised not of direct pressure on the opposing side but of new revelations, fueled mainly by new information about the interests of both sides, and possible actions. These confrontations are not only about wages but a range of business policies that affect profits for capital as well the interests of labor. The most important among these are policies that affect employment itself—expanding or cutting the number of jobs, eliminating, changing, or transferring production, merging, or splitting companies or plants—and also policies that pertain to the conditions of particular work positions—the difficulty and hours of work, physical and mental strain, the work environment, and other conditions. Direct use of power and violence only comes when rational decision making as the method for correctly determining interdependence and related interests fails.

Resolving false conflicts means addressing mutual relations. In business dynamics, it is a continuous process that cannot be limited to the issues of a single organization. It relates to broader economic issues, not just those within a particular industry, but the general problems of the national economy. The resolution of the problems of a particular company often depends on policies that fall under the jurisdiction of the government, or on information that the company itself does not possess. In cases where government policies can resolve a situation, it acts as a direct participant. Often a company loses the ability to survive and cannot find a solution on its own. Workers suffer the most in such cases, and the government will look for solutions. It cannot take the position that the state is not a business partner and therefore has no role in the economic matters. This is the excuse generally used by neoliberals. If it has no chance of survival, letting a company fail is sometimes a reasonable decision. But the government cannot act as if the situation is not its concern. Such cases have social consequences for which the government is responsible. It may not be responsible in each individual case, but the general social situation is made up of many individual and specific cases. By engaging in saving individual companies, the government is providing solutions for society in general.

The success of a national economy depends not only on business performance, which is in the hands of companies. It also hinges on the cooperation of workers. This cooperation is not simply the passive fulfillment of prescribed obligations. With the active participation and commitment of employees of the company who accept the company's goals as their own, business results can be substantially improved, and the resolution of problems facilitated. Employee satisfaction depends not only on identification with company goals but also on the acceptance of the goals and policies of the state. The state, as we have seen, is a participant in the national economy because it complements labor and capital by creating elements that are directly or indirectly embedded in all products and services—even though they are not expressed as a specific input but rather as an unspecified expenditure of the state budget. Therefore it is important that employees not only identify with the goals of the company they work for, but also with the general policies and goals of the state.

That is why the state should not act as a representative for a particular side in this three-sided relationship. Social legislation should contain—and this is a concept retained from the socialist past—an element of supporting and protecting the weak and disadvantaged in society. This was once the role of labor in its conflict with capital. Today the situation has changed due to increasing interdependence. Labor has gained power and has a formally recognized position. Social legislation, insofar as it deals with conditions in the economy, plays the role of arranging relations between participants so as to achieve the best possible outcome for the national economy. That is why social legislation also deals with the role of capital in business activities. Capital, in its business function, also needs to be protected by law, albeit mostly indirectly. The interests of companies often conflict with the socially justified interests of workers. A social or welfare state is not automatically the protector of labor. It must also protect capital in its business role. Even companies may also need a form of welfare, which indicates that the state's role is to find the right balance among participants.

Workers' co-management of companies is an anachronism from a historical period when efforts were made to establish labor as a partner in the economy to counterbalance capital. Workers' representatives on the boards of companies (which represent owners) can point out problems in the relationship between labor and capital, and propose solutions. They are supposed to have the same representational role and tasks in the management of the company as management itself. Thus workers can directly change what occurs in the company, and ensure the transparency of adopted measures. It is an important responsibility that can contribute to resolving issues arising from the relationship of the two sides at various levels of business. However, they cannot decide on issues that relate to the position and status of the company, or business measures that affect the company's performance, and it is precisely these issues that have the potential to cause the most substantial conflicts between labor and capital. These issues can be the most significant to workers, and their representatives in management bodies do not have the authority to present the will and views of the workers. It is the owner who decides these matters, personally or in the form of shareholders. In other words, the representatives of labor have the legitimacy to represent the interests of labor on issues that directly affects the rights and position of workers. They have no legitimacy to act on other issues that relate to general business performance and therefore cannot speak on behalf of the owner.

If no agreement is reached on issues directly related to workers' interests and a dispute escalates, workers can always resort to extreme methods that publicize the conflicts of interests: namely, industrial action. Strikes are the most extreme tool available to workers' when all other means fail. However, strikes are not organized by workers' representatives in management but by their trade unions. It is hard to imagine workers going on strike because their proposals for improving a company's performance were not heard. That would be the concern of the owner. Co-management means co-ownership. It comes from the rights originating in ownership, and is therefore not a way to solve the conflicts between labor and capital.

These conflicts can only be resolved on the level of the state, which has the legitimacy to interfere in matters of ownership. States define the status of property in their constitutions, and the Slovenian constitution, for instance, stipulates that property also has a social role. Legislation may intervene in the extent and use of property as well as guarantee a suitable relationship between labor and capital. Actual co-management only takes place if it delineates the limitations of ownership and the extent of its rights. Co-management on the company level emerging from the rights of workers as co-owners is a contradiction in terms. Workers can only act as co-owners if they become stockholders, which would change their mentality and approach. Stockholders do not behave like workers. If the two roles are combined in the same person (i.e. internal ownership), it leads to a hybrid situation that has advantages and weaknesses, and functions differently in circumstances that emphasize one role or the other.

Appendix

Slovenian Research Agency has contributed to the translation of this book. To meet the terms of Agency's policy, two reviews have to be published in original.

Bogomil Ferfila[1]

At the New Crossroads je sestavljena iz dveh delov. Gre za prvi prevod knjige dr. Franceta Bučarja Na novih razpotjih v tuj jezik – angleščino. Sam prevod je pospremljen s kritičnimi znanstvenimi študijami. Te se vsaka posebej osredotočajo na določeno problematiko, ki jo Bučar v knjigi obravnava. Podobno kot finančna kriza leta 2008 pričujoče delo mednarodno akademsko diskusijo naslavlja z vprašanji in vlogo etike v politiki, ekonomiji in družbi. Prevod knjige Franceta Bučarja, v angleščino omogoča mednarodni javnosti, da se seznani z idejami oblikovanimi v do sedaj nepoznani in ne reprezentativni kulturi in okolju.

V knjigi dr. Bučar razgrne in analitično razčleni današnje družbene probleme, hkrati pa se z njimi sooči na unikaten način. Ključno vlogo pri tem igra Bučarjeva sistemska teorija, ki v središče postavi človeka; etika v njegovi sistemski teoriji pa predstavlja osrednjo povratno zanko. Etika zanj ni le del analitičnega orodja pač pa tudi pot do reševanja odprtih družbenih vprašanj.

Delo ima dvojno akademsko vrednost. Bučarjeva sistemska teorija namreč predstavlja nov mejnik v mednarodnih družboslovnih vedah. Njegova kritika znanstvenega pozitivizma pa preide v sintetiziranje med pozitivizmom in interpretivizmom, česar v današnji znanosti, obsedeni s pink ponkom med tezami in antitezami, močno primanjkuje.

V tej kratki recenziji se želim dotakniti prvega – Bučarjeve sistemske teorije – saj pooseblja tudi drugo točko – združevanje kvantifikacije s kvalitativnimi dimenzijami.

---

[1] Bogomil Ferfila is full professor of Political Science at University of Ljubljana, where he is the chair of American Studies Program.

Sistemska teorija je produkt pozitivizma in je zaživela v začetku 20. stoletja, ko je hiter napredek znanosti klical po večji sistematizaciji vedenja. Najprej se je pojavila v naravoslovju[2], sledila je kibernetika[3], nato družboslovje[4] ter celo humanizem[5]. Vsaka sistemska teorija mora opredeliti svoje elemente in njihovo strukture, ter naravo njihovih odnosov. V teh dveh spremenljivkah je Bučarjeva sistemska teorija unikum.

Prvi, ki je v politologijo vpeljal sistemsko teorijo, je bil David Easton. Njegov sistem je bil preprost, saj so ga sestavljali – vnos (input), obdelava vnosov znotraj sistema, proizvod (output), povratna zanka, in okolje – medtem ko so ostali procesi znotraj sistema ostali neopredeljeni.[6] Pomanjkanje slednjega je vodilo v t.i. problem 'črne škatle'. Eastonovo teorijo je dopolnil Karl Deutsch, ki je predstavil bolj kompleksno teorijo, ki je obravnavala tudi odnose med elementi sistema.[7] V kolikor je Easton poudarjal zgolj strukturne elemente sistema, so Deutschevi nasledniki zanihali v drugo skrajnost ter predstavljali sistemske teorije, ki so se bolj ali manj ukvarjale s procesi. Tako je sistemska teorija postala sinonim za kibernetiko in komunikacijske študije, kjer je vloga posameznika minimalna. Eden izmed najbolj znanih tovrstnih avtorjev je Niklas Luhmann.[8] Nekateri govorijo o Luhmannu kot o anti-humanistu, saj je nekoč dejal, da ga ljudje ne zanimajo.[9]

Bučarjeva sistemska teorija je antipod Luhmannovemu ter nekako predstavlja vrnitev in nadgraditev Deutscha. Posameznik je ključni element Bučarjevega sistema, saj slednji upravlja podsisteme in sistem sam. Da razumemo kako torej deluje sistem, moramo razumeti posameznika, ki s sistemom upravlja. Kar se tiče interakcije med podsistemi, Bučar postreže z normativno preskripcijo: etika je tista, ki mora uravnavati odnose med podsistemi. Posledično to zahteva, da imajo upravljavci podsistemov etično zavest. Ko aplicira svojo teorijo v realno politiko, ja za Bučarja etičnost nacionalni interes.

Poleg znanstvene vrednosti ima publikacija tudi velik političen in diplomatski doprinos. Gre namreč za publikacijo v angleškem jeziku objavljeno pri uveljavljeni mednarodni založbi, ki bo svetovni znanstveni srenji predstavila misel velikega Slovenca. Pričujoča knjiga je torej sredstvo t. i. javne diplomacije, s katerim se Slovenija predstavlja svetu.

---

[2] von Bertalanffy, Ludwig. 1928. *Kritische Theorie der Formbildung*. Berlin: Gebrüder Borntraeger.

[3] Wiener, Norbert. 1948. *Cybernetics: Control and communication in the animal and the machine*. New York: Wiley.

[4] Parsons, Talcott 1951. *The Social System*. London: The Free Press.

[5] Banathy, Bela H. 1968. *Instructional Systems*. Palo Alto: Fearon Publishers.

[6] Easton, David. 1965. *A framework for political analysis*. Englewood Cliffs: Prentice-Hall; Easton, David.1953. *The political system*. New York: Knopf.

[7] Deutsch, Karl W. 1963. *The nerves of government; models of political communication and control*. London: The Free Press.

[8] Luhmann, Niklas. 1977. Differentiation of society. *Canadian Journal of Sociology/Cahiers canadiens de sociologie*, 2(1). Pp. 29–53.

[9] Luhmann, Niklas. 1995. *Social systems*. Palo Alto: Stanford University Press.

Vse navedene karakteristike knjige so izpostavljene tudi v študijah, ki so priložene prevodu knjige. Študije so napisali slovenski znanstveniki, ki delujejo v mednarodnem prostoru. Interdisciplinarni nabor avtorjev – politologi, ekonomisti, pravniki in naravoslovci – odraža interdisciplinarnost dr. Franceta Bučarja in njegovih del.

Peter Rožič[10]

Če je leta 1989 izšel do sedaj edini prevod Franceta Bučarja v angleščino, je torej pred nami šele drugi prevod katerega koli dela tega slovenskega intelektualca. Če je Slovenija ob koncu 80-ih s prevodom njegovega prvega dela – Reality and the Myth (Resničnost in utvara) – v mednarodni skupnosti promovirala svoje težnje po osamosvojitvi in samostojnosti, pa prevod in znanstvena študija Bučarjeve knjige Na novih razpotjih (At the New Crossroads) promovira slovensko misel in raziskovalce v mednarodni skupnosti.

Dr. France Bučar je avtor, ki koncepte problematizira. Medtem ko drugi te koncepte obravnavajo kot dane – na primer človekove pravice kot refleksija etičnega napredka – se Bučar tovrstnih temeljnih vprašanj loti kritično. Osrednje vodilo avtorja pričujoče knjige Na novih razpotjih je, da za ustrezne odgovore na pereča družbena vprašanja najprej opravi dobro diagnozo. Knjiga tako bralca izzove k premisleku o temeljih družbe, države in znanosti. Ob tem pa knjigo orisujeta tudi dve pomembni karakteristiki: Bučarjeva sistemska teorija, ki predstavi izvirno aplikacijo etike v znanstveno raziskovanje, ter njegovo združevanje znanstvenega pristopa s praktičnimi političnimi izkušnjami pri reševanju vprašanj.

Bučar izvor sodobnih družbenih težav pripisuje pomanjkanju etične drže. Zato se bom v tej recenziji osredotočil prav na njegovo razumevanje etike. Korenine vprašanj, s katerimi se sooča knjiga, je pozitivistična kvantifikacija. Po njegovem želi družba nadeti številko vsemu, tudi psihološkemu (inteligenčni kvocient) in duhovnemu (človekove pravice). Čeprav Bučar priznava doprinose pozitivizma – inovativnost, povečanje blagostanja in produktivnosti – le-ta ne more odgovoriti na najbolj osnovna človekova vprašanja. Ta so vedno etične narave. Za Bučarja etika predstavlja takšen vir oz. motiv posameznikovih dejanj, ki ima drugačno logiko kot kvantifikacija. V tej kritiki pozitivizma se Bučar razkrije kot intelektualec posebne vrste. Ne spušča se namreč v moraliziranje, prav tako ne ustvarja neke nove ideologije. Knjiga preprosto s sintetiziranjem raje ponudi oprijemljive rešitve.

Za razvoj Bučarjeve post-moderne etike je ključna sinteza med nacionalnim (tradicionalizem) in individualnim (modernizem) političnim pristopom. Avtor nadaljuje misel Maxa Webra ter njegove etike odgovornosti.[11] Posameznik se mora zavedati posledic svojih dejanj. Slednja so etična, v kolikor so posledice etične.

---

[10] Peter Rožič is a visiting professor of Political Science at Santa Clara University.

[11] Weber, Max. 1919. *Politics as a vocation*. Dostopno: http://anthropos-lab.net/wp/wp-content/uploads/2011/12/Weber-Politics-as-a-Vocation.pdf (10 oktober 2016).

Ker je takšno držo 'etičnega imperativa' težko pridobiti, še težje pa zahtevati od navadnega smrtnika, Bučar cilja na elite. Elite so namreč tiste, ki upravljajo s pod-sistemi v družbi in državi. V kolikor so etične, je tudi družba in sistem etičen. Takšno Schumpeterianskost[12] Bučar dopolni z vlogo etike kot korekcijskega mehanizma znotraj sistema. S tem predstavi zanimivo dopolnilo h Habermasovi diskurzivni etiki.[13] Dodatne dimenzije Bučarjevega razumevanja etike lahko iden-tificiramo v globalnem etosu Hansa Künga[14] in Levinasove [15] etike drugega. Če v medosebnih odnosih glavnega agensa predstavlja človek, takšno entiteto v medn-arodnih odnosih predstavlja narod. Kakor je umor posameznika neetično dejanje, tako je tudi umor naroda neetično dejanje. S tem Bučar ne izreka anateme nad družbo in politiko, pač pa na novo etično in politično ovrednoti posameznika in narod. Slednji dve predstavljata Bučarjevo absolutnost, ki ju je moč doseči le preko odnosnosti do drugega.

Takšno razumevanje etike Bučar aplicira na politične procese znotraj EU, na globalizacijo in na Slovenijo. Zanimivo je, da so zaključki aplikacij sila podobni. Posameznik ne sme negirati svoje lastne kulture in nacionalne identitete; gre namreč za ekvivalent umoru individuuma ali naroda. Glavni moment Bučarjeve etike je torej ohranitev istovetnosti posameznika in naroda. Takšno gonilo politične aktivnosti vodi do redefinicije drugega, ki nasprotnika spremeni v objekt sobivanja. Posledično Bučar preuredi globalizacijsko 'top-down' logiko, ki zago-varja 'globalno državljanstvo', v 'bottom-up' logiko, ki temelji na kulturni edinst-venosti posameznika in naroda. Bolj ko si Španec, bolj si Evropejec, in bolj ko si Evropejec, bolj si kozmopolit. Tako Bučar tudi ponudi paralelo kozmopolitkemu patriotizmu Habermasa.[16]

Pričujoča študija Bučarjeve Na novih razpotjih s strani uveljavljenih znanstve-nikov v Sloveniji in tujini predstavlja sveže razumevanje etike ter inovativno aplikacijo takšnega razumevanja. Dejstvo, da knjiga izhaja v angleščini, pa pomeni tudi, da bo le-ta dostopna številnim zainteresiranim bralcem, kar bo pripomogli tudi k promociji slovenske misli in slovenskih avtorjev širom sveta.

---

[12] Schumpeter, Joseph A. 2013. *Capitalism, socialism and democracy*. London: Routledge.

[13] Habermas, Jurgen. 1990. *Moral consciousness and communicative ethics*. Cambridge: MIT Press.

[14] Küng, Hans. 1991. *Global responsibility: In search of a new world ethic*. New York: Crossroad.

[15] Levinas, Emmanuel. 2001. *Alterity and transcendence*. New York: Columbia University Press.

[16] Habermas, Jürgen. 1997. *A Berlin republic: writings on Germany*. Lincoln: University of Nebraska Press.